DISCARDED

WOMEN, MEN, & THE PSYCHOLOGY OF POWER

Hilary M. Lips

A SPECTRUM BOOK PRENTICE-HALL, INC. Englewood Cliffs, New Jersey 07632

Library of Congress Cataloging in Publication Data

Lips, Hilary M.
  Women, men, and the psychology of power.

  (A Spectrum Book)
  Bibliography: p.
  Includes index.
  1. Power (Social sciences) 2. Women–Psychology.
3. Men–Psychology. 4. Sex role. I. Title.
HM136.L53   302.3'6   81-11922

ISBN 0-13-962332-9 {PBK}

ISBN 0-13-962340-X

Hilary M. Lips, Ph.D., is the coauthor of *The Psychology of Sex
Differences*, published by Prentice-Hall. She is a regular contributor
to professional journals and is currently doing research on the
psychology of pregnancy and other sex-related differences.

A SPECTRUM BOOK

10 9 8 7 6 5 4 3 2 1

Printed in the United States of America

Editorial production/supervision and interior design
  by Cyndy Lyle Rymer

Manufacturing Buyer: Barbara A. Frick

Cover design by Velthaus & King

Prentice-Hall International, Inc., *London*
Prentice-Hall of Australia Pty. Limited, *Sydney*
Prentice-Hall of Canada, Ltd., *Toronto*
Prentice-Hall of India Private Limited, *New Delhi*
Prentice-Hall of Japan, Inc., *Tokyo*
Prentice-Hall of Southeast Asia Pte. Ltd., *Singapore*
Whitehall Books Limited, *Wellington, New Zealand*

CONTENTS

PREFACE

Power is a concept that evokes strong emotional reactions. People fear it in others, but often covet it for themselves. In recent years a spate of books, workshops, and training programs has appeared, each one claiming to provide the key to gaining and holding power. Women particularly have been deluged with suggestions about ways to become more powerful in relation to men. Yet, despite the uproar about power, systematic thinking and concrete re-research on the topic have rarely been brought together in a comprehensive way.

There is no doubt that power is an important issue and that power inequities can prove to be sources of strain at every level of social interaction. In particular, it is clear that, in an age when both sexes are seeking increased freedom and flexibility, an understanding of power is vital to the redefinition of our roles as women and men. Many of us seek intimacy in special relationships with members of the other sex—intimacy that, by definition, implies trust and shared vulnerability. Yet differences in men's and women's access to and use of power continually subvert this intimacy or turn it into a charade. Many of us seek friendship or colleagueship with members of the other sex, often to find that the equality supposed in these relationships is constantly challenged by learned sex-role patterns of dominance and submission. As long as we do not acknowledge or understand the role of power in woman-man relationships, there is little hope that we can change these relationships for the better.

The task of this book is to examine male-female power relationships, using the theory and research of psychology. The book is written from a perspective that is both feminist and social-psychological. From the feminist perspective, women have less access than men do to most kinds of power, and most male-female differences result from this fact. From the social-psychological perspective, the maintenance of any relationship requires the cooperation of both parties, and within a relationship each individual, even the most oppressed, has some source of power. Both themes run throughout the book.

The book begins by examining the attitudes toward and images of power that pervade our culture. It goes on to look at four major frameworks within which psychologists have studied power: the power motive, strategies of interpersonal influence, feelings of effectiveness and control, and the power structure of dominance. Each of these chapters examines the theoretical issues and research findings and confronts the implications these may have for women and men in our present society. Three chapters focus on the issue of power as it relates to three important areas: sexuality, the family, and organizations. Here, the concepts described in earlier chapters are applied to an understanding of specific problems. Finally, a chapter on male-female intergroup relations focuses on the social context that provides the backdrop for individual woman-man relationships. An epilogue presents conclusions, unanswered questions, suggestions, and possible new research directions.

When Kate Millett wrote her incisive theoretical analysis of the male-female power relationship, in *Sexual Politics,* she accused psychology of having little to offer in the way of research that would aid in the understanding of this relationship. In the intervening years, psychology has come a long way. It is my hope that the reader of this book will come away excited both by the variety and fruitfulness of the approaches to power that psychologists have already used and by the breadth and importance of the frontier that lies ahead.

To the women of The Evanston Women's Liberation Center,
with whom I learned a great deal about power

ACKNOWLEDGMENTS

Four people collaborated with me in writing chapters for this book. Lillian M. Esses, a specialist in the field of family therapy and an assistant professor in the Department of Psychology at the University of Manitoba, was an obvious choice as author of the chapter on power in the family. Nina L. Colwill, who has been teaching courses in the psychology of sex differences for years and who coauthored a book on that topic with me, is an assistant professor in the Departments of Psychology and Business Administration at the University of Manitoba. Her strong interest and background in the area of sex roles made her an ideal coauthor for the chapter on power and sexuality. The chapter on power in the organizational context is coauthored by Gary W. Yunker, an organizational psychologist whose specialty is leadership and management, now an associate professor in the Department of Psychology at Jacksonville State University. Finally, Leslie Campbell, a philosopher who teaches Women's Studies at the University of Winnipeg, shared with me the writing of the chapter on the images of power and powerlessness. I am immensely grateful to these four people, whose expertise and hard work substantially enriched the book.

Two people deserve special acknowledgment for reading and commenting on the manuscript. Nina Colwill read the entire manuscript and offered numerous useful suggestions. Katherine Schultz read many of the chapters as they were completed, and her critical comments always helped me as I struggled through revisions. Both people provided support as well as constructive criticism. Without them, the task of writing this book would have been considerably less interesting and more onerous. I also wish to thank the following people, who reviewed various chapters: Wayne Andrew, Steve Davis, Barry Kelly, and Barry Spinner.

Special appreciation is due to Sue Frenette, who typed the final version of the manuscript, and to Barbara Latocki, who typed much of the first draft.

Finally, I send a note of thanks to my students, who provide me with a continual challenge to think out and communicate my ideas.

The author also wishes to thank the following sources for permission to reprint the material found on the following pages: 24, from *The Power Motive* by David G. Winter. Copyright © 1973 by David G. Winter. Reprinted by permission of The Free Press, a division of Macmillan Publishing Co., Inc., New York. 44, from *In Times Like These* by Nellie Clung. Copyright © 1972 by the University of Toronto Press, Toronto. Reprinted by permission. 70, from *Agatha Christie: An Autobiography* by Agatha Christie. Copyright © 1977 by Agatha Christie Limited. Reprinted by permission of Harold Ober Associates, Inc. 72 and 110, from *The Second Sex* by Simone de Beauvoir. Copyright © 1952 by Alfred A. Knopf, New York. Reprinted by permission. 86, from *The Descent of Woman* by Elaine Morgan. Reprinted with permission of Stein and Day, Pub., and Souvenir Press Ltd., 98, from *Body Politics* by Nancy M. Henley. Copyright © 1977 by Prentice-Hall, Inc. Reprinted with permission. 110, from "A Case of Sexual Dysfunction," by Sam Julty. *Ms.*, November 1972, pp. 18, 20–21. 132, from "Marriage is the Message," by Carolyn Heilbrun. *Ms.*, August 1974. Copyright © by *Ms.* Magazine. 158, excerpt from *The Managerial Woman* by Margaret Hennig and Anne Jardim. Copyright © 1976, 1977 by Margaret Hennig and Anne Jardim. Reprinted by permission of Doubleday & Co., Inc. 166, Table 4 is an adaptation of Figure 8 from "The Manager's Role" (p. 59) from *The Nature of Managerial work* by Henry Mintzberg. Copyright © 1973 by Henry Mintzberg. Reprinted by permission of Harper & Row, Pub., Inc. 176, from *Men and Women of the Corporation* by Rosabeth Moss Kanter. Copyright © 1977 by Rosabeth Moss Kanter. Reprinted by permission of Basic Books, Inc. 186, from Sexual Politics by Kate Millett. Copyright © 1969, 1970 by Kate Millett. Reprinted by permission of Doubleday & Co., Inc.

IMAGES OF
POWER &
POWERLESSNESS

1

Hilary M. Lips and Leslie Campbell

Power tends to corrupt, and absolute power corrupts absolutely.

Lord Acton, 1887

When anima and animus meet, the animus draws his sword of power and the anima ejects her poison of illusion and seduction.*

Carl Gustav Jung

*R. F. C. Hull, trans., *The Collected Works of C. G. Jung,* Bollingen Series XX, 9, II, "Aion: Researches into the Phenomenology of the Self," copyright © 1959 by Princeton University Press. Reprinted by permission.

Humanity's concern with the issue of power reaches back to our earliest written history. As McClelland (1975) points out, our myths and religious writings are saturated with expressions of concern about power and power relationships. They are also filled with images of what it means to be powerful: Apollo driving his sun chariot across the sky; Jehovah speaking from a burning bush, moving with his people as a pillar of fire, sending plagues to punish his recalcitrant subjects; Jesus healing the sick with a word and casting out devils with a stern command; Mohammed leading his followers into battle. There seems to be nothing new in people's fascination with the exploits of real or mythic figures who could demonstrate their power by reshaping their world, whether by a literal moving of mountains or by the ability to command the loyalty and obedience of large numbers of people. What is relatively new is the notion that power—the capacity to have an impact on one's world—is not the exclusive prerogative of a few gods, monarchs, and sorcerers. "Power to the people," the popular battle cry of revolutionary movements, has been heard often enough in recent years to constitute an almost meaningless cliché. Nonetheless, ever since the first uprising of peasants against a monarch, movement after popular movement seems to have been fueled by people's desire to take more control over their own lives and to share in the shaping of their environment; both to prevent others from wielding excessive power over them and to exercise their own power. The women's liberation movement emerging in many parts of the world is no exception. The issue of power is at the movement's very core. Because of this movement, many women are now involved in resisting control by people or institutions to which they themselves have little or no input. They are also learning how to get and use many kinds of power for themselves.

Even outside what is usually considered the political arena, power relationships involving women and men have been complex. The well-worn notion that there is a "battle of the sexes" implies that power struggles are an expected part of male-female relations in many areas. The feminist argument that the "personal is political" acknowledges this notion, but so do people who insist on male superiority and female subservience. For people on all sides of the issue, as well as for those whose main concern is simply to get their spouse to stay within the budget or to stop spending so much time away from home, the exercise and appearance of power in male-female relationships are of central importance.

For psychologists, the subject of power has been an intriguing one, although a specific concern with female-male power relationships is relatively recent. Yet, psychology's approach to the study of power has taken a number of diverse paths. A review and some integration of these various psychological approaches to the subject of power and the application of the approaches to male-female relationships are the tasks of this book.

PSYCHOLOGY AND THE STUDY OF POWER

Psychology approaches the study of power on at least five different levels, all of which can be related more or less directly to the "image" of power. Most directly, power can be studied from the point of view of person perception as a *quality that is attributed by one person to another.* When is a person viewed as powerful? What does one have to be or do to acquire a powerful image? This is the focus of this chapter. Second, power can be studied as a *source of motivation to act.* This approach is discussed in Chapter 2, where we see the stereotypic images of the power-driven person are not always sufficient to detect power-motivated behavior. Psychology also studies power as a *social influence process,* by examining the various strategies that people use to get their way or to exert power over others. Chapter 3 reviews this approach and argues that the modes of influence people use, as well as their success rate, shape both their own and others' images of them as relatively powerful or powerless. A fourth approach used by psychology identifies the feeling of power as a *trait or state of the individual* and focuses on the causes and correlates of this feeling. As seen in Chapter 4, people differ in their definitions of what it means to feel powerful; a person may well feel powerful even though he or she does not conform to another's image of a powerful person. Finally, as described in Chapter 5, psychology looks at power from the viewpoint of *social structure,* by studying the origin and maintenance of dominance hierarchies and status differences in social groups. Here again, the image of power is relevant, as it turns out that maintaining one's position in a status hierarchy is in many ways a matter of maintaining a certain image. Society's images of power and powerlessness, then, provide a framework that links all the various psychological approaches to understanding power. Now let us examine those images.

POWERFUL IMAGES

In the 1950s, three researchers developed a method for measuring the shades of meaning that people attach to certain words and concepts (Osgood, Suci,

& Tannenbaum, 1957). Using what is known at the "semantic differential" technique, they asked people to rate the meaning of various words on huge lists of bipolar adjectives. These ratings were analyzed to uncover the underlying dimensions that people used in their reactions to the various words. The analyses led to the conclusion that people's responses tended to cluster around three major dimensions—called evaluation, activity, and potency by the researchers—and a number of minor ones. The potency dimension was made up of adjectives such as strong-weak, large-small, and heavy-light. It is of special interest here because its ubiquitous presence in people's ratings of words and concepts implies that something very much like power is one of the main yardsticks used to characterize a large variety of images. Power, it seems, is an important component of people's evaluation of the roles, activities, and other people that they encounter.

If the dimension of power stands out in the assessment of virtually all images, it becomes especially obvious in particular instances. Certain kinds of people or figures, for example, are routinely described as powerful, and an examination of these types can lead to an appreciation of the many aspects of power.

Perhaps the largest number of human notions of power have found expression in the images of gods. The Judeo-Christian image of God is of a being who is all-powerful by virtue of being everywhere, seeing and knowing everything, and being able to change anything. God is usually seen as a kind of ultimate patriarch whose power, because it is supernatural and without limits, is unchallengeable by human beings. Some of the awe that people accord to this kind of supernatural or spiritual power is also given to those who are believed to have a special link to it—priests, prophets, gurus, faith healers, witches, sorcerers, mystics. Such people are viewed as having access to a kind of spiritual power that is mysterious to everyone else, and they derive their influence over others from this perception.

Another source of power is physical strength and skill, a quality that is part of many images of powerful people. The champion boxer or wrestler, the world class runner, jumper, or discus-thrower, the "fastest gun," and even the person who simply looks too tough to tangle with are surrounded to some extent with an aura of power.

In the areas of politics and economics, people who hold formal authority and who control vast resources are certainly seen as powerful. When people envy others in such positions, it is usually not for the quality of their jobs, but for the speed with which, so it appears, that everyone does their bidding.

Still other people are viewed as powerful because of a certain personal magnetism, attractiveness, or charisma that allows them to charm others. Celebrities or "stars" are often seen as deriving some of their power in this way.

Individuals who have access to information, particularly information that others do not have or cannot understand, and that can have important effects, are also seen as powerful. Various experts, healers, and fixers are treated with respect in our society, and the image of the "mad scientist" wreaking some kind of total havoc on an uncomprehending world has been popular in horror movies for years. Clearly, specialized knowledge is seen as a source of power.

Although all these images are stereotypic, they provide some clues about the reasons for attributing power to a given individual. All of them describe individuals who, because of certain attributes, are able both to act more autonomously than others and to exert more influence than others do on their environment. Often the perceived power of an individual derives from a combination of these qualities. For example, the head of state in a particular country may be seen as a spiritual leader and may be very charismatic, as well as having formal authority. These qualities form the bases on which that person's power rests. If such a person is discredited as a spiritual leader, for example, some of the power will be lost, even if the person's behavior remains exactly the same. The bases of power are discussed in more detail in Chapter 3, but for the time being it is important to remember that others' *perceptions* of an individual are crucial to that person's ability to exercise power.

GENDER AND THE IMAGES OF POWER

In reviewing the list of stereotypic images of power just discussed, most readers will find that the examples of powerful people brought to mind are male. The image of God in Christian, Jewish, and Moslem cultures is definitely male, and most people who are thought to have spiritual power by virtue of a special link to God are men. In the majority of religions, women are barred from positions as priests, ministers, rabbis, mullahs, or shamans. Indeed, as discussed later, history records that women who did show evidence of some special link with the supernatural were more likely presumed to have forged an alliance with the devil than with God, and were executed as witches. Some women have, however, managed to be taken seriously in this area and have left their mark on the world's religions (for example, Mary Baker Eddy, the founder of Christian Science; Saint Teresa of Avila, the eminent Catholic mystic; Ellen White, the founder of the Seventh Day Adventist Church). For the most part, however, although various societies have attributed all manner of magical and mysterious powers to women in connection with menstruation, pregnancy, and childbirth, such powers have rarely in recent times given women the kind of "middle-person" legitimacy between God and the community that has been granted to male priests and medicine men.

Examples of people who are seen as physically powerful are also generally male. Although some of us can, with some effort, come up with the names of champion (and undeniably strong) pentatheletes Diane Jones Konakowski and Jane Frederick, most of our images of the physically strong are not female. Few people worry about a woman coming up behind them on a dark street.

In politics and economics, when most people think of a president, prime minister, chairman of the board, bank manager, or corporation owner, they think of a man—despite the fact that women can, and do, hold these positions. And in the realm of expertise, female doctors, lawyers, professors, auto mechanics, plumbers, and accountants are still trusted less than their male counterparts by many people, and are not even acknowledged to exist by many others.

Perhaps only in the realm of power based on attractiveness, charisma, and personal magnetism do female power images compete with male ones. A beautiful, charming woman is said to be able to "wrap a man around her little finger," just as a suave, handsome man is thought to be able to influence women to "lose their heads" and act against their better judgment. In the performing arts, where success often requires a combination of beauty, charm, and talent, many women have achieved considerable power.

The high proportion of male to female powerful images is not at all surprising when considered in the light of research on sex stereotypes. A large body of research in psychology has shown that men and women are often thought of as opposite sides of duality—men are strong, independent, worldly, aggressive, ambitious, logical, and rough; women are weak dependent, passive, not worldly, not ambitious, illogical, and gentle (Broverman, Vogel, Broverman, Clarkson, & Rosenkrantz, 1972). The most positively valued traits for males have to do with competence; those for females are concerned with warmth and expressiveness (Broverman et al., 1972;

McKee & Sherriffs, 1957). Portrayals of males and females based on these stereotypic notions bombard us through the media. In books written for children, boys have long been portrayed as doers and inventors; girls (if portrayed at all) are watchers from the sidelines and users of boys' inventions (Key, 1975), although most publishers of children's books, especially since the mid-1970s, are consciously trying to change such images. Women in women's magazines are generally portrayed as passive, and ambitious women are depicted as ending up lonely and bitter (Flora, 1971; Franzwa, 1975). In popular songs, women are pictured as passive, dependent, emotional, and sentimental, while men are more likely to be sexually aggressive, nonconforming, egotistical, and adventuresome (Chafetz, 1974; Marks, 1979). On television, similar stereotypes predominate in children's programming (Levinson, 1975; Sternglanz & Serbin, 1974; Feshbach, Dillman, & Jordan, 1979), commercials (McArthur & Resko, 1975), and adult programs (McLaughlin, 1975; Finz & Waters, 1976). In fact, we are surrounded with messages that males can be powerful, but females cannot, or that women's only effective source of influence is beauty and sex appeal.

These messages from the media, like other varieties of social prejudice, have such a self-fulfilling quality that it is difficult to say how and when the stereotypes got started and how the cycle can be broken. Moreover, the issue of power is so intertwined with the issue of gender in these stereotypes that it becomes impossible to separate the two. Are women seldom elevated to positions of power because they are stereotyped as weak and passive, or are they stereotyped as weak because they rarely are seen in powerful positions? Both processes probably operate together to form a vicious circle. In fact, a number of researchers and writers have argued that sex differences and power differences are irretrievably confounded with each other because females are automatically given lower status than males (for example, Hacker, 1951; Henley, 1977; Janeway, 1974; Unger, 1978).

The notion of an automatic male-female status differential will surface repeatedly in this book, as it seems to be one of the keys to understanding power relationships between men and women. The term *status* refers to an individual's position in a hierarchy of power relations within a social group. People tend more or less automatically to attribute a relative status to others, and this attributed status is based both on achievement and ascription. While achieved status is based on the role one performs and how well one performs it, ascribed status is based on personal characteristics, such as age, class, race, sex, and appearance. Research shows clearly that the ascribed status of females is consistently lower than that of males, and the effect is so strong that when women are seen to be "invading" a particular high-status occupation, the rated status of that occupation drops significantly (Touhey, 1974).

If people use sex as a status characteristic, they are likely to attribute different statuses to males and females performing the same roles. Thus, for example, a male bank teller may be ascribed more status than a female bank teller (perhaps it is assumed that *he* is a management trainee). The higher status person is more likely than the lower status one to be listened to, treated with respect, and have his or her advice followed. Moreover, this theory suggests that a woman in a high-status role finds herself in a position of *status incongruity,* in which the high achieved status of her role conflicts with the low ascribed status of her sex. Others who meet her may feel uncomfortable with this double status message and may not know how to treat her, or they may resent her implied attempt to interfere with the social structure by trying to raise her own status. This phenomenon may be partially responsible for the traditional distaste with which powerful women have been viewed, as discussed later in this chapter.

MALE AND FEMALE IMAGES OF POWER

Do women and men hold different images of power and powerful people? Research suggests that, although both sexes do generally attribute more power to males than females, women may show this pattern less strongly. In one study (Lips, 1981), 562 students taking introductory psychology were asked to list and describe the most powerful person they knew. Of 166 males who responded by listing someone whose sex could be identified, 151, or 91 percent, named a male; only 15, or 9 percent, named a female as the most powerful person they knew. Among the 209 females whose response could be coded for sex, 145, or 69.4 percent, listed a male and 64, or 30.6 percent, listed a female as their choice for the most powerful person. Thus, as a group, the females seemed to find it easier than males to view women as powerful, but the predominant tendency for both sexes was, nonetheless, to think of men when thinking of powerful figures.

Some interesting differences appeared between males and females in the types of individuals they chose as powerful others. Although members of both sexes showed some tendency to name their fathers as powerful people (24.4 percent of the males and 28.3 percent of the females did so), only the females showed any appreciable tendency to name their mothers (16.5 percent of the females, but only 2.2 percent of the males). Also, 17.9 percent of the females listed a friend as the powerful person; only 11.8 percent of the males did so. Finally, there was a greater tendency among the males (23 percent) than among the females (10.6 percent) to choose an individual not personally known to them as their most powerful person.

Although these findings indicate that both sexes tend to see the male rather than the female as powerful, they also suggest that there may be some differences in the images of power held by women and men. Such differences and their implications merit further study.

Research on sex stereotyping and on gender and power images, then, suggests that men are more likely than women to be seen as powerful and strong; women are more frequently associated with powerlessness and weakness. Real life is never quite as simple as the stereotypes that depict it, however, and powerful women and powerless men *do* exist. What response greets these "exceptions" to the rules? Experience tells us that they are viewed with distaste, treated with ridicule (the "hen-pecked husband") or hostility (the "castrating bitch"), and, if possible, dismissed. Clearly, the idea of weak men and strong women implies a threat to the existing status hierarchy and creates a lot of discomfort. The next section examines some of the ways in which this discomfort is manifested with regard to powerful women.

Many people who are trying to restructure the relationships between women and men in the direction of greater equality find the issue of power to be problematic. While trying to break free of sexual stereotypes, they are torn between the desire to increase their power and the distaste they feel for the idea of imposing their will on others. Those involved in the women's movement, for instance, often question the ethics of building up power that can be exerted over others, sometimes fear and mistrust powerful individuals within their own ranks, and are wary of becoming part of powerful institutions. The image of power, although attractive, is in many ways a dangerous one. In the following section we examine, from a philosophical viewpoint, some of the thinking about power and the place of power in the relationship between the sexes that has characterized Western society. Here we can see that ambivalence toward power, and particularly toward powerful women, is certainly nothing new.

POWER AS A DOUBLE-EDGED SWORD

Viewed from an ethical standpoint, power is a very complex concept. Since it can be labeled as either good or evil depending on the context, power is often the object of ambivalent reactions when presented in the abstract.

In its positive sense, power is viewed as something good because it enables the power holder to do (intentionally) something perceived as valuable. The powers, for example, of aptitude and determination necessary to succeed in medical school are viewed in a positive light, as is the power of Jesus to heal the sick.

But this condition of power as a good—that of being productive of valued ends—cannot stand alone. For power, if it is to be thought of as a good, must be achieved and exercised in ways deemed worthy of respect as well. Thus, in general, to command admiration for one's power, one must be viewed as having achieved power through legitimate means. For example, the power of a civil servant may be seen as evil if it is suspected that the position of power was obtained through political connections. Similarly, although the power of an athlete is usually praised and celebrated, if it is discovered that an athlete's muscular power has increased due to drug use, the power becomes the object of contempt.

Besides the manner of achievement, the manner in which power is exercised seems to be involved in an ethical evaluation of the power concept. The frequently heard phrase "abuse of power" testifies to the importance of this consideration. Although a person may have rightfully gained a position of power and may use it to further valuable ends, if its exercise is seen as undemocratic, tyrannical, ruthless, devious, manipulative, or even mysterious, the result is a very negative image of power.

In general, then, there seem to be three central considerations involved in ethical evaluations of power: the *source* of or means by which it is gained, the *manner of its employment,* and the intended *effects* of its use. Power can be termed a "double-edged sword" because of the wide variety of ethical connotations attached to particular powers in relation to these three considerations. In the abstract sense, power as a good can be defined as the ability to realize valuable intended effects without resort to unethical means of achieving or exercising that ability. And, logically speaking, power as an evil in the abstract sense is simply the negation of this definition. Hence, any power that is directed toward something judged evil or undesirable, or that is viewed as undeserved or exercised in a malicious or otherwise immoral manner, will, in all probability, have a negative, evil image.

This analysis helps to explain why people so often differ in their evaluations of particular powers. There are those, for instance, who claim that any power advantage resting on material wealth is undeserved and hence evil, while others view such power as deserved and praiseworthy if gained through hard work, or even if inherited. It also helps to explain the similarities in many people's reactions to some examples of power. The sinister nature of the power exerted by such leaders as Adolf Hitler, Charles Manson, and Jim Jones is a matter of fairly general agreement. These men appear to us as evil geniuses and mesmerizers, who caused others to lose sight of what is deemed good sense and to surrender their self-control. Their power seems to have been based on a strange charismatic type of personality, and perhaps on certain needs of their followers, rather than on a legitimate authority (such as knowledge or moral character). In fact, on all three counts, this type of power seems evil: it has destructive effects, is undeserved, and its employment seems to rest on what could be called psychological coercion.

Power's dual image is brought out clearly in a consideration of human views of nature. Nature the bountiful, the life-giver, the healer, the beautiful—all are images of nature as a good and powerful force. We often praise and rejoice in nature when it acts in accordance with human needs. But nature is also a potent source of danger and destruction. Natural disasters such as floods, droughts, hurricanes, earthquakes, and volcanic eruptions make us painfully aware of humanity's limitations in controlling nature. From the human perspective, the results of such natural powers are evil, and so nature seems a cruel monster as well as a bountiful mother.

It is interesting to note here that natural phenomena are often referred to as female. The more unruly acts of nature, in particular, seem to conjure up visions of women. Only recently have the names of hurricanes, once all female, been changed to include, on a rotating basis, male names as well. Some theorists account for the identification of nature as female in terms of androcentric, or male-centered, culture and male resentment of natural and female powers that are not of the bountiful-mother type. Although such powers may be reluctantly admired, ultimately they are viewed as a challenge to male authority, a challenge that should be conquered, tamed, or subdued. (The evil image of female power is discussed at greater length in the next section.)

The evil potential of power is often cited in relation to its effects on the power holders themselves. In fact, the phrase "power corrupts" is treated by many as though it represented an absolute truth. The cliché is applied particularly to organizational and political power, and to most it appears well confirmed if corruption is defined loosely as any change for the worse morally. The endeavors known as "empire building" and the documented sadistic treatment of inmates by staff at prisons and mental institutions (for example, Chesler, 1973) are viewed as concrete expressions of the corrupting influence that power can exert on those who wield it.

Many thinkers have argued against absolute acceptance of the notion that power corrupts. Some claim that if power is sought after and used as a means to a noble end, or if it is used only in conjunction with other virtues such as love and justice, power need not corrupt (for example, Tillich, 1971). In the political arena, philosophers have often urged various institutionalized checks and restraints so that the final policies of a governing body represent a "balanced" view (for example, Russell, 1938; Girvetz, 1963). The plethora of committees that emerge in so many Western organizations may be a response to the ingrained idea that power must be spread around if corruption is to be reduced or at least made less damaging. In general, fear of this evil aspect of power has played a significant role in the demand for democratization in all our institutions—family, school, workplace, government.

Feminist groups constitute a good example of what happens when power is viewed with suspicion. Initially, many such groups actively avoided having formal leaders in order to avoid the negative effects of power. After a time, however, a more sophisticated approach gained ground, and it was recognized that a lack of structured leadership can sometimes pave the way for unchecked tyranny by informal "leaders" (Freeman, 1973). However, some feminists still voice skepticism about those in power, even when the powerful are also of feminist persuasion. Especially disfavored is domination or power over others (for example, Rich, 1976). Power to transform society and to control one's own life are viewed as valuable aims, distinct from domination. Thus, many consider power corrupting when exercised over others, but liberating when channeled into the constructive changing of self and society. Admittedly, however, it is difficult to draw a clear line here: it is questionable whether the transforming power can be attained without, in some sense, power over others.

The concept of power has become the subject of a critique in which feminists are playing a large part. It is argued, for example, that power over others should be avoided because that power is somewhat addictive. Those who gain power are seen as losing sight of their original values and concerns, or at least as making such values and concerns subsidiary to maintaining or increasing personal power. Political campaigns make many people cynical because politicians, caught up in a drive for power, say what they think voters want to hear, rather than presenting their genuine beliefs. Such observations give rise to the idea that many people, having had a taste of power, cannot or will not give it up. The negative associations attached to the label "power hungry" also point to this dark side of power. It appears, then, that the "evil edge" of the power concept contains recognition of the damage that power can wreak, not only on those influenced by it, but also on the power holders themselves.

POWERFUL WOMAN, POWERFUL MAN: A DOUBLE STANDARD?

The dichotomy in the power concept is particularly apparent in the way that powerful women, as opposed to powerful men, are viewed in the popular imagination. At first glance, a double standard seems to operate here: powerful men are far more likely than powerful women to be thought of in a positive light, with admiration and reverence. A closer look reveals that the double standard is actually somewhat more complex. The way in which the power is exerted and the purposes for which it is used have an important bearing on the evaluation of the powerful person. A man, for example, who uses power in an open, direct, or confronting way, for purposes of self-assertion, showing strength, or winning, is likely to be evaluated more positively than is a woman using power in similar ways. On the other hand, a man who uses his power to promote compromise or understanding may be taking a larger risk of being evaluated as weak and of losing his power than would a woman. Historically, for instance, male politicians whose international strategy has been to "bomb the hell out of them" have been extremely popular, while those who have become known as peacemakers (such as Woodrow Wilson, Neville Chamberlain, George McGovern, or Jimmy Carter) have been regarded as weak or even emasculated with the sexual slur that they "have no balls." The *content* of the negative or positive evaluation reveals the double standard: a woman such as Mother Theresa of Calcutta, using power in a nurturing or selfless way, may be viewed positively as both strong and feminine; a woman using power in a more selfish, assertive, competitive, or domineering way risks a negative evaluation that includes loss of femininity. A man using power in a selfish, assertive, competitive, or domineering way may sometimes be personally disliked, but he is often admired, and he certainly risks no impugning of his masculinity. A man who uses his power in a compassionate and caring way does take such a risk.

The evil associated with assertively powerful women is a common theme in literature and other media. A stereotype in vogue in the early 1980s, and utilized a great deal in television programs, is that of the career-minded woman who loses sight of all noble values and feminine virtues in the competitive struggle for success. The late 1970s movie *Network*, featuring Faye Dunaway as a very powerful television executive, is a good case in point. The executive is portrayed as being so obsessed with power that she would stop at literally nothing to increase her station's ratings. Another media stereotype is that of the woman who, placed in a position of control over others, becomes completely domineering and smothering in her exercise of authority. Ken Kesey's (1962) "Big Nurse" in *One Flew Over the Cuckoo's Nest* is a well-known illustration.

Why is it that power in the hands of a woman is often judged and portrayed as sinister and dangerous? Possibly part of the reason is that women often exert their power in a different manner than men do. As discussed in Chapter 3, women may rely on less direct forms of influence than men because they have less access to traditional avenues of power and have been encouraged to use "feminine charms and wiles" to realize their desires. But when the successful use of power is covert or manipulative, as it is with such methods of influence, we are likely to view the power wielder as duping others, and we judge the person's behavior as unfair. Think, for example, of the stereotype of the scheming woman attempting to persuade her husband to buy her something. She is not openly assertive, she is devious. Her power, although pitiful, is judged harshly.

Such supposed differences in the styles of power exertion do not, however, account for the negative reaction to and portrayal of women who are powerful in the same way as men are powerful—women such as England's Prime Minister, Margaret Thatcher. Journalists often refer to Thatcher as "the iron maiden" and "Attila the Hen." Such epithets, even if they were masculinized, would not be applied to a man behaving in a similar fashion, and one cannot help but suspect that their use represents an uneasy attempt to trivialize or make ridiculous the notion of a woman holding so much formal power. Although powerful male politicians are often caricatured, their masculinity is seldom called into question in public, while slurs upon the femininity of a powerful female politician are frequent. The masculinity of male politicians is, on the other hand, questioned only if they appear weak, as in the case of Senator Edmund Muskie, who lost popularity in the 1970s after an incident in which he cried in public.

The explanation for the adverse reaction to politically powerful women may lie in an analysis of the concepts of man and woman in our androcentric world. Simone de Beauvoir (1952) uses the characterization of woman as "the Other" to demonstrate that the story of the world, our values, and concepts have been determined from the male perspective. She suggests that woman is always defined in relation to man, and that whenever a woman tries to behave in a fully human fashion, she is accused of trying to act like a man.

De Beauvoir's analysis is not inconsistent with the notion of status incongruity discussed in the first part of this chapter. A person (woman) with low ascribed status who gains higher achieved status through a particular role may be ridiculed and accused of trying to emulate members of a group with higher ascribed status (men) simply because her increase in achieved status threatens the ascribed status differential between the two groups (women and men). These accusations may come from both women and men, as both sexes have been well trained in the ideology that de Beauvoir describes. In fact, many women have been, and continue to be, strong proponents of the idea that women should be subordinate to men, as witnessed by the popularity of the "Total Woman" movement. The situation is reminiscent of the hostility directed toward black Americans in the early days of the civil rights movement when they tried to "act like whites" by sitting at the same lunch counters, riding at the front of the bus, and demanding the same education and occupational advantages.

The sexual stereotypes discussed earlier also reinforce the idea that a woman acting in a powerful way is behaving like a man. Since femininity has been associated with such qualities as weakness, passivity, dependence, emotionality, irrationality, subservience, the body and temptation, while masculinity has been associated with potency, action, independence, rationality, domination, the mind, and moral purpose, men who exercise power typically risk no reduction of their manliness in the eyes of others. Women with power risk being viewed as unwomanly or unfeminine. The concept of "power" just does not seem to fit or mesh with the concept of "woman." When the two concepts are forced together, the result is the contradiction of the unwomanly woman. It is hardly surprising, then, that powerful women are subjected to extremely pejorative labels: castrating bitch, ball-breaker, iron maiden, witch.

The witch is, in fact, an excellent historical case of the patriarchy's response to female power.

The Powerful Woman as Witch

As far as we know, people began to be persecuted as witches in the thirteenth century. With the publication of the *Malleus Maleficarum* (*Hammer Against Witches*) in 1486 and its sanctification by Pope Innocent VIII, the witch hunt became especially vigorous. Historians estimate that anywhere from one to nine million people, the vast majority (85 percent) of them female, were put to death for being judged guilty of witchcraft or died in the process of (and as a result of) judicial proceedings (Dworkin 1974). Feminist theorists compare it to the Nazi holocaust (for example, Ruether, 1975; Raymond, 1978).

The *Malleus Maleficarum* argued that women were particularly susceptible to witchcraft due to their light-minded, fickle, lustful natures (Sprenger & Kramer, 1971). Men were thought to be immune to the curse of witchcraft by virtue of the fact of Jesus's maleness. The authors were obsessed and deluded about female sexuality, and they painted vivid fantasies of women engaging in erotic debauchery with Satan. They also provided thorough instructions on trial procedures and the extraction of confessions through extraordinarily sadistic forms of torture, such as the witches' chair, thumbscrews, the rack, starvation, beatings, and spikes.

Accusations that brought women to trial for witchcraft fall into three main categories: sexual crimes (such as copulation with the devil or causing a man to be impotent), being organized (meeting in groups), and possession of magical powers affecting health. In their book *Witches, Midwives and Nurses: A History of Women Healers,* Barbara Ehrenreich and Deirdre English (1973) argue that many of those accused and condemned were simply peasant women who had power—power to heal through their knowledge of herbs and other "folk remedies" and midwifery. The fact that these women healers existed at a time when the medical profession was becoming a respected field of masculine endeavor is cited to explain, in part, the resentment they aroused. Because they commanded respect among the peasantry, these wise women angered authorities in the medical field and worried and annoyed rulers in both the church and state. As Ehrenreich and English say, "The real issue was control: Male upper class healing under the auspices of the Church was acceptable, female healing as part of a peasant subculture was not" (p. 11).

Mary Daly (1978) cites the abandonment, in the sixteenth century, of the legal distinction between "good witch" and "bad witch" as evidence of the patriarchy's resentment of all female powers—even those directed to good purposes such as health. Speaking of the status of the victims, Daly says, "They constituted a threat to the rising professional hierarchy precisely as possessors of (unlegitimated) higher learning, that is, of spiritual wisdom and healing—and of the highly independent character that accompanies such wisdom" (p. 195). Shedding further light on the reasons behind the witch craze and on the types of women selected as witches, scholar H. C. Erik Midelfort (1972) claims that the small witch trials "served a function, delineating the social thresholds of eccentricity tolerable to society, and registering fear of a socially indigestible group, unmarried women . . . until single women found a more comfortable place in the concepts and communities of western men, one could argue that they were a socially disruptive element, at least when they lived without family and without patriarchal control" (pp. 195-196).

Thus, these women healers and/or nonconformists were seen as dangerous because their power was felt as detrimental to established male status and authority in the state, church, and medical fields. They were also seen as dangerous because of their sexuality. Remember that women have been stereotypically depicted not only as weak, but also as mysterious, and that sexuality and personal magnetism are the only sources of power routinely attributed to women. The image of the witch combined the notion of mystery with that of "devouring" female sexuality, and the result was no doubt very frightening. Men's fear of female sexuality (and their own) led to the depiction of the witch as a woman who lusted after the devil and who derived much pleasure from magically removing "the male organ." The male fear, in fact, seems far better suited to the label "castration complex" than anything given us by Freud!

Clearly, the fear and hostility toward powerful women is not "natural," but cultural. Not all cultures have been similar to the Judaeo-Christian one in their reactions to women seen to have supernatural powers. In a few societies, such women are or have been known as sorceresses and treated with respect similar to that accorded male sorcerers. For example, MacCormack (1977) describes the sacred society of women in the Sherbro and Mende cultures in Sierra Leone. Initiates into the society learn to take control of their reproduction and sexuality and to heal various illnesses. Women in commanding roles in this society are treated with reverence and respect, and they exert significant political force. In another example, studies of the ancient Navajo culture found that the "medicine man" or chanter—the most powerful religious figures—could be either a man or a woman (Downs, 1972). Finally, Castaneda (1977) in *The Second Ring of Power*, which might be termed a semifictional account of Yaqui Indian religion, describes some truly awesome sorceresses.

The witch craze serves as an excellent, although perhaps extreme, example of how, in a culture that stresses male authority over women, power's dark side is overemphasized when it is wielded by a woman. This belief in male authority is a strong element of our own culture, as demonstrated by the depiction of powerful women in our religious and mythological heritage, and in popular culture today.

Anyone reasonably well acquainted with Greek and Roman mythology and the Judeo-Christian tradition can verify that women, to a greater degree than men, appear as agents of evil. Eve in the biblical story of "The Fall" and the Sirens in Homer's *Odyssey* share in the same image—the temptress who tests men's ability to resist evil. Women, especially attractive ones, are thought to be dangerous and hence evil because men are distracted by them from the path of righteousness. In Christianity, for example, since the highest achievement was to be in spiritual communion with a noncorporeal god, whatever distracted a man from contemplation of the godhead was viewed as despicable. Normal sexual desire caused men to be attracted—and therefore distracted—by women, and hence to view them and to portray them in myth as dangerous and evil. This male perspective also accounts for the frequency with which the clergy have admonished women to dress modestly. As de Beauvoir (1952) says, "In a religion that holds the flesh accursed, woman becomes the devil's most fearsome temptation" (p. 110).

Many historians and feminist theorists have claimed that prior to the establishment of patriarchal religions and gods, there existed goddesses as the chief objects of worship (for example, Campbell, 1959; Harrison, 1963; Levy, 1963). Adrienne Rich (1976) argues that goddess worship was due to the mystery and profound reverence surrounding female procreative power and its important fertility associations. In tracing the origins of patriarchal society, Rich cites as crucial the moment "when man discovers that it is he himself, not the moon or the spring rains or the spirits of the dead, who impregnates the woman; that the child she carries and gives birth to is *his* child, who can make *him* immortal, both mystically, by propitiating the gods with prayers and sacrifices, when he is dead, and concretely, by receiving the patrimony from him" (p. 44). She argues that this recognition was responsible, in part, not only for the rise of the patriarchal family with its emphasis on sexual possession, monogamy, and the economic dependence of women, but also for the demise of the great goddesses. As male authority became more firmly entrenched, goddesses began to change character and to lose status through gaining a more powerful husband or son, and sometimes their worship was forbidden. In general, the goddess image changed from benevolent earth-mother types (Demeter, Cybele, Artemis) to temptresses (Pandora, Hera) and destructive mothers (Gaea, Kali, Medea, Clytemnestra). Again, it is not un-reasonable to conclude that androcentrism, or even misogyny (hatred of women), lies behind these negative images of female power.

The contention that society views a female power holder more nega-tively than a male power holder is further supported by present-day examples. Consider, for instance, the images of the mother. Although the role of mother is one in which women's influence, and thus power, is accepted, a mother must be careful to be a "giver," serving others, sacrificing her own interests, and deriving her satisfaction from her family's achievements in order to be revered. If the mother, however, is one who dominates her children, or if she demands some concrete recognition of her own needs, her power is perceived less positively. Even when she is self-sacrificing, she may be portrayed as life-sucking and castrating—as in the novel *Portnoy's Complaint* (Roth, 1967). When in a more self-asserting role, she may be considered unreasonably selfish and neglectful of her children's welfare—an image that proponents of day care have repeatedly tried to counteract. The fact that the term "maternal depriva-tion" is still used in reference to neglected children testifies both to sex-role stereotypes regarding the care of children and to the evil power associated with women as mothers.

Another brief example comes from the women's movement. Feminists long ago became aware of the fact that obstacles to women's achieving power are great not only because of the changes implied in and for women, but be-cause of the necessity for a drastic change—reduction, sharing, or de-emphasis of power—for men as well. Since this change is highly distasteful and upsetting to many people, it is not surprising that feminists are often portrayed by the media as strident, hostile women who desire and demand more than the equality they deserve.

A final example of society's views of powerful women can be found in their fictional treatment in literature and films. Here, the powerful woman is often depicted as something to be conquered or a prize to be won by the hero. Initially she resists the man's charms and advances, but, ultimately, she sub-mits. If she does not, her refusal is explained as the result of her problems with sexuality and emotions (she is a lesbian or frigid). The most blatantly sexist scenarios show an initially assertive woman persistently refusing a man's attentions until he physically imposes an embrace upon her, pinning her to the floor/wall/bed. She tries "in vain" to fight him off . . . and then, secretly wanting to be "taken," she melts in his arms. This is a male-centered fantasy, but one that, because of our patriarchal culture, both men and women have been programmed to expect as normal.

Thus, a series of examples suggest that in a male-centered society the image of the powerful woman is full of danger and challenge. When a woman rejects the more limited and passive roles consistent with the female stereotype and openly attempts to exercise power in her life or over that of others, she risks losing femininity in the eyes of others—women as well as men. She becomes a threat to a social structure that emphasizes the superior status of men and is, therefore, likely to be perceived and portrayed as evil and dangerous.

SUMMARY

Power, the capacity to have an impact on one's environment, is introduced in this chapter as a complex concept. We see that psychologists have approached power from several different directions, to all of which the image of the powerful person has some direct relevance. We see that the perception of a person as powerful can rest on a number of different bases, and that men have more access to most of these bases than women do. In line with this, research shows that stereotypical masculinity is more congruent with an image of powerfulness than is stereotypical femininity, and that higher status is routinely ascribed to men, not to women, in our society. Furthermore, both males and females seem to find it easier to think of men than women as powerful, although the strength of this pro-male bias is somewhat diluted among women.

From a philosophical point of view, power can be a problematic issue, producing both attraction and aversion. Although power is thought of as good and even necessary when it is acquired legitimately and used benevolently for good and useful ends, it is viewed as evil when these conditions are not met. A number of examples suggest that the dark or evil side of power tends to be overemphasized when the power holder is a woman. The image of the powerful woman as evil may be due to one or all of several reasons. A woman exercising power may be seen as threatening to a social hierarchy in which men are ascribed higher status than woman. A powerful woman may behave in a way that is considered unfeminine and, hence, with which other people have not been trained to cope. Because other people do not know how to relate to her, she may suffer rejection and even on occasion be hated, scorned, or feared because she is "unnatural." A powerful woman who exercises power in the so-called feminine modes of trickery, deceit, or manipulation may be held in contempt because such tactics are considered unfair. And, finally, women's power is sometimes attributed to nonrational mysterious, magical, or strong emotional forces associated with sexuality and reproduction, the use of which gives them an "unfair advantage" over men.

The acquisition and use of power, then, although difficult, problematic, and filled with moral dilemmas for members of both sexes, is a source of particular ambivalence for women. The negative image of the overtly powerful women lies at the heart of many of the gender differences in power-related behavior (and the theories about such behavior) that will be discussed in the chapters to follow.

MEN, WOMEN, & THE NEED FOR **POWER**

2

*Individual*s, *especially if they are prominent in public life, almost never say that their actions are motivated by a desire for power; instead they talk of idealistic abstractions such as "service," "duty," "responsibility," or perhaps "legitimate power." This has led some psychologists to conclude that, just as sexuality was repressed and denied during the nineteenth century, so today power strivings are repressed and achieve only disguised expression through defense mechanisms such as distortion, displacement, projection, and rationalization.*

David Winter

It is a truism that certain people seem to need, even crave, power. Indeed, in the history of psychology's concern with the concept of power, the need for power, or power motive, is apparently the first aspect of power to have been studied.

Psychoanalysts Alfred Adler and Karen Horney both wrote of a striving for power that served as compensation for feelings of inferiority. Adler (1927) developed the concept of the "will to power"—a striving that he felt could be found in any person who felt inferior. Since Adler saw society as valuing masculinity over femininity, he felt that power was frequently equated with masculinity, and hence will to power was often especially marked in women. Horney (1942) also discussed a neurotic need for power stemming from feelings of anxiety and inferiority.

In the above conceptions, the power that is sought seems to be some kind of superiority, but another personality theory (Sullivan, 1947) defined the power motive as an impulse toward feelings of ability. Later definitions have described the goal of a power motive as the satisfaction derived from influencing another person (Veroff, 1957), the maintenance of a satisfactory level of control in relations with other people (Schutz, 1958), and the drive to influence others in face-to-face interactions (Uleman, 1966, 1972).

Perhaps the two most commonly accepted definitions of the power motive today in psychology are those of David Winter and David McClelland. Winter (1973) stresses *social* power, and thus defines the power motive as the striving "to produce effects (consciously or unconsciously intended) on the behavior or feelings of another person" (p. 10). McClelland (1975), taking a somewhat broader perspective, argues that "the *goal* of power *motivation* is to *feel powerful,* and that influencing others is only one of many ways of feeling powerful" (p. 17). As we will see in the following section, feeling powerful, when defined and measured by researchers, seems to boil down to the feeling that one is having an impact on the environment.

MEASURING THE POWER MOTIVE

There are many possible ways of trying to measure the strength of a power motive. One may, on the one hand, simply ask a person, "How important is it to you that you hold power over others?" This method has the advantage of being straightforward and the disadvantages of being prone to either dishonesty on the part of the respondent or misunderstanding because questioner and respondent do not share a definition of power. Alternatively, one may observe the individual's behavior. How many obstacles is he or she willing to overcome to obtain power? This method has a great deal of merit as long as the observer and the individual in question agree that "having power" is a crucial aspect of the goal that is being approached. The sheer amount of behavior one might have to observe to determine individual differences in the power motive might, however, be quite staggering.

Psychologists interested in the study of motives such as power have noted that a major difficulty in measurement is that people are not always aware of their own motives, of why they behave as they do. More simply put, people do not always seem to know what they want or why they want it. Thus, the power motive is now usually measured by the Thematic Apperception Test (TAT), which presumably is able to detect and assess even unconscious strivings for power.

The TAT, developed by Murray (1937), involves showing a subject an ambiguous stimulus and requesting that she or he make up a dynamic story about it. The stories are thought to indicate conscious and unconscious motives of the storyteller. Winter (1973), building on the work of several other researchers, adapted the TAT for the measurement of the power motive. A series of pictures is shown with a slide projector to subjects in groups, and the subjects are then asked to write stories about what they see in each picture. Stories are scored using a standardized system developed by Winter. (For a detailed description of the development and use of this scoring system, see Winter [1973]). The subject's score, based on the results for the entire series of stories, is called that person's level of need for power, or *n* Power.

Researchers who use the TAT to measure the strength of motives assume that: (1) a motive can be more or less aroused in an individual depending on circumstances, and therefore can be experimentally changed or manipulated; (2) the same motive is stronger in some people than others; and (3) a person with a habitually strong motive will respond to the TAT in the same way as will a person whose motive has been experimentally aroused. So, the scoring system to arrive at *n* Power, or a person's level of need for power, was developed through a series of experiments in which some subjects were exposed to conditions thought to arouse the power motive and others were not.* The differences in story themes that reliably appeared between aroused

---

*Some of the conditions used to arouse the power motive included being assigned the role of the psychological experimenter (Uleman, 1966), viewing a demonstration of hypnosis (Uleman, 1966), viewing a film of the inauguration oath and address of President John F. Kennedy (Winter, 1967), and imagining a situation where the leader of one's action group has been arrested and the group is deciding what to do (Watson, 1969).

and nonaroused subjects were thought to characterize high and low *n* Power. And taking that assumption further, these same differences in story themes were thought to characterize persons who were habitually high or low in *n* Power.

What kinds of differences in the stories they tell indicate persons high in *n* Power? According to Winter (1973), "Power Imagery is scored if some person or group of persons in the story is concerned about establishing, maintaining or restoring his power—that is, his impact, control or influence over another person, group of persons, or the world at large" (p. 250). Specifically, a person concerned with power can be expected to use three general themes in the stories: someone showing power through powerful actions; doing something that arouses strong positive or negative emotions in others; or showing concern for reputation or position. The general theme of powerful actions can include forceful behavior such as assaults, threats, or insults; sexual exploitation; taking advantage of another's weakness; giving unsolicited help, support, or protection; trying to control another person by regulating behavior or living conditions or by seeking information; trying to influence or persuade another; and trying to impress some other person or the world at large. Each story is scored according to the number of different power imagery categories it contains, and then the scores for all the stories are added up to determine the *n* Power score.*

THE POWER MOTIVE
IN MEN AND WOMEN

Almost all of the original research on *n* Power was done with male subjects. This practice parallels that followed in early research on the achievement motive (McClelland, 1958; McClelland, Atkinson, Clark, & Lowell, 1953). The danger in this exclusive reliance on male subjects is that male and female response patterns may differ, as indeed happened in the research on achievement motivation. When this happens there is a mistaken tendency to define the male response as the norm, and the female response as deviant.† Ignoring

*Some researchers have questioned the usefulness of the *n* Power score, arguing that it cannot be proven to measure actual need for power and that it is unreliable. For a discussion of these issues see Winter (1973).

†When the sexes appear to differ on some characteristic or in their response to a given situation, one can argue just as easily that it is the men who are deviant. Preferably, one can argue that the factors influencing the response are not understood and that an adequate model would explain the behavior of both sexes.

the potential pitfalls of this approach, however, researchers have used male subjects to develop and refine the scoring system for *n* Power, and they have only recently turned their attention to the power motive in females. Therefore, any discussion on female *n* Power is limited by a relative scarcity of information.

Levels and Arousal of *n* Power

The few studies that do report *n* Power scores for both male and female subjects suggest that there is no difference in *n* Power level between men and women under neutral conditions. Moreover, Stewart and Winter (1976) show that *n* Power can be aroused in women using the same procedures as those that work for men—watching a demonstration of hypnosis or listening to excerpts of famous speeches by powerful men. And these procedures produced the same increase in *n* Power scores for women as for men. Furthermore, the stories written by women in response to TAT pictures showed no other (nonpower) themes that were not present in the stories written by men (Winter & Stewart, 1978). Thus, these arousal procedures seem to have the same effect on the power motivation of both women and men.

Although the results indicate that *n* Power can be aroused in women and men by the same experiences, one might think that particular experiences would be associated with *n* Power arousal for each sex. There has been very little research on this question, but one researcher (Stewart, 1975, cited in Winter & Stewart, 1978), thinking that the experience of providing food from their own bodies to dependent infants might arouse feelings of power in nursing mothers, studied the effects on fantasy of nursing a baby. The study revealed no differences in *n* Power between the nursing and control mothers. Other experiences unique to women or men could be studied. Would women respond with increased *n* Power scores to accounts of pregnancy and birth? Would women's or men's *n* Power be aroused differently in response to descriptions of certain sexual scenes? At present, this is unexplored territory.

Correlates of *n* Power

Winter and Stewart (1978) note a distinction between two aspects of the *n* Power score—*Hope of Power* and *Fear of Power*. These concepts represent the approach and avoidance sides of the power motive. Hope of Power implies a tendency to hope for and seek power; Fear of Power is a tendency to fear, mistrust, and avoid power. A person's overall *n* Power score, which represents the total concern with or motivational importance of power, can be broken down into these two categories. Winter and Stewart find, however, that Hope of Power is usually so tied in with overall *n* Power that the two are frequently not separated by researchers. On the other hand, fear of power is not as highly correlated with *n* Power, is not correlated at all with hope of power, and seems to predict different behaviors. In examining the correlates of, or kinds of behaviors related to, the power motive, then, Fear of Power is considered separately.

Hope of Power and n *Power.* As we know, the two sides of *n* Power have been investigated much more thoroughly for men than for women. However, Winter and Stewart (1978) indicate that, at least in some respects, *n* Power predicts similar behaviors for both sexes. For example, in both women and men high *n* Power is associated with acquiring formal institutionalized social power through leadership roles or offices, or through careers such as business executive, teacher, psychologist, or member of the clergy, which involve direct, legitimate interpersonal power over others.*

Winter's (1973) research on college males shows that those high in *n* Power tend to use a variety of tactics to increase their power—writing letters to the university newspaper, gravitating toward positions and locations of inherent power, and taking extreme risks (McClelland & Watson, 1973) to increase their visibility; and they are very concerned with building loyal alliances with friends and expanding their network of social contacts. Jones (cited in Winter & Stewart, 1978) found that, in discussion groups made up of previously unacquainted students, members high in *n* Power talked more and were voted by the others as having most clearly defined the problems, most encouraged others to participate, and most influenced other participants. They were not, however, characterized as offering the best solutions, working hardest, or being best liked. Here again, high *n* Power males seem to increase visibility by speaking up and participating. Unfortunately, no comparable research is available for females.

The overlapping areas of competitiveness and aggressiveness as they relate to *n* Power have also been investigated for men only. Researchers surmise that a power-motivated man would be more likely to aggress or compete to achieve a goal. Although this prediction may have intuitive appeal,

---

*Direct legitimate power involves having the authority to influence others openly (discussed in more detail in Chapter 3). Winter and Stewart note that the important aspect of the careers that correlate with *n* Power seems to be the opportunity to direct others on an individual, immediate basis.

its support from research is slim. Several studies relate n Power to participation in competitive sports and to attendance at games, watching games on television, or reading sports magazines (Winter & Stewart, 1973). Power motivation has also been linked with the frequency of arguments reported (McClelland, 1975) and with such aggressive acts as yelling in traffic, destroying objects, and insulting store clerks. No comparable data is available for women. There is, however, some evidence that women and men sometimes differ in their approach to competition, as we will discuss later.

The behavior of both women and men high in n Power has been investigated in terms of symbols that indicate prestige. For college students of both sexes, the power motive is associated with such "prestige" possessions as television sets and tape recorders, and, for males and females in several economic groups, the power motive is also related to the number of credit cards carried (McClelland, 1975; Winter & Stewart, 1978).

Studies have found that, for males, Hope of Power is positively related to drinking behavior (Winter & Stewart, 1978). McClelland, Davis, Kalin, & Wanner (1972) demonstrated that drinking itself seemed to increase the levels of men's power motive. For women as for men, the power motive is related to drinking history and to consumption of alcohol in a simulated social drinking setting (Wilsnack, 1974). However, there is no evidence that women's n Power scores increase after social drinking. It is supposed that drinking correlates with n Power because alcohol may free the person to feel powerful through fantasy (McClelland et al., 1972). Other behaviors that are thought to help a person feel powerful, such as drug use and risk taking, also are linked with n Power for male subjects. Again, comparable research has not been done with women.

One area in which n Power appears to predict very different behaviors for the sexes is that of male-female relationships. According to Winter and Stewart (1978), men high in n Power have difficulty in their relationships with women and tend to hold an exploitative view of women. Winter (1973) reports that high n Power men tend to have more sexual partners, to prefer wives who are dependent and submissive, and to be interested in pornographic magazines. Slavin (cited in Winter & Stewart, 1978) reports that college men high in n Power showed a tendency to write stories in which women were harmful to men, a tendency that was strongest among high n Power men who were also immature.* Among these immature men, n Power predicted a

*The immature men were "pre-Oedipal," according to the researcher's definition. To be classified in this way, a subject had to report that he resembled his mother more than his father and to not use castration imagery in describing death.

pattern of negative behaviors toward women: having attitudes of male domi-nance about the ideal type of wife, feminism, and female work roles; with-drawal from women; and being directly aggressive toward women.

According to Winter and Stewart (1978), when male college students were asked to draw male and female figures, *n* Power was associated with an emphasis on female breasts and with drawing bizarre, distorted female (but not male) figures. McClelland (1975) found that highly power-motivated men tended to be separated or divorced from their wives. In a study of dating couples (Stewart & Rubin, 1974), Hope of Power among the men was in-versely related to their own and their partner's satisfaction with the dating relationship and positively related to the tendency to anticipate problems in the relationship during the next year. Men's Hope of Power was also negatively related to scores that assessed their love and liking for their part-ners. Finally, a two-year followup showed that couples in which the man scored high in Hope of Power were much more likely to have broken up and much less likely to have married than couples in which the man scored low in Hope of Power. Since the husband's *n* Power is inversely related to the wife's career level in marriages that do last (Winter, Stewart, & McClelland, 1977), one might wonder if power-motivated men find it difficult to tolerate the amount of power sharing that can result from their wives' pursuit of indepen-dent careers.

Converging evidence suggests, then, that high *n* Power men exhibit difficulty and exploitation in their relationships with women. Do power-motivated women show similar tendencies in their relationships with their partners? Apparently not. In the study of dating couples by Stewart and Rubin (1974), the women's Hope of Power scores were not related to their own or their partner's reported satisfaction with the relationship or to their measured love or liking for their partners. Similarly, there was no relation-ship between a woman's Hope of Power score and the tendency for the couple to break up. In an attempt to explain the rather contradictory findings for highly power-motivated women and men, Stewart and Rubin suggest that ". . . whereas men learn to seek power by means of short-term, serial con-quests of women (the Don Juan syndrome), women are more inclined to seek lasting relationships with men as power or prestige 'possessions.' As a result, women high in power motivation may be relatively unlikely to report difficul-ties or to want to dissolve an intimate relationship. Another possible explana-tion is that power-motivated women may be better able to manage conflict than power-motivated men, reflecting a general tendency for women to be socialized to resolve conflicts and to reduce interpersonal tension" (p. 309).

Although their explanations for the behavior of power-motivated women are based on speculation, Stewart and Rubin have touched on an important issue—the way the power motive is expressed by men and women may be tempered by the differing social expectations and roles for the two sexes. We will discuss this point in more detail later in this chapter. Gender characteristics and career and life-style choices would also seem to influence power expressions.

Fear of Power. The avoidance side of the power motive involves sensitivity to power and power relationships, combined with a negative feeling about them. It may include both a negative reaction to others holding power as well as a discomfort with one's own power. Research evidence suggests that Fear of Power derives from the experience of powerlessness. For males, at least, being the youngest member of a relatively large family is connected with high scores on Fear of Power. Comparable data for females are not available, leaving some interesting questions to be answered. Do females experience more powerlessness than males in their early years? Their lesser physical size and strength, along with society's widespread attitudes of male superiority, suggest this is a serious possibility. If women have more experience of powerlessness, are they, then, higher than men in Fear of Power? This is still an open question. As we will see in a later section, there is evidence that women and men differ in their orientation toward power, and some might interpret women's sometimes more accommodative and cooperative behavior in experimental game situations as congruent with a high Fear of Power.

Fear of Power is related to a variety of behaviors for both women and men. Winter and Stewart (1978) report that college students high in Fear of Power tend to view power or authority with distrust and suspicion, and they are protective of their own autonomy and independence. Such students seem to spend time alone, prefer less-structured aspects of academic life (seminars over lectures, papers over exams, freedom of choice over rigid requirements), disregard academic deadlines, and deny the influence of peers over them. They also carefully guard information about themselves, even to the point of lying. Research also suggests that individuals high in Fear of Power use their power to help others: lending their possessions, sharing their knowledge, equalizing the power or resource difference between the helper and the helped. On the other hand, some evidence suggests that situations calling for strong action are met with very high arousal or anxiety and are handled poorly by high Fear of Power individuals. Winter and Stewart suggest that such individuals feel more comfortable and are more effective when acting to help others than when acting for personal gain.

Research is really only beginning, but the results to date suggest that the behaviors accompanying Fear of Power are similar for men and women. It remains to be seen whether this "avoidance" side of the power motive can be useful in understanding some of the differences in the ways women and men handle power.

Gender Roles and the Power Motive

If women and men both have a need for power, must this need always be expressed in similar ways? As noted earlier, research on n Power suggests an association with some different behaviors for women and men. Perhaps social pressures to act feminine or masculine lead to different expressions of the power motive. Indeed, there is some evidence that, for women, the power motive interacts with sex-role concepts or style of self-definition. Winter and Stewart (1978) say that "Among women who are self-defining, . . . [the power motive] . . . predicts behavior in ways closer to the male pattern, whereas among socially defined women, the style traditionally associated with the female role, power motivation predicts power behaviors that are congruent with (and constrained by) that role" (p. 413.)* McClelland (1975) also argues that women in the traditional feminine role develop ways of expressing the power motive that differ from those used by men. The traditional feminine life-style, he says, encourages women to express their power motivation by gathering strength and resources for the purpose of helping others.

However, these authors seem to ignore the possibility that the *male* pattern of power motivation may be affected by gender role. (Perhaps they do not see as wide a variation in male as in female life-style patterns.) It seems quite probable, however, that within each sex there is wide individual variation in the way n Power is expressed, and that some of this variation is related to our socially defined gender roles. Thus, for example, a woman in the traditionally female occupation of homemaker may have less opportunity than a man in the traditionally male occupation of football coach to express n Power through sports or physically aggressive acts, and more opportunity

---

*In the above context, a "self-defining" woman is one who does not allow herself to be defined by traditional social demands. The research referred to here defines self-definition as the attribute that distinguishes college women planning a career from those planning marriage and family without a career.

to express it through acts of nurturing. On the other hand, a man in the less traditionally masculine occupation of artist or musician may have few opportunities to express his power motivation in either aggressive acts or nurturing. In fact, when labeling behaviors or careers as "masculine" or "feminine," it quickly becomes apparent that one of the key aspects of the meaning of these terms is related to the expression of power. The "most masculine" behaviors include elements of toughness and overt dominance, while the "most feminine" ones involve softness and nurturance. This pattern follows the stereotypes of masculinity and femininity discussed in Chapter 1.

Winter (1973) argues that the power motive is connected to the relationship between the sexes on a level that goes deeper than occupational and social roles. Using a blend of psychoanalytic theory and mythology, he says that, for males, the need for power stems from an ambivalent relationship with the mother. The mother is said to be alternately a source of satisfaction and frustration, eliciting both dependence and rage on the part of the son. Although a certain amount of ambivalence is inevitable in any caretaker relationship, Winter suggests that it may be especially pronounced in certain cases. The mother may mix rejection and pleasure in such a complex way that the child cannot develop an unambivalent attitude toward her. She may do this as an act of retaliation against her husband, father, and men in general for her own suppression at their hands. The male child, unable to form a consistent attitude toward his mother, grows up with ambivalent feelings toward women in general. The ambivalence is expressed in a tendency toward sexual dominance and exploitation of the women with whom he forms relationships. Indeed, Winter feels that the archetype of the power motive is the mythical figure of Don Juan—the legendary seducer of women who derived his greatest pleasure from tricking them and leaving them dishonored.

If there is any truth to Winter's argument, the power motive in men is directly related to adult sex roles (the woman as the primary caretaker of children) and the resentment-producing suppression of women by men. However, there is very little evidence for or against his argument, except for the data showing a correlation between male n Power and difficulties in male-female relationships. Furthermore, the argument does not discuss the possible sources of the power motive in women, who, as we have seen, show an average level of n Power equal to that of men. One might argue, of course, that highly power-motivated women experienced similar early ambivalent relationships with their mothers. If this early ambivalence is the source of the power motive, one would, following Winter's logic, expect highly power-motivated women to show difficulties in their relationships with other women rather than with men. Although research indicates that women high in Hope of Power seem to have no special difficulties in their dating relationships with men (Stewart & Rubin, 1974), there is no information at all to assess their relationships with other women.

There may be another explanation why highly power-motivated men may have a tendency to exploit women and highly power-motivated women do not show a tendency to exploit men; the difference may stem from women's financial dependence on men and their risk of pregnancy. Women's exploitation of men may take the form of a "love 'em and hook 'em" philosophy rather than the Don Juan "love 'em and leave 'em" motto. Alternatively, because of men's greater physical strength and greater access to resources, women may simply find them too dangerous a group to exploit; men, on the other hand, may find women an easy group to exploit for precisely the same reasons. Unfortunately, this explanation leaves unanswered the question of how highly power-motivated women and men get that way in the first place.

Much more research on the power motive in women and men is necessary before these issues can be clarified. At the present time what is known about *n* Power in women and men is only enough to provide a few tantalizing clues about the ways in which power interacts with gender role.

INTERACTING IN POWER SITUATIONS

The power motive is defined as a desire to have an impact on one's environment and/or the people in it. Many situations that involve interacting with other people give the individual the opportunity to have such an impact by influencing others, being seen as important, competing and winning, and enhancing visibility. Although the role of power in interpersonal situations is examined throughout this book, the focus here is particularly on *task-oriented* interactions, or working together.

Why include this discussion in a chapter dealing with the power *motive*? First, although there is little research linking *n* Power to behavior when people perform tasks together, many behavioral aspects of *n* Power (seeking visibility and prestige, forming alliances, display, aggression, competition) might be expected to emerge in such situations. And second, research suggests a wide variety of ways in which people try to have an impact on others when they work together. An examination of these different approaches to feelings of power points to some of the directions in which the power motive can be channeled. For instance, a person can often achieve as much impact on others by cooperation as by competition, by sharing resources as by accumulating them for display or status, and by working with others to get a task accomplished as by getting one's own way.

Strategies in Experimental Games

A substantial body of research backs up the idea that there are some differences in the ways women and men approach working on a task with a group. The conclusions come from the study of game situations in which participants attempt to accumulate points in cooperation with or in opposition to one another, and from experiments in which participants in a task are asked to allocate rewards to themselves and others as payment for performance.

In three-person game studies by Bond and Vinacke (1961) and Vinacke (1959), women and men showed different approaches to forming coalitions. Men formed coalitions, or alliances, with other players only when doing so would help them to win the game and to maximize their own gains. Women, on the other hand, formed alliances even when they could have won the game alone. They seemed concerned with achieving the best outcome for all players, so that each player would have a share of the final prize. These differences hold in later research for both single-sex and mixed-sex groups. Worthy of note is the fact that women do as well as or better than men in terms of total points earned, despite the fact that their strategy is what Vinacke calls an "accommodative" rather than an "exploitative" one.

A similar difference in the level of concern with "coming out on top" sometimes seems to characterize the behavior of women and men where rewards are concerned. Early research with groups indicated that, when men were asked to distribute a reward among themselves, they tended to follow a distribution rule based on equity: the allocation of rewards or payment on the basis of perceived performance or input to the task. Women, however, tended to favor a more equal distribution of rewards, regardless of input (see Sampson, 1975, and Deaux, 1976 for reviews of this literature). These results are usually taken to mean that women are often more concerned with interaction of people in a situation, while men emphasize the material rewards. In other words, women and men use different interaction strategies because they have different interaction goals; women choose to safeguard relationships by de-emphasizing status differences even where this means accepting smaller rewards.

The idea that women and men sometimes differ in their goals when interacting with others is supported by research in other areas of social psychology. For example, Stein and Bailey (1973) demonstrated that affiliation with others is an achievement goal for women, and the study by Aries (1976) of small discussion groups showed that all-male groups tended to develop status hierarchies and competition quickly, while females avoided hierarchies and emphasized equal participation. Different situations, however, may affect interaction goals and thus have a great impact on the behavior that individuals choose. Under the proper conditions, then, both males and females may favor equity or equality (Kahn, 1979; Kahn, Nelson, & Gaeddert, 1980). For example, Zanna and Bowden (1977) showed that both women and men allocated rewards equally when relating to others as persons, but they allocated equitably when relating to others as positions or roles. However, when the situation is ambiguous, sex differences still appear. So, Zanna and Bowden found that when the situation was defined as relating to *neither* person nor position, traditional males allocated equitably and traditional females allocated equally.

It appears that under certain conditions women and men, although both concerned about their impact on a situation, may focus on different aspects of that impact. Men may show a tendency to seek impact by winning over others in terms of resources or status. Women may seek impact by becoming well liked and forming friendships. Either goal could reflect the presence of the power motive as well as of other factors.

Perspectives on Ways of Being Powerful

The study of the power motive and its expression points to the conclusion that many behaviors can lead to the experience of power. In this section, we will discuss several perspectives that challenge the stereotype of the power wielder as a dominant exploitative, and competitive individual.

Goodchilds and Johnson: a focus on the task. Although much of their own research on power has focused on dominance, or the successful exertion of influence over others, social psychologists Goodchilds (1979) and Johnson (1979) have recently called for a new emphasis in research on power. Both maintain that an important part of the experience of power is the accomplishment of the task at hand, and they suggest that it is this sense of accomplishment that deserves urgent research attention.

Goodchilds (1979) says that power can be thought of in terms of three "gettings": getting one's way, getting along with others, and getting things done. The first two may often be perceived as conflicting, she argues, but a focus on the third goal often dissolves the conflict. Instead of viewing power as the influence one person exerts over another, then, power could be seen as "an interactive product of persons and resources and situation and action" (p. 3), all combining to produce a desired outcome. Anyone who has worked successfully with a group of others to reach a fund raising goal, to get a new institution off the ground, or to elect a political candidate is well aware of how heady this type of power can be. And, as Johnson (1979) indicates, the key to this experience of power is the confidence that the task to be accomplished is a good and important one.

Can a person find satisfactory expression of the power motive through the group experience of accomplishing a task, or must satisfaction involve striving for impact as an individual? Research so far has concentrated on the individual's need for a sense of effectiveness, but it is possible that this sense could be achieved through collective accomplishments. More research may settle this question. In the meantime, Goodchilds and Johnson have helped to expand the notion of power and how it may be experienced.

Ruth Benedict: synergy. Although she did not focus on power as such, the great anthropologist Ruth Benedict (1970) provided some clues to its use in what she called high-synergy societies. High synergy refers to a situation in which any individual's wealth and accomplishments tend to be mutually beneficial to the whole society and to that particular individual. In a highly synergistic society, the more rewards or resources a person gains, the greater the benefits that accrue both to that individual and to the rest of the society. By contrast, in a low-synergy society, any advantage achieved by one individual is always to the detriment of others in the society.

According to Benedict (1970) and Maslow (1971), one synergistic way for an individual to display power and achieve status is to show off his or her generosity. Indeed, in some societies, the member with the most status is the one who can give away or lend the most goods. Maslow describes the Sun Dance ceremony of the Blackfoot Indians, in which the rich men of the tribe ritually gave away all their accumulated possessions. Such societies have built-in cooperative reward structures, such that an advantage to any one member tends to become an advantage to the whole society. This is not to say that such a social group is noncompetitive. There may, in fact, be a great deal of competitiveness surrounding the display of power through gift-giving. It may also be that the ceremony generates a good deal of resentment among those who are forced to be only recipients because they have nothing to give.

However, the end result of this kind of power display by an individual is that the entire group is materially better off. Under the right conditions, the expression of the power motive by an individual can have some positive results for others.

McClelland: the power of giving in traditional India. McClelland's (1975) analysis of traditional Indian society shows how a culture can be structured so that the major acceptable way to express the power motive is through giving. Although such a system may initially strike some of us as ideal, McClelland's portrayal suggests that it is not without its problems.

According to McClelland, who achieved these insights by analyzing children's stories and other Indian documents, a person in traditional India is thought to accumulate merit and status in proportion to the amount she or he gives to others. One demonstrates moral superiority by being interested in giving rather than receiving. The paradox that one must first accumulate resources in order to give them away causes some conflict, and attempts to gain wealth or position are often rationalized by the thought that this will allow the individual to be more generous. Giving to another also creates or preserves a relative status difference between the giver and the receiver or between two givers; the most generous giver is demonstrating superiority. Thus, there may be unacknowledged contests for dominance in a relationship, waged through mutual attempts to "outgive" the other. McClelland cites the conflict that sometimes occurs in Indian society between a new wife and her husband's mother. The mother has achieved her moral status, and thus her power over her son, through a constant display of giving and self-sacrifice on his behalf. When the new wife moves into the household, as is the custom, her own display of giving and self-sacrifice toward the husband challenges the mother's status. A fierce power struggle may result, with both women trying to gain control over the husband through displays of superior moral merit.

Another aspect of this particular system of power-through-giving is that one cannot win recognition by seeking it, but only by being modest and self-effacing—while hoping someone will notice and commend one's humility! One seeks power by pretending not to seek it. The danger here, of course, is that modesty may work altogether too well, and no one may indeed notice one's self-sacrifice. If one does not extract an expression of appreciation or gratitude for one's humble generosity, then one has not successfully exerted power. This refusal to openly acknowledge one's need to express power through giving is in strong contrast to the example of the Blackfoot Indians mentioned earlier. In the Blackfoot culture, giving is done ritually, and the giver struts, boasts about his wealth, and is anything but self-effacing about his generosity.

The covert attempt to gain power by acting generous and humble is certainly not limited to traditional India. It can be recognized in a kind of "martyr syndrome" that frequently appears in relationships in North America. The parent who exerts control over children by sacrificing so much for them that they are forever bound by a mixture of guilt and gratitude or the spouse who forces the partner to guess his or her preferences while steadfastly maintaining that he or she has none may both be expressing their power needs in unacknowledged ways. This kind of situation may create confusion and resentment precisely because the parties involved do not admit that a need for power is being expressed or that a power struggle is going on. Social psychologists have referred to this unacknowledged kind of power exertion as manipulative or indirect (see Chapter 3), and in Western society it is stereotyped as a feminine power mode. Yet, McClelland's (1975) research indicates that this approach to power is just as prevalent among men as among women in traditional Indian society, and thus suggests that culture rather than sex dictates the ways in which power is sought.

The three examples described in this section point to the fact that, although many people may be motivated to some extent by a similar need for power, its forms of expression can vary widely. The popular stereotype of the power-motivated person as one who gives orders, accumulates and keeps vast personal wealth, and strives for high personal visibility and fame is obviously too narrow. To predict or understand how a power-motivated man or woman will behave, it is necessary to look at the culture and immediate social situation in which that person functions.

SUMMARY

We have seen that the power motive can be defined as the need to feel that one is having an impact on one's environment. To a certain extent, this motive can be aroused by external events and its presence can be assessed by a projective test. Research suggests that men and women show equally strong n Power under arousal conditions and that many of the behaviors associated with n Power are similar for men and women. However, in the area of cross-sex relationships the implications of *n* Power seem to be very different for the two sexes. Highly power-motivated men show difficulties and a tendency to exploitation in their relationships with women; highly power-motivated women seem to show no such pattern in their relationships with men. This difference may well be linked to the sociopolitical context in which male-female relationships take place: the general control of concrete resources by adult males and consequent dependence of females on them for survival, combined perhaps with a pervasive control of personal emotional rewards by adult females, particularly in the mother-child relationship. An understanding of this particular difference in the behavior of high *n* Power women and men may eventually prove to be a key factor in sorting out the reasons for the perennial conflict between the sexes.

In any given situation, the power goal of having an impact may be reached in a variety of different ways. Research suggests that a person may achieve feelings of power by winning, by gaining respect and liking, by accomplishing an important task, by giving away possessions, or even by being pointedly self-sacrificing and modest. Thus, a power-motivated person can express this motivation in many ways, depending on the social circumstances. In the next chapter, we explore in detail the variety of "power styles" that men and women may adopt in their search for impact on their interpersonal environments.

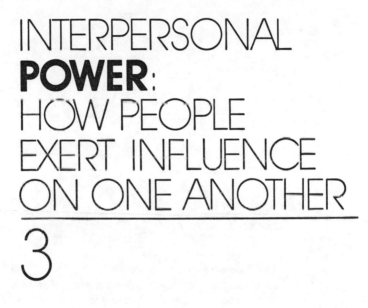

INTERPERSONAL
POWER:
HOW PEOPLE
EXERT INFLUENCE
ON ONE ANOTHER

3

The hand that rocks the cradle rules the world.

Old saying

The "womanly way" is to nag and tease. Women have often been told that if they go about it right that they can get anything. They are encouraged to plot and scheme, and deceive, and wheedle, and coax for things. This is womanly and sweet. Of course, if this fails, they still have tears—they can always cry and have hysterics, and raise hob generally, but they must do it in a womanly way. Will the time ever come when the word "feminine" will have in it no trace of trickery?

Nellie McClung
Manitoba suffragette, 1915

In many circles, "power" is a dirty word. There is a tendency, often seen especially among some of us who consider ourselves feminists or humanists, to disclaim any desire to have power over other people. We argue that each person should have control over his or her own life, and we shrink from the notion of one person or one group controlling another. In our rush to do away with the concept of power, we have sometimes set up, in our own groups, political structures in which permanent leadership has no place. Sometimes these experiments have been successful; at other times they seem to have paved the way for what Jo Freeman (1973) calls the "tyranny of structurelessness." In such a group, many timid souls may watch in helpless, horrified fascination as the group, in which there is no official leader, becomes dominated by an unofficial leader: the person with the loudest voice, the least compromising opinions, and the highest tolerance for conflict. The group, not really understanding how it is happening, may be browbeaten into unhappy submission, wondering if this is what democracy is all about. The point here is *not* that leaderless groups do not work. Rather, it is that the absence of an "official" power holder in a particular situation does not necessarily mean that no one in that situation has power over the other participants.

It is useful to remember that our interactions with others are virtually filled with behaviors related to power and influence. How can I get my students to behave in the way I want them to? How does my coworker always manage to manipulate me into taking public positions with which I am not comfortable? Much of our everyday activity is concerned with trying to exert influence on the people with whom we interact and with responding to pressures of influence directed at us by others. As it relates to interaction among people, psychologists have defined social power as the ability to get others to do what one wants them to do, despite resistance. In fact, the range of behaviors through which one person can move another indicates the amount of power that first person holds in the interaction (Thibaut & Kelley, 1959). Thus, in social psychological terms, *power* is the capacity to affect another person, and *influence* is the use of that capacity. *Control* refers to the successful use of power (Cartwright, 1959).

POWER IN THE CONTEXT
OF SOCIAL EXCHANGE

According to social exchange theory, the capacity of one person to influence another's behavior depends on the first person's control over outcomes or payoffs for the second person (Homans, 1974). Thus, a parent can influence a child to eat vegetables by threatening to withhold dessert. If to the child the rewards of eating dessert outweigh the unpleasantness of eating the vegetables, she or he will probably eat the vegetables, and the parent's exertion of power will have been successful. On the other hand, if the parent cannot offer any inducement or threat that makes the child view eating vegetables as the less costly of two alternatives, the parent will be unable to influence the child's behavior.

It is important to remember that, in any interaction, *both* parties have some control over each other's outcomes. Thus, one person can never have complete or ultimate control over another. In the parent-child example, for instance, although the parent may control access to dessert, toys, television, approval, and so on for the child, the child controls certain outcomes for the parent. By being slow, stubborn, cantankerous, or loudly miserable, the child has the capacity to ruin the parent's dinner and may, therefore, greatly increase the costs to the parent of insisting that the vegetables be eaten.

Who wins out in such an interaction? According to social exchange theory, the outcome is determined by *the principle of least interest.* This principle holds that the party who is least dependent on the other for reward has the greater power in such an interaction. Theoretically, then, if the child sees missing dessert as more costly then the parent sees loss of peace and quiet at the dinner table, the child will eventually give in. However, if the parent is particularly desperate for peace and quiet, the child may well win this skirmish.

Unless one is dealing with an exchange between two strangers who will in all probability never see each other again, it may often be a mistake to consider a single exchange in isolation. The person who has the greater power in a *relationship* with another person is the one who gets least out of the exchanges taken as a whole; that is, the person who needs the relationship least has the most power (Homans, 1974). This generalized power difference between two people may sometimes have an impact on specific exchanges, an impact that could not be predicted merely by stating the immediate rewards and costs to the participants. The parent-child conflict, for instance, takes place in a relationship in which the child almost certainly is much more dependent on the parent for a variety of outcomes, such as food, clothing, shelter, entertainment, love, and approval, than the parent is on the child. The parent also has what Lacey (1979) calls "agenda control," which the child does not have. The child may be able to choose between the outcomes of eating or not eating the vegetables, but it is the parent who decides when dinner will occur, and even whether it will occur at all. Thus, although the child may have the power to win in a particular social exchange with the parent, an awareness or fear (realistic or not) of possible far-reaching consequences may stop the child from exerting this power. In judging power in ongoing social relationships, then, one should consider both the specific exchange and the general power differences between the two people.

The social exchange theory describes power as a matter of negotiation; both parties rationally weigh the costs and rewards of various outcomes that can be brought about by the other person and decide whether to change their behavior. Admittedly, however, emotion can sometimes overwhelm rationality, or people do not see all the possible costs and rewards attached to particular outcomes. Thus, this "payoff" system rationally constructed by the social scientist may often fail to predict the outcomes of social exchange. The criminal cornered by police may try to commit suicide rather than be taken, even though many people would consider death to be a much higher cost than prison. The person who has what Thibaut and Kelley (1959) call "fate control" over another—in the sense, for example, of having the final decision about that person's promotion—may exercise that power without carefully considering the ways in which the supposedly "controlled" person can make life miserable once he or she decides that there is no hope of *ever* getting promoted. Indeed, the very fact that we find it so difficult to control the behavior of others points out that we and they are often being less than totally rational. It also suggests that, even when being rational, people frequently disagree on the perceived value of various outcomes in an exchange. Ultimately, regardless of the degree of control one has over another person's outcomes, one has no power over that person unless she or he values those outcomes.

INTERPERSONAL POWER STRATEGIES

Psychologists argue that the exertion of power is always based on the principle of least interest, but they have also shown that the capacity to influence another person's outcomes can be based on a variety of different factors and can be communicated in many ways. There are many ways of getting a person to comply with your wishes; people, indeed, have developed an astonishing number of methods for getting their way. This section is concerned with these methods, the various ways to exert influence over another.

Several psychologists have tried to understand the complex processes of power by classifying various ways that people try to exert influence. Once established, these influence categories can be useful tools in the study of power. One can, for example, investigate the comparative effectiveness of different categories, how often they are used by various groups of people, or the impact they have on what people think of the power user. Influence categories can also help to analyze the power relationships in which we all participate. Perhaps we can best understand the potential of such categories by examining three major ways of classifying interpersonal power: its bases, the processes by which it is exerted, and the dimensions along which its use varies.

Bases of Social Power

In the late 1950s, two social psychologists attempted to categorize the bases on which the exercise of power rested. French and Raven (1959) defined the basis of interpersonal power as the relationship between two persons that was the source of one person's power over the other. They listed five possible bases on which one person's power over another might rest: reward power, coercive power, legitimate power, referent power, and expert power. Whether a base exists and how strong it is depend on certain aspects of the way the power user is seen by the other person.

Reward power. One person's power over another may be based on his or her perceived ability to reward the other. The larger and more important the rewards one person can give another, the more likely the second person is to do what the first asks, or to try to please that person. Thus, if person A's affection and approval, or the ability to grant a promotion or a raise, is important to person B, it forms a basis of reward power that A has over B. It is B's perception of A's ability to reward him or her that becomes a source of power for A over B.

Coercive power. Power over another person may also rest on the threat of punishment for noncompliance. To the extent that person B regards person A as willing and able to administer important negative consequences, person B will try to avoid those consequences by doing what A wishes. Thus, if I am terrified of your anger, or if I see that you can withhold an important letter of recommendation for me, this aspect of our relationship gives you a source of power over me.

According to Homans (1974), the emotional consequences of reward power and coercive power may be quite different. The person who has been coerced is often frustrated and angry; the one who has been rewarded may feel a happy sense of accomplishment. Homans suggests that those who use coercive power must always guard against the anger of the coerced. This is one of the major costs incurred by users of coercive power. He also notes that, whereas the giving of a reward indicates that the power user has exerted power successfully, the administration of punishment indicates that the power user has *not* exerted power successfully; hence, the other person is being punished for noncompliance. In such a case, the person's power base of coercion has not been converted into power because the desired behavioral response did not occur—the coercion did not work.

Legitimate power. This is the most complex basis of power. It stems from the values that an individual holds about how she or he should behave and who has a right to influence her or him. Using these values, one person can exert power by invoking some code of behaviors that is accepted by the other. For example, a child may influence his father to accompany him to the father-son banquet by pointing out that this is part of the expected role of a father. (This works only, of course, if the father's set of values also says that this *is* part of his father role.) Or one friend may get another to provide help by reminding her of a previous promise to do so. One has a legitimate right to expect help if it has been promised. (Again, this works only if the other person also places value on keeping one's word or one's promise.) Thus, in a variety of ways one person can influence another by pointing out that for some reason he or she has a legitimate right, acknowledged by both persons, to expect the desired behavior.

Referent power. This is based on the other person's liking for or identification with the power user. If a child wants badly to be like her mother, this gives the mother a source of power over her. Because the daughter wants to be like her mother, she may assume her mother's attitudes or behaviors, regardless of any rewards and punishments from the mother for such imitation. Similarly, a person may conform to the standards of a particular reference group to which he or she is attracted without being directly rewarded by the group for doing so. French and Raven (1959) claim that the person being influenced is often unaware of the "referent" power being exerted by the person or group. Presumably, although they do not suggest this, anyone else (not the reference person) can exert influence by reminding the target person of the behavior that is necessary to become like the important person or group. For example, someone who knows nothing about tennis may influence the behavior of an aspiring young tennis player by telling her that Billie Jean King follows a certain dietary or exercise regimen.

Expert power. One person's power over another may be based on what is seen as his or her knowledge or expertise in a given area. In health matters, many of us are particularly susceptible to the influence of a person who has earned a medical degree. We presume that such a person's opinion is informed and accurate. It is often this presumption of expertise, rather than the content of the advice, that gives doctors, lawyers, accountants, and others a source of power in dealing with their clients.

The five bases of power are all what might be called source-dependent. Their presence and strength depend on qualities that the target person specifically sees in the source person. However, Raven (1965) notes a sixth basis of power, which is not source-dependent. *Informational power* is based on the content of the influence message rather than on the person who delivers it. If someone influences us by presenting an argument that sounds logical, reasonable, and acceptable, we have responded to informational power. So it follows that a person with access to many such facts and arguments may have a large source of informational power.

French and Raven stress that it is seldom possible to identify a single power base from which an influence attempt stems. More commonly, they say, several bases of power may be behind a given attempt to change a person's attitude or behavior. Their theoretical analysis allows for a beginning answer to the question *"Why* does one person have power over another?"

The Processes of Power

If French and Raven's analysis concerns the question of *why* one person has power over another, a later line of research centers on the question of *how* such power is exerted. Given potential power over another, how will the power holder try to communicate that influence to the other person?

Tedeschi, Schlenker, and Bonoma (1973) describe a two-way method of classifying the kinds of influence used in two-person exchanges. The first distinction is between open and manipulatory types of influence. Second is the distinction between influence attempts in which one person controls or mediates rewards and punishments and influence attempts in which this control is held by a third party. These two dimensions interact to form four possible categories of influence, as shown in Table 1.

TABLE 1: The Modes of Influence*

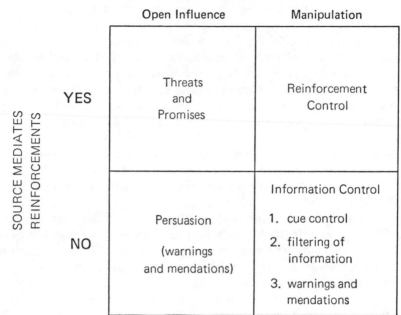

		Open Influence	Manipulation
SOURCE MEDIATES REINFORCEMENTS	**YES**	Threats and Promises	Reinforcement Control
	NO	Persuasion (warnings and mendations)	Information Control 1. cue control 2. filtering of information 3. warnings and mendations

An *open* type of influence is one in which the influencer does not try to hide his or her attempt to exercise power. In contrast, *manipulatory* influence is covert. The influencer attempts to disguise his or her intent and behaves as if the other person is unaware of any influence attempt. When a person controls the reinforcements in a situation and also uses open influence, he or she tries promises and threats—"If you do a good job on this project, I'll put you in for a promotion"; "If you insist on behaving this way, I'll leave you." However, a person who wants to use open influence, but does *not* control the reinforcements for the other person must rely on the persuasive tactics of predictions and warnings—"If you insist on behaving this way, your wife will probably leave you." The effectiveness of such an approach will depend on how much credibility or expertise the influencer has.

Manipulation, being covert, is somewhat more complex. If the influencer controls the rewards and punishments and also uses manipulatory influence, she or he relies on reinforcement control. Flattery or favors may

*Types of influence modes available to a potential source. From Tedeschi, J.T., Schlenker, B.R., & Bonoma, T.V. Conflict, power and games. Chicago, Aldine, 1973, p. 88.

make the other person feel obligated to cooperate. The influencer may use subtle, nonverbal indications of disapproval if the other person does not respond as the influencer intends. The person who uses manipulatory influence, but who does not have or does not wish to use reinforcement, instead uses various kinds of information control. This may include cue control, filtering of information, and manipulative use of warnings and positive predictions. Cue control involves knowing the target person's habits well enough to know that certain stimuli or cues generally bring about a certain behavior pattern. For example, a child who knows that her parents respond with guilt and protectiveness when she shows signs of being ill may use a cue of illness to influence them to stay at home for an evening. As her parents get ready to leave, she "develops" a sore throat or a headache. The parents, caught up in their habitual response of guilt and protectiveness to this cue, may decide to abandon their plans.

A person using information control may also filter, hide, or distort information in order to influence the target person. This tactic disguises the intent of warnings and positive predictions. For example, an influencer may present a prediction in such a way that she or he appears to be arguing against her or his own interest—"If you decide to enter the competition, you'll probably win over me, but I think it's a great idea for you to enter." Or the influencer may arrange for the target to overhear "leaked" warnings—"I've heard rumors that if she tries to get that policy adopted, a lot of the committee members are just going to stop cooperating with her." Both strategies can be quite effective.

The Nixon tapes. Thomas Bonoma (1975) used the methods we have been discussing to analyze the Watergate tapes in terms of power interactions between former President Richard Nixon and his aides. The analysis was done partly to check on two popular but conflicting hypotheses about Nixon's behavior: (1) he was a weak, indecisive president who could not use power effectively and he was manipulated by his advisors; or (2) he was a highly effective power user who simply made decisions favoring his own personal status and security. The researcher was able to show that the president did exert considerable power in his interactions with his subordinates, relying heavily on coercive and threatening types of influence.

The Dimensions of Power

Social psychologist Paula Johnson (1976) says that the exertion of power can vary according to three dimensions: directness-indirectness, competence-helplessness, and personal resources-concrete resources. She suggests that these dimensions can aid in understanding the use of power in general, and also, that they may provide a key to understanding the differences sometimes observed in the ways women and men use power.

The *directness-indirectness* dimension is similar to the open-manipulatory distinction made by Tedeschi et al. (1973). A person who operates near the "direct" end is open about any attempt to influence another; people who work near the indirect end are covert, even sneaky. These differences show up, for example, between the person who tells his friends he would rather go out for hamburgers than Chinese food, and the one who, while claiming no preference, subtly steers the hungry group toward McDonalds!

The *competence-helplessness* dimension distinguishes between the exertion of power through strength and competence or through weakness. It is easy to see how power can be based on strength and competence. A person who is big and strong or who is an expert can easily order a weaker or less expert person around. But how can power be exerted through weakness? The answer is easy; in fact, weakness or helplessness as a method of influence is very common, although rarely acknowledged. It is used *indirectly* by people who "simply can't" learn to drive and have to be chauffeured everywhere; by people who are so persistently incompetent at any task they are asked to perform against their will that it becomes easier not to ask them for help; or by those who exact guilt and compliance from others with refrains such as "Don't worry about me. It's not important that I'm lonely and miserable. It's important that you go out and have a good time." Helplessness is used more *directly* by people who simply ask for help, citing weakness, illness, or incapacity as justification. Often, as Johnson points out, helplessness is used as a form of legitimate power. When people are helpless or ill, others may feel that such people have a right to make certain requests that would otherwise be illegitimate.

Johnson's third dimension shows that the *resources on which the exertion of power* rests can range from the *concrete* to the very *personal*. Resources are what the power user has to back up influence attempts; the storehouse of possible rewards and punishments. Concrete resources, such as money, knowledge, and physical strength, are independent of relationships and they can be used to back up influence attempts in many situations. Personal resources, on the other hand, depend on a specific relationship. Liking, love, and approval are personal resources; they are effective only in certain relationships. If someone does not care whether you like her, your personal resource of affection will not give you much of a basis for exerting power over her.

Johnson points out that any of these kinds of influence can be effective in the right situation, but over the long run some of them may have unwanted effects for the user. The continual use of indirect forms of power, for instance, may disguise one's influence potential all too well! Even though the influencer may constantly get her way, others, who do not see her as the source of influence, may not regard or treat her as a powerful person. Therefore, despite the fact that this indirect influencer is successful, she does not gain in status and may, in fact, feel no gain in self-esteem. The effective direct influencer, on the other hand, may reap rewards in respect, admiration, fear, or ingratiation because she is thought of as a powerful person.

The use of helplessness to influence others also carries dangers. The person who acts helpless and weak much of the time may be looked on with contempt or resentment, even by those he or she effectively influences. The price of relying on this type of power may be chronic low self-esteem. There may also be dangers in too much use of competence and strength as a source of influence. The person who has never shown weakness may be disbelieved rather than helped if he or she ever does have to try to influence from a position of helplessness.

Finally, the use of personal resources as a main power base may leave a person feeling somewhat insecure, since personal resources are effective only with certain people in certain relationships. If a person is forced to deal with new people, or if the relationship changes, his or her power may literally evaporate. Power based on concrete resources is generally effective in more situations, but there too, the power stems only from the "perceived value" of the resources. One cannot bribe someone to whom money is unimportant!

SEX DIFFERENCES IN THE USE OF POWER

As we have seen, the stereotype persists in Western culture that women and men use different methods to get their way. Women are thought to rely on tears, sex appeal, and general deviousness; men give orders, shout, threaten, and hurt people. To some extent this stereotype can be seen as an exaggeration and distortion of reality, but, in fact, do some such sex differences exist?

Some observers say that sex roles in society seem to interact with the type of power used by women and men. Anthropologist Michelle Rosaldo

(1974) notes, for example, that women in many cultures share a common lack, not of all kinds of power, but specifically of the legitimate power of authority. They wield considerable influence behind the scenes, often through their husbands, brothers, and sons, but this influence is both covert and unacknowledged. The open exercise of power by women has been seen—and in large measure continues to be seen—in virtually all cultures as disruptive and illegitimate. History is filled with examples of men reminding women of their great hidden power in order to keep women from competing for open positions of power and authority.

> [Woman should] inspire in her home a vision of the meaning of life and freedom . . . This assignment for you, as wives and mothers, you can do in the living room with a baby in your lap or in the kitchen with a can opener in your hand . . . I think there is much you can do about our crisis in the humble role of housewife. I could wish you no better vocation than that.*

Jessie Bernard (1972) makes a similar point about hidden power when writing of marriage in North America. She suggests that women do not necessarily have less power than men in the marriage relationship. Rather, she argues, the wife and husband often conspire to hide the wife's power. Again, cultural requirements dictate that the woman's use of power be covert.

Johnson (1976) says that women's use of power is more often indirect, helpless, and personal while men's use is direct, competent, and concrete. Her suggestion derives from the fact that women simply have less access than men do to concrete resources and competence, as well as to positions of authority.

Combining her three dimensions with French and Raven's (1959; 1965) six bases of power, Johnson makes specific points about stereotypes surrounding male and female use of power. Reward and coercion, she suggests, are expected to be used in a direct, concrete way by men and in an indirect, personal way by women. Men have the resources and social approval to offer or withdraw money, for example. Women offer or withdraw love, friendship, and sexual rewards. Men may make more open threats and promises; women are expected to use more reinforcement control, such as ingratiation. Referent power, says Johnson, is regarded as appropriate for both sexes, but, since it is primarily personal, it may be especially appropriate for women. Expert power, based on superior skills, knowledge, and trustworthiness, is concrete,

*Adlai Stevenson (cited in Friedan, 1963, p. 54.)

competent, and usually direct, so it may be viewed as singularly appropriate for men. Informational power is thought to be used directly by men and indirectly by women. Legitimate power has several facets. The power of legitimate position or authority is usually expected of males. Legitimate power based on the expectation of reciprocity (for example, "You owe me a favor") is expected to be used directly by males. However, legitimate power based on the expectation of social responsibility—or legitimate helplessness— is strongly stereotyped as feminine.

Johnson also reports some support for her idea that people expect women and men to exercise power differently. Using a questionnaire that outlined a hypothetical situation (one student trying to get another to change his or her opinion on a legal case), fifteen different methods or types of power were presented. For each method, the respondents were asked to indicate whether they felt the influencer was male or female. Results showed that concrete coercion and competent legitimate, expert, and direct informational power were significantly more expected of males than females. Personal reward and sexuality were seen as significantly more characteristic of females. Johnson's results, then, support the idea that her supposed male sources of power are strongly linked with males in peoples' expectations. However, only two of the several proposed female sources of power were more strongly expected of females than males. These results, suggests Johnson, can be explained through the notion that power (*all* power) is thought of as essentially a male domain. Men are expected to use the "masculine" power strategies such as coercion, but they may also use other strategies that seem appropriate. Women, on the other hand, are expected to stick to the less aggressive forms of power, and they are usually considered "out of line" if they adopt direct, competent, concrete influence methods. This explanation, of course, requires further study to be verified.

Men and women are *expected* to use power differently; but, in reality, do they? Are there actual differences in behavior in power use situations? Some studies give us preliminary answers to this question. In one study, Johnson (1974) gave male and female group leaders an opportunity to choose one of six power messages to persuade their group to work faster at a given task. Strong differences did emerge between males and females in the messages they chose. Males frequently used the message based on expert power—the "do it this way because I know how" urging. Females avoided it; they often used the helpless power message—the "help me, I don't know how to do it" plea—which males without exception rejected. Johnson's results also showed that any of the power methods—except helplessness—tended to raise the self-esteem of the user. The use of helplessness was linked with a reduction in self-esteem.

Falbo (1977) set out to examine the relationship between sex and sex role, and social influence. She believed that sex-role typing would prove more important than sex in accounting for the differences in methods of social influence. Falbo's subjects completed the Bem Sex Role Inventory (BSRI; Bem, 1974). This self-report inventory measures the extent to which people see themselves as having certain traits that research has shown are stereotyped as socially desirable for either women or men. Persons who see themselves as having many of the so-called masculine traits and few of the feminine ones on this test would be classified as Masculine. Those who see themselves as having many of the feminine and few of the masculine traits would be classified as Feminine. Subjects who report a good balance of masculine and feminine traits are Androgynous. A fourth label, Undifferentiated, indicates those low on both the feminine or masculine traits. Equal numbers of males and females falling into each of the first three categories were chosen for the experiment.

Falbo asked each of her subjects to spend ten minutes writing an essay on "How I Get My Way." The essays were coded for the presence or absence of the following methods of influence: assertion, tears, emotional change, subtlety, and reasoning. The results lent some, but not total, support to Falbo's hypothesis that sex-role typing accounts for more differences in influence strategies than sex. Persons of either sex who were classified as Feminine on the BSRI were more likely to report using tears, subtlety, and mood changes, and less likely to use assertion than were persons classed as Masculine. A significant sex difference was found for reasoning; more females than males reported this strategy. Sex-role differences were also found in the number of types of influence that were reported; Masculine persons reported fewer strategies than Androgynous or Feminine ones.

Although Falbo's results demonstrate the importance of sex-role typing in the use of influence methods, they cannot be used to show that sex differences in these methods do or do not exist. Great care was taken to include in the experiment equal numbers of both sexes who scored in each of the Masculine, Feminine, and Androgynous categories. This probably obscured any sex differences, since in the real world the ratio of females to males scoring as Feminine is quite high, as is the ratio of males to females scoring as Masculine. The results do imply however, that whatever sex differences do exist in these behaviors, they are the result of sex-role learning.

Carleton Cann (1979) tried a direct behavioral test of sex differences in types of influence. She placed women and men in a simulated work situation; they were to supervise workers in another room and were allowed to communicate with them by written messages. The supervisors were allowed to threaten and/or reward the workers, and were instructed simply to influence them to increase production. Cann found that male and female supervisors did not differ in the methods used in this situation; both sexes relied heavily on persuasion and reward. However, men made *more* attempts to influence than women did, and men also tended to see their own behavior as more powerful and aggressive than women saw theirs. At the end of the experiment, the women indicated a significantly lower desire than the men to play the role of manager again.

Cann's study did not show sex differences in methods of influence, but it may indirectly provide a key for understanding any differences that do exist. The key is related to legitimacy, as discussed earlier. Both men and women in the study were given equally legitimate positions of authority from which to exert influence. In the real world, however, that is seldom the case. Men, as we know are routinely ascribed higher status than women. Husbands are regularly viewed as the "heads" of households, and men are usually the ones placed in charge of organizations varying from businesses to armies to countries. These positions tend to reinforce and increase men's high status, and men are often viewed as superior to and more informed, more intelligent, more capable, and more logical than women. Consequently, when a man is trying to influence a woman, he is very often operating from a legitimate position either of explicit authority or implicit superiority. A woman trying to influence a man, on the other hand, is often working from a subordinate position. Given this, it would not be surprising if women and men often relied on different strategies for exerting influence. Indeed, even when women are given positions of authority over men, the incongruity in status and the conflict with social norms for exerting power are often enough to make everyone uncomfortable. Women may try to reduce the discomfort by being unobtrusive in their authority roles. This seems to be the case in the Cann study, where women supervisors expressed a lack of comfort in their roles and used fewer influence attempts than men did.

It seems safe to say that in an influence situation, the more legitimate power the influencer holds, the more direct she or he is able to be (Lips & Colwill, 1978). Whether the legitimacy stems from position, role, social norms, or previous agreements, the results should be the same. Thus, women, who are so often lacking in legitimate power relative to men, will frequently be indirect in their influence methods (unless, of course, they are using legitimate helplessness).

But what if the social situations were reversed? In a situation where women had legitimacy on their side, would men employ indirect influence techniques? Let's look at an example. Over the past five years, a woman has worked to put her husband through graduate school. Now he has a good job, and, according to a previous agreement, it is her turn to pursue advanced training in her own field. The husband, who was happy enough with their pact when it was made five years ago, now is dissatisfied with his wife's plans. He feels that they can now afford to have a family. He likes the image of himself as a successful businessman, coming home at the end of the day to a happy wife, a clean house, and two or three adoring children. Yet, if he tries to influence his wife in this direction now, the normal legitimacy that such a demand would have (after all, this is still the most socially accepted pattern for women to follow) would be lacking because of their original agreement. Therefore, the husband might be very indirect in his influence methods. While verbally reinforcing her plans and their agreement, he might at the same time begin to speak sadly and longingly of babies when she is around, joke pointedly with her mother about her lack of "maternal instinct," leave magazine articles around the house that discuss the dangers of putting off childbearing, and so on. If confronted, he is likely to deny any attempt to influence her. After all, fair is fair, and they *do* have an agreement.

If the above scenario sounds familiar, it may be because variations on it are being played out in countless families as women and men struggle to redefine their roles. Women returning to school or paid work after many years of staying home and looking after their families often speak unhappily and bitterly about husbands (and children) who, while verbally reinforcing their efforts, indirectly sabotage them in countless ways: by refusing to adjust the family vacation schedule to mother's new needs, by making a scene about how dirty the house is on the night before her crucial exam, by being totally incompetent at any housework they are asked to do, by insisting that PTA meetings and baking cookies for the class are still mother's jobs, by having nervous breakdowns, and by, in countless ways, laying on guilt about "neglected" family responsibilities. These are situations where legitimacy is confused. The woman may feel somewhat tentative in her new role and anxious not to let her family suffer, even though she thinks she has made a legitimate decision. The man may feel anxious to be fair and reasonable, but unhappy about the disruption in his life-style. The man feels he cannot openly assert his wishes because they are unfair and, hence, illegitimate. The woman, feeling that her actions are not only reasonable but also agreed to by her mate, is confused and angered by the double messages she receives from him. Such situations, if not dealt with constructively, lead to widening rifts between the partners.

The amount and kind of power held by an individual depend not only on that person, but on the target person and on the particulars of the situation as well. In a family, for instance, a woman may feel that, although her status gives her little legitimate authority in dealing with her husband, it does give her such authority relative to her children. Thus, the influence methods she uses in dealing with her husband and her children may differ markedly. Little research has been done on this, but much more should be, since power is obviously a situational as well as a personal characteristic. One study (McGillin, 1979) tried to judge how differences in personalities and situations affected power use by persons having a discussion. The results showed, first, a significant connection between sex and sex-role typing and assertiveness—the amount of time spent talking and the number of interruptions allowed. Males were more assertive than females overall, and assertiveness was also significantly related to sex-role classification on the BSRI. Androgynous persons were most assertive, followed by those classified as Masculine, Feminine, and Undifferentiated. Second, the target person was also important to the exercise of power. Androgynous women were more assertive with men than with women. Also, although women who were not strongly stereotyped as Feminine were more generally powerful than those who were, the highly Feminine women were powerful (more effective as influencers) when dealing with men, although low in power when dealing with women. Clearly, then, the kind and amount of power used when two people interact depends not only on who is doing the influencing but also on who is being influenced.

EFFECTS OF POWER
STRATEGIES ON THEIR USERS

It is rare for a behavior to have only a single, intended consequence. As pointed out earlier, influence-directed activities may have consequences, not only in terms of obtaining compliance, but also in terms of the influencer's self-perception and satisfaction and the way he or she is regarded by others. Research by Kipnis (1972), for example, shows that the control of power affects the power holder's self-perception and perception of the less power-ful. Males who had control of power devalued the worth of subordinates' performances, attributed the cause of subordinates' efforts to the power of the holder, not to the subordinates' motivation to do well, and viewed subordinates as objects of manipulation. These findings led Kipnis to con-clude that, in a sense, power does corrupt the person who wields it.

The ways in which we use power may actually increase or undermine our resources for future power use. It is dangerous, for example, to use threats or promises that cannot be carried out. The credibility lost on these occasions reduces the power of the influencer because it makes future threats and promises less effective. It is also inadvisable to use legitimate power out-side the range for which it is prescribed (French & Raven, 1959). For exam-ple, an employer who tries to dictate behavior in an employee's personal life may be seen as overstepping legitimate authority. This would have the probable effect of decreasing the employer's legitimate power and attractive-ness. Also, it is possible that someone who exerts more power than is neces-sary to gain a certain degree of compliance will be disliked, leading ultimately to a decrease in power.

The ways in which one uses power can also have an important effect on how powerful the power user *feels*. This is discussed more fully in Chapter 4, but it is worth noting that a heavy reliance on the indirect, helpless, and personal modes of influence may leave an individual with low self-esteem and very little sense of effectiveness.

Finally, the reliance by certain groups on particular power tactics may have some long-range social consequences in terms of stereotyping and trust. The politician who promises lower taxes and the salesperson who insists that "that outfit is *you*" are acting so much within the stereotypes of how such people exert influence that their sincerity is almost automatically doubted. People who become known as manipulators quickly lose the trust of their colleagues, and perhaps this is partially responsible for the stereotype that women do not trust other women. Women have been taught to be indirect, helpless, and even seductive in their attempts to influence men, both because they have had few of the alternatives provided by authority or money, and because men, who like to believe that women are dependent on them, seem to fall for it. But when women use these influence methods on other women, they are simply not as effective. Women who rely on indirect, personal types of influence may prefer the company of men because they know how to operate successfully with them. This behavior, in turn, may well cause resentment among other women, both because it reinforces a stereotype of women as dependent and/or manipulative, thus undermining their efforts to deal directly and competently with men, and because it implies that women are not worthwhile companions. An understanding of the implications of using various types of power, then, is crucial not just to an understanding of relationships between women and men, but also to an understanding of relationships among women. Further, such knowledge is also crucial for comprehending male-male relationships; if both men accept the strong, aggressive power stereotype, they may be unable to communicate any uncertainties, vulnerabilities, and weaknesses that are actually present.

SUMMARY

The power of one person over another is most easily understood to result from the ability to control the other's outcomes. In any social exchange, each person has some control over the outcomes of the other, and the principle of least interest predicts that the person who is the least dependent on the other for rewards—who needs the exchange or the relationship least—will have the most power.

Power can rest on one or more of the bases of reward, coercion, legitimacy, expertise, personal or reference group attraction, and information. It can be exerted in a number of ways, many covert and not at all apparent at first glance. A belief exists that men and women use power differently, and more research is needed to examine the extent to which this belief is grounded in reality. There is reason to think that the type of influence a person adopts has consequences not only for influence effectiveness, but also for self-esteem and social relationships. The strategies that seem to require the largest toll in self-esteem are those that are generally attributed to women. Women might do well, then, to avoid falling continually into the "womanly" influence methods scathingly outlined by Nellie McClung in one of this chapter's opening quotes.

A knowledge of the many ways in which power can be used should make one less vulnerable to unwanted influence and more honest about one's own influence strategies. The reader should not be able to be fooled by the situation described in an early example, in which someone who says she is not leading the group is clearly dominating it with coercive power. It should be clear that one solution to such a problem would be to enact some ground rules to guide participation, thus giving the rest of the group legitimate power to control such a person. Armed with a basic understanding of interpersonal power, people are less likely to be victimized in their relationships.

Even people who are equally effective at influencing others may differ in how powerful they actually feel. In the next chapter, we will look at the psychological state or trait of feeling powerful.

FEELING
POWERFUL

4

Question: When have you felt most powerful?

Answer: At the birth of my child . . .
When I am supervising someone . . .
When I accomplish something . . .
When I beat someone up . . .

Responses to a questionnaire on power

Author's Note: Portions of this chapter appeared in Lips, H. M. "Women and power: Psychology's search for new directions," *Atlantis,* 5 (1), 1979, pp. 1–13.

How often do people who hold powerful positions seem not to have a real sense of their power? How often do people underestimate their own power? How often do people actually give their power away in situations where they feel unable to use it? Such occurrences are frequent enough to suggest that holding power in some objective sense is not enough to make a person effective. It is also necessary that she or he define and experience the situation in a certain way—that she or he *feel* powerful.

What determines whether we feel powerful in a given situation? Some of the issues described in previous chapters are obviously crucial. How do we perceive our own power resources as compared to those possessed by others in the situation and to those required for success? How much practice have we had at employing various influence methods? What is our status relative to those with whom we are interacting? Another important set of factors includes the habits we have formed in perceiving and interpreting situations. Do we generally think of ourselves as pawns of fate or as having some measure of control over what happens to us? Are we conscious of our ability to make choices in many situations? Are we used to taking credit for our successes? How, in general, do we perceive our strengths and weaknesses? This chapter examines the ways in which these various social and personal factors may work together to influence an individual's feeling of powerfulness in a given situation.

POWER AS A STATE OR TRAIT

According to Minton (1967), power occurs at two levels—manifest and latent. Attempts to gain or use power through social influence and power strategies (as discussed in Chapter 3) represent power at the manifest (visible or obvious) level. The latent (or hidden) level of power, discussed in this chapter, includes individual feelings of power and readiness to apply manifest power.

Minton's term "latent power" was a new one at the time, but previous researchers had noted that individuals could differ in terms of felt powerfulness-powerlessness and that experiences could affect such feelings. White (1959), for example, described a feeling of "efficacy" accompanying an individual's experience of competence in interaction with the environment. Lewin (1936), writing about the individual interacting with restraining forces of the environment, developed the concept of "space of free movement," which seems to be the same as individual power in both the manifest and latent sense. Heider (1958) discussed power as part of the "attribution of can"—the individual's perception that he or she rather than the environment is responsible for effecting outcomes or changes. Beginning with such analyses, the issues of perceived power and control have emerged as central in psychological research. Although we cannot complete an exhaustive review of research in this area, we can outline some main concepts and their relevance to male-female relations.

Locus of Control

Psychologists tend to define control as the successful use of one's influence in a given situation (Cartwright, 1959). They are also quick to point out that what a person sees as the amount of control she or he exerts, either in a given situation or in life in general, is not always accurate and may, indeed, differ drastically from reality. Rotter (1966) proposed that people's generalized beliefs about how much control they have over their own outcomes are reflected in their behavior. He developed a scale to measure the extent to which people believe in internal or external control. A person who scores near the "internal" end of this scale tends to believe that he or she controls his or her own fate to a large extent and is said to have an internal "locus" of control. Someone who scores near the "external" end of the scale tends to believe that he or she is controlled by external forces to a large extent and is said to have an external locus of control. People in these two groups are often referred to as internals and externals.

Although life is not so simple that everyone can be neatly classified as an internal or an external,* the variations shown on Rotter's scale seems to be important for predicting other factors. For example, internals are more effective than externals at seeking and using information relevant to personal decisions (Phares, 1968; Seeman, 1963; Seeman & Evans, 1962), and at changing other people's attitudes (Phares, 1976); internals are more likely to view their own task performance as the result of skill rather than luck (Phares, 1976); internals are less susceptible to social influence (Ryckman, Rodda & Sherman, 1972); and they score higher than externals on a variety of achievement tests (Phares, 1976). These results do not, of course, prove that a

*A person can score anywhere on a continuum from high internal to high external. Researchers often compare the one-third of their subjects who score nearest the internal pole with the one-third who score nearest the external pole.

belief in internal control *causes* certain behaviors. Indeed, the cause-effect relationship could possibly work in the other direction; for example, effective information-seeking could lead to an increased belief in internal control. Nonetheless, it is clear that people differ in their general beliefs about the extent to which they control their own lives, and these differences are paralleled in a number of behaviors.

One's locus of control may relate to how powerful one feels and the ways in which one uses power. It seems likely that the more external one's general orientation, the less likely one is to feel powerful (that is, to feel able to have a potential impact) in any particular situation. Moreover, research has shown that if, in a specific situation, a person is made to feel that she or he has no control over outcomes, she or he will eventually stop trying to influence the situation. This phenomenon has been called "learned helplessness" (Seligman, 1975).

Unfortunately, learned helplessness tends to extend beyond the specific situation in which it was learned. This happens when the person attributes a particular failure to a global rather than a specific cause (Abramson, Seligman & Teasdale, 1978). The individual is left with a feeling of ineffectiveness and, hence, an unwillingness to try to control outcomes in other situations. Thus, for example, someone who repeatedly fails in the attempt to find employment may attribute the failure to an inability to appear competent to others, and may gradually develop a lack of self-confidence. This may overlap other areas, such as relations with others and decision-making. This effect is all the more probable if the individual believes that the inability to appear competent is not related to her or his qualifications or self-presentation, but rather to something arbitrary such as discrimination by sex or race. In this case, the individual sees the outcome as both global and completely unrelated to her or his own actions or achievements—a prime condition for the development of learned helplessness.

Sex differences in locus of control? Do women and men differ in their feelings of internal and external control? Maccoby and Jacklin (1974) report that until high school age there is no consistent difference between the sexes in perceived locus of control, but at college age and beyond women are more external than men. In one study, which examined locus of control in five different countries, women in all five cultures were more external than men

(McGinnies, Nordholm, Ward, & Bhanthuonnavin, 1974).* These findings are consistent with a number of others not using this scale, which show that men and boys consistently describe themselves as more powerful and stronger than do women and girls (Maccoby & Jacklin, 1974).

Why should women feel less powerful and less in control of their fate than men do? To some extent, these beliefs are probably a reflection of the way they have been trained and treated. For example, historically, women have been expected not to plan their lives, but to wait in readiness for whatever fate awaits them in the form of a husband. Agatha Christie's (1977) description of this "readiness" in her autobiography is reflective of a message that many young women still continue to receive.

> The real excitement of being a girl—of being, that is, a woman in embryo—was that life was such a wonderful gamble. *You didn't know what was going to happen to you.* That was what made being a woman so exciting. No worry about what you should be or do—Biology would decide. You were waiting for The Man, and when the man came, he would change your entire life. You can say what you like, that is an exciting point of view to hold at the threshold of life. What will happen? . . . The whole world was open to you—not open to your *choice,* but open to what Fate *brought* you. You might marry *anyone;* you might, of course, marry a drunkard or be very unhappy, but that only heightened the general feeling of excitement (p. 131).

Psychologists, too, have picked up this theme. Erik Erikson, for instance, theorized that a young woman's identity was intimately bound up with her search for the right man (Erikson, 1974).

Besides the fact that women seem to be taught not to *try* to take control of their own lives, when they do try certain forms of control, the outcomes tend to be unrelated to their efforts. Research shows that women's

---

*Research shows that sex role bias may influence responses to the I-E scale. If subjects are instructed to respond in a "masculine" way they obtain high internal scores, but score as more external if instructed to respond in a "feminine" way (Hochreich, 1975). Studies which find sex differences using this scale, then, must be cautiously interpreted. Moreover, it is now clear that a person's overall score on this scale does not tell the whole story. Strickland and Haley (1980) showed that, even when males and females obtained similar total scores, they differed significantly in their responses to particular items. It appears that men and women express their expectancies for control on different scale items and in different ways. Until the I-E scale is revised to eliminate sex-biased items it will be difficult to separate the effects of sex role stereotypes from the effects of gender on the scores.

work tends to be undervalued because a woman has done it rather than because of its quality (Deaux & Taynor, 1973; Goldberg, 1968; Pheterson, Kiesler, & Goldberg, 1971), and that women's success is attributed more often than men's to luck or chance (Deaux & Emswiller, 1974; Terborg & Ilgen, 1975). Women are less likely than men to be chosen for management positions, and jobs traditionally filled by women are likely to be lower paid than those traditionally filled by men. Employment and income statistics show that discrimination against women is alive and well in North America (and elsewhere)!

A person or group whose outcomes are frequently linked to factors over which they have no control (such as sex, race, or physical appearance) rather than to behavior or achievements is vulnerable to feelings of external control and learned helplessness. In today's social situation, women very often find themselves in this position. Furthermore, there is danger that as some aspects of the situation change to favor a certain amount of affirmative action, women who feel they are hired because they are women (instead of *not* being hired because they are women) will still feel that their outcomes are tied more to their sex than to their skills or credentials. This danger can be alleviated somewhat if the woman is treated as a competent, valued member of the staff rather than as a necessary token. However, many women would probably agree that as long as gender is going to be used as a determining factor in whether they are hired, they would prefer to have it work for rather than against them!

In general, it seems that the sex difference in feelings of control is linked to a social situation in which women very simply have less control over their own outcomes than men do. A change in this real-life situation is what will enable the majority of women to gain a stronger sense of internal control.

The body and sense of control. Some analysts have made much of the notion that women, because of menstruation, pregnancy, and menopause, have less control over their own bodies than men do, and hence women perceive themselves as more vulnerable and less in command of their fate. For example, Nancy Friday (1977) discusses the onset of menstruation as something that "turns us back . . . to that earlier time when we were unable to control our bodies. Suddenly we are back in touch with emotions we haven't felt in years, the primitive shame that went with wetting our bed, bad odors, soiling our clothes" (p. 145).

Of course, women are not the only ones whose bodies may betray them at inconvenient moments. Any man who has ever gotten an erection at a time when it was more embarrassing than useful or who could *not* get one at a time when he wished to will testify to that! Neither male nor female bodies are as easily controlled as we might wish.

Pregnancy, however, does have a serious potential to limit a woman's control of her body. Until recently, most sexually active women lived with the anxiety that one or more unplanned pregnancies would disrupt their lives, interfering with the course they had set for themselves, and introducing irrevocable factors in the form of helpless infants requiring care. Under these conditions, it is not surprising if women felt (or feel) little sense of internal control. A popular women's movement slogan is that women must gain control over their own bodies. It is under this banner that women have agitated for greater access to contraception and abortion so that they will be decreasingly subject to unplanned pregnancies. It cannot be denied that such access is crucial in increasing women's perceived and actual control over their lives.

One could still argue that the experience of pregnancy, planned or not, makes women aware of a sense of vulnerability and external control that is not often felt by men. Simone de Beauvoir (1952), for instance, writes of the experience of pregnancy as one in which the woman cannot help but feel a rather dramatic loss of control over her body.

> A new life is going to manifest itself and justify its own separate existence, she is proud of it; but she also feels herself tossed and driven, the plaything of obscure forces . . . Ensnared by nature, the pregnant woman is plant and animal, a stockpile of colloids, and incubator, an egg; she scares children proud of their young, straight bodies and makes young people titter contemptuously because she is a human being, a conscious and free individual, who has become life's passive instrument (pp. 466–467).

However, it is not necessarily true that a woman always experiences pregnancy in this way, nor that, if she does, the sense of lack of control permeates the other areas of her life. Furthermore, there is another side to the reproductive coin: women sometimes say that they have felt at their most powerful at the birth of a child. Thus, the idea that women must necessarily feel less powerful and more externally controlled than men because of the way their reproductive functions are divided seems overly simplistic.

Freedom and Personal Responsibility

Implicit in any definition of power is that it includes a certain freedom to act and to decide how to act. Powerlessness, on the other hand, connotes a situation in which one has no choices, but is acted upon by external forces. We characterize learned helplessness as the feeling of a person who is convinced that she or he can make no impact on a situation. A person may or may not feel free to act in various ways, but senses that these actions make no difference to what happens. There are, however, times when a person's very freedom to act or to choose is threatened by some external force. For example, a person may be offered a job, but may be strongly urged by a spouse not to take it, as in the case of a housewife who wants to return to paid work but whose husband objects. Here, the initial reaction is not helplessness but what is called reactance, a concept that can shed a considerable amount of light on the use, experience of, and reaction of power.

The reactance theory, from Brehm (1966), says that people are motivated to protect their behavioral freedom if it is threatened. Research shows that people may react against a threat to or a restriction of freedom in several ways: by trying to reassert or regain the threatened freedom, by anger and hostility toward the person or institution threatening the freedom, and/or by an increased attraction toward what is threatened. The particular reaction that a person chooses depends on how effective that person thinks the choice will be in regaining the freedom and how safely it can be used. Of course, for *any* of these reactions to occur, the person must believe that he or she was originally free to choose the threatened alternative. If the housewife in our example has never felt that she had a right to take a paid job, she will probably experience helplessness rather than reactance in the face of her husband's objections.

Since reactance is often a response to an attempt at social influence, examining it is important to the question of power. When someone tries to influence us, what method of power is likely to produce the most reactance on our part (and hence the least influence)? When we do comply with an influence attempt, why do we think we are doing so? To what extent do these reasons relate to a feeling of power or powerlessness? These questions are only now beginning to be investigated fully, but there are indications that different styles of influence produce different reactions in the person toward whom that influence is directed.

Rodin and Janis (1979) suggest that in some circumstances the person who is the target of expert and coercive power use may experience feelings of lessening personal control. This person may feel a threat to freedom and may be motivated to regain control by disregarding or flaunting the given advice or instructions. Rodin and Janis say that this reaction may be the reason why large numbers of patients do not follow the advice of their doctors. Furthermore, they note, when persons comply because of expert, coercive, or reward power that is exerted on them, they tend to attribute their compliance to external reasons. They are less likely to see themselves as having personal responsibility for or control over their actions. Thus, these methods of influence seem to encourage a sense of powerlessness in the target person in some situations.

Are there ways of influencing people that do not leave them feeling a loss of freedom, control, and personal responsibility? Past research indicates that if the external incentive used to convince people to perform a behavior is very small, they are likely to see themselves as having internal reasons for their actions (Collins, 1969). Cynically stated, if you give people the illusion that they have choices—that they are not being bossed, coerced, or bribed—at the same time channeling them in a subtle and careful way toward a particular decision or behavior, you can influence them without producing a sense of reactance or helplessness. This method involves the indirect or manipulatory style of power. On the other hand, you can be direct but noncoercive, giving the person a real rather than an illusory choice. In this case, your "success" rate may be lower, but the person to whom you direct the influence attempt will not feel that his or her freedom and control are diminished, regardless of the outcome.

Rodin and Janis suggest that the use of referent power, which is based on seeing the power holder as likeable, admirable, and accepting is unlikely to threaten feelings of internal control. If, for instance, I do something that you request because I like and admire you, then I see myself as acting because of my internal feelings rather than any external limits. So, although you have influenced me (and, therefore, have exerted power over me), I do not see myself as being controlled; I see myself as choosing to do something for someone I like and admire. Of course, if you have tried to induce my feelings of liking and admiration specifically to have this power over me, the process becomes, in its own way, a manipulation.

What does all this mean in discussing male-female power relationships? For one thing, it helps us to understand the effects of the differing power styles thought to be used by women and men in some situations. We know that women are said to rely heavily on indirect, personal types of power, while men are more likely to be direct and concrete. It is as if women unconsciously try to avoid provoking reactance in the other person when exercising influence, while men make no such effort. This analysis is oversimplified, of course, yet it does give some insight into why members of two groups who differ in access to resources may differ in power strategies. The individual who has access to many resources with which to back up demands can afford to be direct enough to arouse anger, hostility, or other reactions. The person who has little or no access to concrete resources with which to bargain and threaten, however, must be much more cautious.

Remember, too, that if in any given male-female relationship, the woman wields power indirectly and personally, while the man is much more direct, the two parties will tend to attribute their compliance to very different reasons. When she complies, the woman will attribute it to external pressure from him, and she will feel little sense of personal control or responsibility for her decision. But when he complies, he may have been manipulated into seeing his behavior not as compliance to her, but as a product of his own decision. Thus, he maintains a sense of control and responsibility, and a difference between them in the sense of power and control is maintained.

Must one always feel powerful at the expense of another's powerlessness? Not necessarily. It is possible, as we have seen to exert influence without robbing a person's sense of personal control, by giving him or her the illusion or the reality of choice. In relationships that aspire to be honest, only the reality of choice is acceptable. However, for people in relatively powerless positions, honesty is a luxury they often feel they cannot afford. As women and men move toward more equally balanced relationships, perhaps we will more often see a give-and-take of influence wherein neither party is continually fighting a loss of freedom or personal control.

Competence, Effectiveness, and Strength

How we *think* about ourselves and our actions often has as much or more impact on our experience as does the actual situation itself. Thus, we may sometimes act in a way that causes others to label us powerful and competent at the same time that we are feeling weak and unsure. Furthermore, the labels we attach to ourselves tend to be self-perpetuating; they form a framework within which we explain our actions. Any change in our power relationships presumes a shift in the kinds of images we form of ourselves and others and the causes to which we attribute our and others' actions. The issues concerning the formation of such images and attributions are particularly important for an understanding of how male and female uses of power differ.

One highlight of a conference workshop on women and power was one woman's discussion of her attempt to maintain an image of herself as strong and powerful just after the birth of her child. Rather than succumb to the traditional vision of the "little mother," she devised an image for herself that was both powerful and appropriate—a lioness.

This story points up both the importance of images in an individual's life and the shortage of powerful images with which women, in particular, can identify. Social psychology has long recognized that females, lacking readily available achieving and powerful women as models, are at a disadvantage in learning certain achievement behaviors. But the problem is now recognized as being more serious; as we saw in Chapter 1, the accepted image of power and the accepted image of femininity in society are often totally imcompatible and mutually exclusive. Feminine images are filled with powerlessness and weakness.

Although the incompatibility of images of femininity and of power have been noted for many years by feminist writers (see, for example, de Beauvoir, 1952), it is perhaps the feminist theologians (such as Daly, 1973; Fiorenza, 1976) who have been forced to confront this incongruity in its deepest sense. God, the ultimate image of power, is perceived in our culture as inescapably male—not just male, but also a father. The strength of the hold that this image has on Western consciousness can perhaps best be gauged by the violence of people's reactions to the idea of women as priests, rabbis, and ministers. Many people recoil from this notion as blasphemous, and some feminists have had to struggle with the "rightness" of this image as they have with no other.

Can our culture develop images of power for women? Some important steps are being taken in this direction. Pressure is being exerted on the media to portray women more often as strong, competent, and powerful. Very slowly, powerful women as role models are becoming more visible. Also, there is an emerging awareness that women have the ability to develop physically strong and competent bodies. Female athletes are becoming more visible, and an increasing number of women are developing a sense of pleasure in their own strength as they take up running, swimming, team sports, or the martial arts. Beginning research indicates that these changes can have a significant impact on women's self-perceptions (Rorbaugh, 1979).

In the area of psychotherapy, women are being encouraged to come to terms with their images of themselves as powerless. Britain (1978), for example, reports on the use of dreams to help women realize the extent to which they have connected femininity with powerlessness. One emerging theme is that of women's being hampered, restricted, tripped, or vulnerably exposed by the "feminine" clothing they find themselves wearing in their dreams. These images occur even for successful professional women. Clearly, the notion of feminine weakness is a difficult one to dislodge.

Why should the idea of femaleness/weakness and maleness/strength be so difficult to dispel? The answer may be at least partially found in the way people explain their experience and behavior. Research suggests that this process of explanation is intimately linked to sex roles and to feelings of effectiveness and power.

According to Weiner, Frieze, Kukla, Reed, Rest, and Rosenbaum (1971), four explanations often given for a person's success or failure are ability, effort, luck, and level of task difficulty. Ability and effort are considered internal factors, originating within the individual. Luck and task difficulty are environmental factors, external to the individual. Furthermore, ability and task difficulty are thought of as relatively stable and unchanging, while effort and luck are unstable factors capable of large fluctuations. Finally, as noted by Elig and Frieze (1975), the explanation for success and failure can also vary because of "intentionality," the extent to which the person is seen as being in control of her or his behavior. Effort, for example, would be regarded as an intentional factor in explaining success, since presumably one cannot make an effort to succeed without intending to. On the other hand, ability, luck, and task difficulty are not intentional factors; they are seen to operate without the person's volition.

The various reasons given for one's own success or failure obviously have logical implications for how one experiences an event and for one's self-image. It may be difficult for someone to maintain a self-image of power or effectiveness, for example, if her successes are continually attributed to unintentional factors. Frieze (1975) explains that a person feels maximum pride and security in an achievement if that achievement is seen as the result of the internal, stable factor of ability, while success attributed to external factors brings less pride. Frieze also points out that if lack of ability is seen as the cause of a failure, there is little tendency to try again, because the person has little reason to believe that failure can be changed to success. Thus, Frieze argues, high self-esteem is theoretically associated with giving internal, stable reasons for success and external or unstable reasons for failure.

Research shows that women and men appear to differ in how they attribute causes for success and failure. Women more often than men show patterns that are the result of, and/or contribute to, low self-esteem. They give external reasons for both successes and failures more than men do, or, even more disturbingly, they may attribute their failures to lack of ability and their successes to external, unstable causes (Frieze, 1975). In general, men rely more heavily on ability and women on luck to explain their successes. Even among highly achievement-motivated women and men, women tend to use effort and luck to explain both success and failure; men rely heavily on ability to explain success and on external factors to explain failure (Bar-Tal & Frieze, 1977).

All this suggests that men and women, even under conditions of equal success, often do not experience success in the same way. Men have learned to claim credit for success and to view it as a source of pride. Women have learned to view success as less susceptible to their own control and, therefore, as less reliable and worthy of praise. This pattern parallels somewhat the findings on sex differences in locus of control discussed earlier, and it may be related to some of the same social factors. Both sets of findings, taken together, show that it is entirely possible for women to maintain a self-image of weakness and powerlessness even when their behavior appears to others to be a demonstration of power and strength.

Changing patterns of attribution. Is it possible to change the pattern of attributing causes for success or failure? We know that thoughts, feelings, and behaviors are inextricably linked so that a change in thoughts or feelings can alter behavior or a change in behavior can cause a shift in thoughts and feelings. Therefore, although one way to change patterns of attribution is to re-educate people in ways of interpreting their outcomes, certain behavioral changes may make new interpretations easier. If the object is to allow women to feel more effective and in control of their outcomes, some specific types of behaviors will help. We will focus briefly here on two of them—direct uses of interpersonal power and developing special abilities or competence.

Johnson's (1976) analysis of the advantages and disadvantages of different power methods, discussed in Chapter 3, suggests that the *way* one exercises power is very closely related to how powerful one feels. She argues that the indirect power user does not receive credit for the influence that she or he exerts because it is hidden. Thus, the individual continues to be treated as powerless and perhaps does not experience the gain in self-esteem that would occur if her or his effectiveness were recognized by others. It seems obvious, then, that the person who wishes to feel more powerful must try to be more open or direct in attempting to influence another. The sensible way to begin, of course, is by being most open and direct in situations where one is relatively sure of being effective. This openness also includes taking proper credit for the use of power. For example, suppose I have worked very hard to get a committee to adopt a certain position, and they do. If someone congratulates me for making my point so well, I am giving my power away if I respond by saying, "It wasn't really me. They were leaning in that direction anyway." Here is a situation that calls for attributing success to one's own skill or effort—in other words, a simple "thank you" will do. In many situations, modesty is the enemy of power.

For people who need guidance is how to become more direct in interpersonal influence, assertiveness training is a possible answer. Now offered in most North American cities, this training encourages direct, honest, nonaggressive expression of one's desires in interaction with others. Although by no means a universal solution to the problem of directness in attempts to influence others, this type of training may give the individual some useful techniques and a new sense of what is possible in relationships with other people.

Unfortunately, although there seems to be much to gain by using direct instead of indirect power, its use by women (and by members of other low-status groups) is often clouded by a "catch-22." Low-status people who try openly to exert power are often misinterpreted, or are characterized as "uppity" and are disliked. For example, as we will see in Chapter 5, Nancy Henley (1977) indicates that a woman who uses nonverbal cues associated with power is often seen as communicating sexual availability rather than power. Thus, for a woman, the use of more direct influence methods is not a simple solution to overcoming a sense of powerlessness. Women should try to develop more directness, but they should also be aware of the possible problems it entails.

Another type of behavior that may increase a person's sense of power is to learn and practice skills that require special competence and strength. This may be especially true of activities requiring *physical* strength. Many people feel that a sense of physical weakness or vulnerability contributes to a more general sense of powerlessness, and that women in particular suffer from this syndrome. Kathryn Lance, in her book *Getting Strong*, calls us "a nation of weak sisters" and argues that by building physical strength women can derive the psychological benefits of increased security, a lessening of physical fear and the sense of being a potential victim, and a general increase in confidence and sense of control. Leanne Schreiber (cited in Rorbaugh, 1979) asserts that society's conventions have steered women away from a sense of physical power toward weakness, and that this sense of physical power must be reclaimed.

> Women have been systematically encouraged to divorce their identities from their bodies and in so doing they have been divorced from the most basic sense of power and the most basic source of power. When you divorce a whole class of people from that very primary sense of their own power, you've created a sort of ruptured identity . . . a very primary disconnection with the world.

Of course, as McHugh, Duquin, and Frieze (1977) point out, even a superb athlete can attribute success in competition to external factors. Competition aside, however, as a woman works herself up to being able to lift heavier weights or run increased distances, it becomes difficult for her to attribute these new-found capabilities to anything but the internal factor of increased strength, brought about by her own efforts.

PERSONAL POWER

The idea that increased physical strength may have an impact on feelings of power, suggests that feeling powerful need not always entail feelings of control over other people. Indeed, power may be felt chiefly *for* the self, and only secondarily, or not at all, may imply control *over* others. This type of power might be called personal, as opposed to interpersonal power.

Carl Rogers (1977), writing on personal power, describes a politics of therapy whose main goal is *not to take power away* from the individual. The system rests on the assumption that individuals have an inner strength that will emerge and develop if obstacles are not placed in their path. Personal power is seen by Rogers as a tendency to grow and to self-actualize. The person would experience power, then, to the extent that she or he was not restricted in this growth.

Writing on the psychology of women, Jean Baker Miller (1977) notes that the traditional concept of power, which implies a winner-loser situation, should be broadened. In that traditional framework, the power of another person is always seen as dangerous, and the quest for power means a struggle between individuals or groups for control over the other. In this competition, any increase in power for one of the parties automatically leads to a decrease in power for the other. Miller suggests, however, that an equally and perhaps more important type of power is the capacity to develop one's abilities. This kind of power implies a lack of constraints by and dependence on others, but not domination of them. It involves a refusal to be controlled rather than control over others. Miller argues that when an individual becomes more powerful in this way, the result is ultimately beneficial to others, too, because it lessens the individual's need to restrict others through domination or dependence.

In terms of feeling powerful, Miller speaks of ways in which we label feelings as weak or powerful. She suggests particularly that a number of so-called feminine weaknesses can and should be "re-seen" as actual or potential strengths; for example, in our society men have been taught to deny and women to cultivate the feelings of vulnerability and weakness that are an inevitable part of the human experience. Miller argues that, although this contributes to the label of women as the weaker sex, the fact that women can tolerate their feelings of vulnerability is actually a strength. Psychological growth, she suggests, may depend on one's reaction to the feelings of vulnerability that one encounters throughout life. If an individual flees from or denies such feelings, he or she loses possibilities for growth. Women, then, can learn to look on their very openness to and understanding of weakness as a strength, as long as they work productively with those feelings rather than wallowing in them. For Miller, feelings of personal power involve a sense of being able to grow and to develop one's abilities, while at the same time not regarding every feeling of weakness as a threat or a defeat.

Adrienne Rich (1976) also writes of a type of power that involves self-expression rather than domination. She labels as *powerfulness* "the expressive energy of an ego which . . . was licensed to direct itself outward upon the world" (p. 55). Feeling powerful in this sense implies feeling the ability and freedom to direct one's expressive energy outward in some creative effort rather than being forced to suppress it. Both Tillich (1954) and Daly (1973) write about a "power of being," which involves a radical recognition, enhancement, and development of the self and which, to be authentic, cannot be separated from the forces of love and justice.

These writings, then, say that one can feel powerful without necessarily feeling control over others. A sense of power in one's self or inner strength is one dimension of the experience of power; the sense of control over others is another. A sense of collective, cooperative power, as described in Chapter 2, may be a third. The extent to which these dimensions may be independent is not clear, but it is reasonable to assume that they are not perfectly linked. For example, it is easy to conceive of a person who wields a great deal of control over others, but who feels little sense of inner strength. It is also possible to imagine that a person with little interpersonal power as an individual could experience a great sense of collective or cooperative power when working with a group toward a goal. Feeling powerful, then, is not limited to interpersonal influence.

Feeling Powerful: Men vs. Women

Much of this chapter has suggested that men have more opportunities than women do for feeling powerful, but certain kinds of questions remain unanswered. Do men and women experience the feeling of power in similar ways? Does power mean the same thing to them? Some preliminary research (Lips, 1979) suggests that there may be considerable differences between the sexes in the way they experience power. The male and female members of an introductory psychology class responded differently in many respects when they were asked, "When have you felt most powerful?" Although both sexes stressed leadership and control over others as an element of power (47 percent of the 15 males and 43 percent of the 35 females), only the females labeled the sense of accomplishment at simply doing something well as a feeling of power (none of the males, but 17 percent of the females mentioned this). Two of the men, but none of the women, mentioned exerting physical force over another person as an experience of power; two of the women said that they had felt most powerful at the birth of a baby. Three of the men claimed that they had *never* felt powerful; none of the women responded in this way. Although the data are insufficient to draw definitive conclusions, this preliminary research suggests that men and women may view power differently and more women than men may be oriented toward what has been described as personal power.

To the extent that men and women operate in different spheres, it is reasonable to expect them to draw their experiences of power from different sources. Rich's (1976) suggestion that many women derive their main experience of power over another person through motherhood seems plausible, for instance. Research that compares the power experiences of women and men in various life-styles may sort out the effects of sex from those of life situations.

SUMMARY

Feeling powerful can involve a number of factors: the sense of personal control over one's outcomes, the feeling of freedom of choice in one's behavior, the ability to see oneself as competent and effective by taking credit for one's accomplishments, and the sense of one's capacity to develop and implement one's abilities. It is apparent that in many of these areas the experience of women in our culture differs from that of men. Women more than men have been encouraged to feel a sense of external control over their lives and, perhaps as a result, less readily take credit for their personal successes. Men tend to use power strategies that enhance their vision of their own effectiveness; women are more likely to use the indirect strategies, which result in less sense of power.

Women influenced by men in a direct, concrete way may find it difficult to maintain a sense of freedom, control, and responsibility about their behavior in relation to these men. Men influenced by women in ways that are mainly manipulative and hidden, on the other hand, maintain (accurately or not) a belief that they are making their own decisions. Even in the area of personal power, women do not seem as free as men to explore and develop the sense of their own abilities.

On the face of it, this picture leaves little hope for the idea of women as powerful human beings or women and men as equal partners in the human race. Yet, in fact, there are signs of optimism. Many would argue that this is one of the most exciting times in history to be a woman in Western culture. All over the continent, alone and in groups, women are experiencing a new sense of their own power. They are moving into new career areas, exercising their relatively new freedom to decide when and whether to marry or to have children, and winning political victories. Some men, too, are finding a new sense of their own power in the lessened financial and emotional dependence of women on them. This is not to say that power struggles between women and men are coming to an end. Indeed, in many ways, the struggles are only beginning. As we will see in the next chapter, the structure of a power relationship can be so rigid and deeply rooted that sometimes even people who wish to change it may find themselves maintaining it through their behavior.

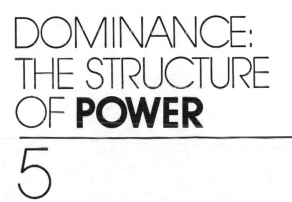

DOMINANCE:
THE STRUCTURE
OF **POWER**

5

The roles they played were based upon a script constructed around a few basic axioms. One was that men were created dominant and would always remain so because of their superior strength and superior wisdom, and because it was the will of God.

Elaine Morgan

Under the general rubric of power, the study of dominance and dominance hierarchies is the only area in which psychologists have traditionally regarded sex as an important variable. The early research on dominance was done with animals, where male dominance over females was reasonably common, and this pattern of dominance behavior was judged to be rooted in biology and evolution. Apologists for male dominance among humans have been quick to adopt a simplistic version of the evolutionary perspective—a precarious base from which they assert, for example, that because male baboons dominate female baboons, it is natural and right for human males to dominate human females. Versions of this argument have been appearing in the popular press for years (Robert Ardrey's *The Territorial Imperative,* Desmond Morris' *Naked Apes,* Lionel Tiger's *Men in Groups* are perhaps the best known). As we will see in this chapter, however, generalizations from animal to human populations must be tenuous at best, and social as well as biological considerations are important to patterns of dominance behavior.

Dominance refers to the imposition of one's will on someone else. Regardless of the particular power methods used, the individual who exerts the most influence when two people interact characterized as the dominant party. In some situations, dominance derives merely from influential behavior; however, usually it is also a matter of rank, position, and relative status. For example, a person of high status can often dominate or exert influence over a lower status person through mere presence, without making any overt behavioral attempt to do so. The study of dominance and dominance hierarchies is an inquiry into the origin and maintenance of stable structures of power relationships.

Research on dominance behavior has occupied psychologists and ethologists for years. This chapter begins with a look at the way dominance has been defined, the assumptions that have guided the research, and an overview of human sex differences in dominance. Then we examine possible evolutionary and biological roots of dominance behavior. Much of the research that concerns this issue has been carried out with various animal species, and the results show a fairly clear link between sex and dominance. This link is not quite so clear however, in studies of human dominance behavior. The social roots of dominance behavior in humans are also examined, and we will see that much of our social structure may lay the groundwork for and encourage male dominance.

PSYCHOLOGICAL RESEARCH
ON DOMINANCE

Psychologists have tried to measure dominance by devising situations in which one individual must defer to another. Thus, in observing animals, a dominant animal is one whose threats result in withdrawal by other animals, who wins out in conflicts over resources, the one toward whom submissive gestures are made, and the one who is typically followed by other members of the group (Maccoby & Jacklin, 1974). In experimental studies, two animals are paired in confrontation over a reward such as food, and the animal who forces the other to give way is called the dominant one. In studies of humans, dominance is measured by the emergence or election of an individual to a leadership position (for example, Megargee, 1969), the number of contributions to a joint decision made by each individual in a pair (for example, Knott & Drost, 1969), the number of challenges to his or her opinion that a person can sustain in a disagreement (for example, Adams & Landers, 1978), the number of times one person interrupts the other (for example, Zimmerman & West, 1975), and other behavioral indications that one person is exerting more influence than another on the interaction and its outcome. Psychologists have also studied the tendency toward dominance by measuring *attempts* at influence in various situations: attempts to control peers, number of orders or suggestions given, and speaking intensity.

Research with animals has established that in many (but not all) species, groups are organized in stable dominance hierarchies, with the larger or stronger animals having higher status and hence more influence (for example, De Vore, 1965). These hierarchies appear to hold in all situations. Knowledge of the positions of two animals in the hierarchy enables the researcher to predict which one will win out in a conflict over food, space, or other resources. Often males and females form separate dominance hierarchies, but female hierarchies appear to be somewhat less stable than those of the male. In a conflict between a male and a female, it is usually the female who defers to the male. The presence of dominance hierarchies provides a structural solution to the problem of who gives way to whom: the animal lower in the hierarchy automatically defers to the dominant animal. This eliminates the need for constant fighting.

One rather basic assumption of the research has been that dominance hierarchies are maintained through the efforts of the dominant animals. However, Rowell (1966) questions this, arguing that the hierarchy is supported mainly by the behavior of subordinates rather than by the high-ranking animals. He claims that hierarchies are a product of environmental stress. Stress has the most devastating effect on the weakest animals, resulting in lowered resistance to disease and behavioral changes such as an increase in behaviors of submission. Because of these changes, these weaker stressed animals assume a low ranking in the group, and it is their behavior rather than the behavior of the dominant animals that maintains the hierarchy.

A second assumption is that dominance hierarchies actually do exist and are important for social organization in *most* animal species. However, applying the concept of dominance so generally can be questioned (Archer, 1971). For example, the emphasis on dominance hierarchies derives mainly from studies of animals confined in spaces much smaller than their natural home ranges. An examination of the variation in dominance behavior among different species suggests that they do not all fit conveniently into general statements about these hierarchies.

The research on human dominance has been guided by the animal studies, under the assumption that similar kinds of hierarchies exist in human groups. This assumption, too, appears overly simplistic. Collins and Raven (1968) suggest that although there are some similarities between dominance in groups of young children and dominance in primate groups, there are important differences. In children, dominance hierarchies are not as stable from one situation to another as are hierarchies in primate groups. Furthermore, they argue, the older the members of the human group and the more complex the social setting in which they function, the less likely that the same rank ordering of power in the group will prove true in all situations. Dominance among human adults, then, cannot be understood in the same way as dominance among subhuman primates.

DOMINANCE AND SUBMISSION
AMONG HUMAN MALES AND FEMALES

Research suggests that human males are more concerned with dominance than human females, and much of their dominance behavior is directed toward one another (Maccoby & Jacklin, 1974). On paper-and-pencil measures of dominance, males tend to score higher than females (Hoyenga & Hoyenga, 1979). The studies of nonverbal communication described later in this chapter also suggest strongly that males are more likely than females to behave in a dominant way.

A number of studies show that when males interact with females they take dominant roles. For example, Megargee (1969) paired subjects who had measured high and low on a paper-and-pencil measure of dominance, and asked each pair to decide which would be the leader and which the follower. Among same-sex pairs, the high dominance person was most likely to become the leader. Similarly, when a high-dominant male was paired with a low-dominant female, the male usually emerged as the leader. However, when a high-dominant woman was paired with a low-dominant man, sex roles apparently took precedence over personality disposition, and the man still became the leader 80 percent of the time. Although under the other conditions it was usually the leader who made the decision to lead, in the high-dominant female low-dominant male situation, it was often the woman who decided that the man should lead. These women truly gave their power away.

A study by Adams and Landers (1978) paired students with confederates* to come up with joint decisions about the relative attractiveness of pairs of pictures. Dominance was defined by the number of challenges to his or her preference that a subject could sustain against the partner. Results showed clearly that males withstood more challenges to their preferences than females did. Sex of the challenger apparently made no difference, however, to the dominance behavior of either male or female subjects. That finding is surprising, but may perhaps be attributed to the experimental procedure. Both male and female confederates apparently had been trained to use the same standard challenges. In real life it is doubtful that males and females would choose identical ways of influencing another's opinion (see Chapter 3).

Finally, a study of small group interaction by Aries (1976) shows that male dominance is not limited to pairs of individuals. When she analyzed the speaking behavior in all-female, all-male, and mixed-sex groups, she found striking differences in dominance between women and men. In the mixed-sex groups, males both initiated more interactions and got more responses than females—behavior considered to indicate dominance ranking in the group. Moreover, the all-male groups established a more stable dominance order over time than did the female groups.

The pattern of male dominance shows up not just in the lab experiments of social scientists, but also in the real world. Studies of organizations

---

*A confederate is someone playing the part of an experimental subject but who has actually been trained by the experimenter to behave in a certain way during the experiment.

(discussed in Chapter 8) show that there is often a reluctance to allow women to take on management positions. (For an extensive analysis of the roles of women and men in organizations, see also N.L. Colwill, in press). Male dominance is also a recurring issue in sexuality (Chapter 6) and in the family (Chapter 7).

If men are more concerned than women with dominance, does this imply that women in general are submissive? Not necessarily. Research shows that women are quite capable of dominance behaviors under the right conditions, and everyday observation indicates that women regularly counter men's attempts to dominate or devalue them. In fact, as Maccoby and Jacklin (1974) suggest, dominance and submission may not even be on the same behavioral plane, but may be independent aspects of behavior.

Research by Eagly, Wood, and Fishbaugh (in press) suggests that some interpretation may be needed to assess the results that show women to be more compliant and able to be persuaded than men. It has usually been assumed that women more often than men change their private opinions to coincide with those of a group in the interest of group harmony. This is one source of the stereotype that women are submissive. However, Eagly's results showed that women's opinions tended to remain unchanged when confronted with a group. Rather it was the opinions of the men that changed—in the direction of greater nonconformity. Eagly and her colleagues suggest, then, that the sometimes observed sex differences in who can be influenced stem, not from greater female submissiveness, but from greater male concern with grabbing the spotlight—one way, of course, of attaining dominance.

Males have greater concern with dominance than females; this appears to be a common finding in human studies. Why? Some researchers view dominance behavior as rooted in biology and evolution. Let us examine this viewpoint. Later, we will look at possible social origins of dominance.

BIOLOGICAL AND EVOLUTIONARY ROOTS OF DOMINANCE

Does dominance behavior have some connection to physical or physiological factors? In animals, at least, there is strong evidence that is does. Furthermore, research suggests that in certain animal species, dominance patterns have evolved because they have helped species to adapt to their environment and thus to survive. These generalizations are probably less true for humans, however, as we shall see.

Dominance and Aggression

Among animals, the major way of asserting dominance is through aggression. Thus, not surprisingly, the physical and biological factors that correlate with or accompany aggression are similar to those which appear in conjunction with dominance. For example, smaller and weaker animals are usually dominated by larger and stronger animals who are more capable of effective aggression. In most species, this means that the males dominate the females (Hoyenga & Hoyenga, 1979). There are exceptions, however. Among macaque monkeys, some females can dominate some males and some females may dominate a whole troop (Washburn, Jay, & Lancaster, 1965). Older females sometimes determine whether a new male will be accepted into the group (Lancaster, 1976). Among patas monkeys, the smaller female may successfully threaten the male, particularly when she is protecting an infant (Hall & Mayer, 1967). Lancaster also reports that among some monkeys such as vervet, langurs, patas, and zeladas, it is quite common for adult females to form coalitions against dominant males who try to monopolize a special food source or frighten an infant. She asserts that even the lowest ranking females will chase a male who has made one of their infants scream.

> A typical sequence might begin with a female screaming and soliciting aid by giving rapid glances back and forth between the adult male and the females whose support she sought. The coalition would then attack, running and usually screaming, at the male. The male would turn and flee. He would run as fast as he could until he reached the nearest tree or rock. He would then run up it and turn to face his chasers who threatened from below. After a minute or so of exchanging threats, the females would then move off, perhaps going back to the food or infant which was the cause of the problem. After that the male might be free to join them, but now on their terms and not on his (Lancaster, 1976, p. 35).

Although these coalitions and attacks do not seem to affect the rank of the male in question or enhance the positions of the individual female members, they do seem to affect the male's behavior. Lancaster reports, for instance, that males become cautious about frightening infants. She describes several instances when, after an infant vervet monkey had screamed, all nearby adult males, apparently anticipating a female attack, immediately left the area. Thus, although the hierarchy itself is unchanged, the potential for dominant behavior by the males in these groups is somewhat tempered by the female coalitions.

Another interesting point about dominance hierarchies is that among some species of monkeys, it is sufficient to know the individual's mother and birth order to know its rank in the group hierarchy (Kawamura, 1958; Sade, 1967). With Indian and Japanese macaques, dominance relations among young monkeys are entirely determined by the relative ranks of their mothers. As Lancaster (1976) explains, this may occur because mothers respond to threats to their offspring in ways that reflect their own rank in the group. If the threat comes from a lower ranking animal, the mother will respond aggressively; if it comes from a higher ranking animal, she may flee with her infant or make placating gestures. Thus, the young monkey learns, through a model, to respond to other monkeys in the group according to their status, while the other group members learn which infants have powerful mothers to defend them. In any case, it is fairly clear that dominance is related to the individual's potential to behave aggressively and/or to enlist help in behaving aggressively.

The level of the male sex hormone, testosterone, relates to aggression levels of both animals and humans (see Maccoby & Jacklin, 1974, and Hoyenga & Hoyenga, 1979 for reviews of these findings) and may possibly relate to dominance. However, testosterone levels may be interpreted as either a cause or an effect of aggression or dominance. This point is made most clearly in a study by Rose, Gordon, and Bernstein (1972), which showed that if male rhesus monkeys low on the dominance hierarchy were placed with females whom they could dominate, their testosterone levels rose markedly. On the other hand, when a male rhesus monkey was defeated in a fight, his testosterone level dropped and remained low.

For humans, unlike animals, aggression and dominance are not as closely related, and so there is less support for a link between human dominance and biology. As already discussed, there are many ways for one person to exert influence over another without relying on actual or threatened physical force, such as by acting submissive or helpless. However, research suggests that, where dominance is defined in terms of aggression, there are some similarities between dominance behavior patterns of young children and primate groups.

Studies in several cultures have investigated dominance hierarchies among groups of four-to-ten-year-old children (Omark & Edelman, 1973; Edelman & Omark, 1975). When children were asked to rate one another in terms of "toughness," there was a great deal of agreement about the toughness hierarchies of both boys and girls. Boys were rated as tougher than girls, and within each sex the hierarchies were reasonably stable (although less so for girls). Pairs of these children, each given a crayon of a different color, were then set to work drawing a picture together. Dominance was measured by seeing which child's color was predominant in the main outline and the available space of the picture. Interestingly, although boys dominated girls in mixed-sex pairs at every grade except kindergarten, in same-sex pairs "toughness" did not particularly predict dominance. The tendency for toughness scores to relate to dominance was significant in only two grades out of five. Thus, the individual child's ranking in the dominance hierarchy did not seem to give him or her a general status of dominance.

Other research suggests that toughness or aggressiveness is only one aspect of dominance in human groups. Characteristics of children described by other children as influential include politeness and pleasantness as well as toughness (Gold, 1958), and among adolescents, leadership in both sexes is related to a variety of qualities such as popularity, attractiveness, athletic skills, and social interests (Marks, 1957). Collins and Raven (1968) note that among adolescents and adults, dominance in any one aspect of a relationship with another does not always mean dominance in all aspects of the relationship.

Dominance and Evolution

Many researchers suggest that dominance hierarchies and sex differences in dominance have helped a variety of species to survive and, therefore, are significant in evolution. Among primates, for example, a stable dominance hierarchy may reduce aggression within the group, as well as providing the group with a protector in the form of the dominant male or males. Furthermore, rank in the hierarchy may be associated with reproductive success. In many species, dominant males have more access to females, both because they can outthreaten other males and because females seem to prefer the higher ranking males (Sugiyama, 1969; van Lawick-Goodall, 1968). Among females as well, dominance may be associated with the number of offspring. This appears to be not because dominance increases females' access to sexual partners, but because the fertility of low-ranking females is impaired through frequent attacks by dominant females (Dunbar & Dunbar, 1977). Reproductive selection, then, would favor the passing on of genes associated with within-sex dominance in both males and females. The evolution of male dominance *over* females is said to stem from the frequent female preference for a dominant male (a preference for a dominant partner that does not appear to be shared by the male), in combination with the dominant male's success at protecting his own offspring (Hoyenga & Hoyenga, 1979).

Dominance does not have the same significance in every species, however, and is not universally associated with reproductive success. As Archer (1971) points out, it is oversimplistic to assume that in all animal species success in one type of fighting activity automatically means top access to all biologically important resources such as food, nest sites, and mates.

There are many evolutionary routes to the survival of the species, and the formation of rigid male dominance hierarchies is just one of a number of possibilities.

Can dominance behavior in *humans* be linked to evolution? Have we evolved sex differences in the tendency toward dominance? These issues have been hotly debated for years.

Some psychologists (for example, Hutt, 1972) have applied a theory to humans that was developed by Wynne-Edwards (1962) to explain the evolution of sex differences in social behavior among animals. Wynne-Edwards argued that behavioral sex differences could be traced to the different roles played by males and females in reproduction. Since the female had to carry (and, in the case of mammals, suckle) the young, it was left to the male to obtain food and to protect the group. This basic division of labor led, over generations, to specialization according to sex in particular behaviors and characteristics (dominance for males, nurturing for females). Applying this type of theory to explain human sex differences is popular with sociobiologists today.

Tiger (1969) has also argued that human male dominance, even in complex social affairs, is the result of evolution. He suggests a species-specific, biologically based pattern that facilitates bonding, or sticking together, among males. Supposedly, this pattern developed as a result of selection in prehistoric hunting groups against females who hunted and males willing to let them hunt. The pattern is a predisposition for men to stick together *and* to exclude women from their groups. Thus, Tiger argues, males have a naturally evolved tendency to dominate political and decision-making groups. Human females, on the other hand, are "biologically unprogrammed to dominate political systems," according to Tiger. They do not have a capacity that is biologically based, as males do, to trigger "followership" behavior among their cohorts, and thus they do not make effective leaders. Tiger's ideas have caused considerable comment, but they remain unproven. His argument rests largely on a comparison of human and baboon societies, and, as already noted, there is much danger in generalizing from any particular species of primate to humans.

There are several basic problems in the attempt to show that male dominance in human societies is rooted in evolution. First, such arguments tend to rest on the notion that male dominance is a universally evolved pattern among our distant cousins, the primates. But this is demonstrably not the case. Second, these arguments tend to assume that male dominance is relatively universal in human societies. However, there is considerable anthropological data to the contrary, beginning with Margaret Mead's (1950) classic study of New Guinea tribes. Her research indicated that the characteristic of dominance could be ascribed to either, neither, or both sexes. Rosenblatt and Cuningham (1976), in reviewing the anthropological literature, suggest the argument that in many societies where male dominance is observed in public, there is actually a fairly even balance of power between the sexes in private and domestic matters.

Although there *may* be an evolutionary basis for human sex differences in dominance, then, the evidence is certainly not unequivocal. Moreover, it is clearly impossible to accept the argument that because a characteristic may have had a selective advantage for the species in the past, it is not modifiable under present conditions. Human dominance behavior obviously can be modified. Moreover, the process of evolution is a continuing one, and different characteristics are favored as our environment changes.

In studying dominance among human beings, we would do well to remember that dominance, rather than being an unchanging personality trait, can just as easily be thought of as behavior in a specific situation. To assess how consistent dominant behavior is within individuals, we must recognize the signals through which dominance is expressed. So, we must examine verbal and nonverbal signals of dominance.

SIGNALS OF DOMINANCE AND SUBMISSION

Ethologists suggest that dominance relations among animals are maintained through behaviors that signal dominance and submission. For example, depending on the species, a dominant animal may snarl, bare its teeth, move toward the other animal, or adopt various other aggressive postures in the effort to get the other animal to back down. Conversely, the nondominant animal may signal submission by backing away, lowering the head or eyes, or even "smiling" (among some monkeys and apes). The submissive gesture diminishes the aggressive potential of the interaction and makes it unnecessary for the participants to fight.

Do humans have similar signals of dominance and submission that help to regulate their interactions? A growing body of research suggests that we have. Investigations of the way people use space, facial expressions, gestures, touch, and body position, as well as the way they regulate their conversations, use language, and arrange their clothing and their environment, indicate that certain behaviors seem to be reliable indicators of power, and they may actually help to establish and maintain power differences between participants in an interaction.

Control over Space

Space plays a part in rank in the dominance hierarchy among animals. Dominant animals are said to have more freedom in the areas they may visit without interference from other members of the group (for example, Hall, 1966; Sommer, 1969); they have larger areas of "personal space" (Hall, 1966) and greater choice of feeding and resting areas (Washburn & De Vore, 1961) than subordinate animals.

Although the research on humans has been somewhat less systematic, there are many indications that control of space does have to do with both dominance and status. Simple observation, for instance, tells us that the higher status people in organizations have the larger and better equipped offices, that parents control more space in the home than children, and that the most privileged members of society tend to control access to the most desirable territory, whether it be beach-front lots or the best seats at the theatre. Rigid, straight body positions that occupy less space are said to communicate fearfulness and low status (Mehrabian, 1972). Furthermore, both formal and informal rules designate the distances that must be maintained between people of unequal status (Hall, 1966; Goffman, 1971), and preschool children keep a greater distance from a child who has previously established dominance over them than from other children (King, 1966).

Males and females tend to use space differently, and the male-female differences parallel high-low status and dominance-submission differences (Frieze & Ramsey, 1976; Henley, 1977). Frieze and Ramsey cite a survey by Altman and Nelson, which indicates that mothers are less likely than fathers to have a special room in the family home. Even when mothers do have such a room, it is more likely than the father's room to be violated. They also note that in many homes fathers have a "special chair," while mothers rarely do, and that women's space in the work world often tends to be more public and crowded than that of the men. (In the work world, at least, sex is confounded with status so that women usually hold the lower status jobs.)

It has been found repeatedly that females yield space more easily than males. Women move out of the way more frequently and earlier than men when being approached or passed on the sidewalk (Dobbs, 1972; Silveira, 1972). Also, in situation after situation, women tend to choose postures and body positions that take up a minimum of space, while male positions are often characterized by a spreading out of the legs or arms (Frieze & Ramsey, 1972; Henley, 1977). Any woman who has been unlucky enough to be assigned the middle seat between two men on a long airplane trip already knows this. Women contract and men expand!

Facial Expression

The face may be a major channel for the display of power or authority. We tend to connect stern or impassive expressions, unwavering stares, and clenched jaws with dominance, while, as Nancy Henley (1977) points out, smiling sometimes indicates deference.

> . . . smiling is a human facial expression also associated with subordinate status. The unctuous Uriah Heep, the shuffling Uncle Tom, anyone seeking to ingratiate is depicted with a perpetual grin. The "nervous" smile, like the nervous laugh, conveys tension more than pleasure, and in many people has had to be held so long and so often that it has become a habit and an etched facial expression. Though little research has been done on smiling, it is understood as a gesture offered upwards in the status hierarchy; indeed, a powerful and successful person may be said to be surrounded by a thousand suns! (p. 171)

Many writers have suggested that women smile more than men, and although there is little hard research to back up this observation, the available evidence tends to support it (Henley 1977). In general, women seem to be more facially expressive than men. Not only do they smile more, they also cry more. Such expressiveness may make them more vulnerable than men, who control their expressions to hide their emotions.

The eyes are thought to be especially important in dominance. According to Henley, two aspects of eye contact are used to define hierarchical position. In the first instance, staring is used to assert dominance, while averting the gaze is a gesture of submission. Studies show that men tend to stare more than women, while women are more likely to drop their eyes than men. In the second instance, a secure dominant position is reinforced and maintained by visually ignoring the other person (such as looking away while the other speaks), while a subordinate person requires considerable eye contact as a feature of attentive listening. Here again, the dominant behavior is more often found in males and the subordinate one in females.

Gestures

Gesture, body movement, and position are also thought to communicate dominance, status, and superiority. Expansive gestures and those associated with relaxation convey superiority, while closed, contracted positions are characteristic of subordinates (Henley, 1977). Dominant individuals may also convey superiority by gestures associated with territorial rights (putting one's feet on the desk), with height (standing up to make a point), or with control from a distance (beckoning or directing by gesture).

In this area, too, there are male-female behavioral differences in which gender and dominance are confounded. For example, Henley (1977) cites research suggesting that women more often than men tilt their heads sideways to indicate attentive listening. This listening position conveys less dominance than one in which the head is erect and facing forward. A similar theme (with a different behavior) is found by Borden and Homleid (1978), who studied the way in which male-female couples position themselves while walking together. They found a strong tendency in same-handed couples for the woman to be positioned on the man's dominant side (on his right if he is right-handed or on his left if he is left-handed). As the authors suggest with wry humor in the title of their article, men seem to be "strong-arming" women.

Touch

Although we tend to think of touch as something that communicates affection, it may convey dominance in many situations as well. Nancy Henley (1977) argues persuasively that dominants touch subordinates more than vice versa, and also that men touch women more than women touch men. To see the role of touch in action in dominance hierarchies, one need only observe the interaction of a group of status-differentiated people (same sex, to avoid confusing the issue). Those who initiate touch are more often the high-status members of the group, while those who receive it are low status. Similarly, although the president of a company may slap the back or put a hand on the shoulder of a new employee, it is clearly inappropriate for the employee to initiate such behaviors toward the company president. They signal a degree of familiarity that is a violation of the president's status (and perhaps, by implication, authority).

According to Henley, the issue is even more complex when female-male interactions are involved. When a woman uses touch to convey dominance (for example, if she is in a position of authority over a man), her signals are often misinterpreted and misread as indicating a sexual advance. This may be because her behavior presents others with a status incongruity (low-status person/high-status behavior), which they resolve by redefining her behavior.

Who Talks? Who Listens?

Dominance can be conveyed by the degree to which one can hold the center of a conversation, the success with which one can interrupt another speaker, and the extent to which one is able to draw a response or discussion of one's own ideas by others. All of these are indications that one is controlling the conversation.

Research indicates that status is related to the ability to control a conversation. For example, adults have been found to interrupt children frequently (Sacks, 1972), and the department chairman was found to be the person least frequently interrupted during the faculty meetings of one department (Eakins & Eakins, 1976).

Sex differences appear in this area as well:

> Not only have men been found to talk more than women in a mixed group, but they attain their greater talkativeness in part by interrupting women or answering questions that are not addressed to them. Men have been found to interrupt women more than women interrupt men. Many women have a difficult time getting and keeping attention in a group. Perhaps because their voices are less powerful they have a harder time getting the floor and a harder time keeping it through interruptions (Eakins & Eakins, 1978, p. 66).

A study that sheds considerable light on the reasons why women may have trouble getting and keeping the floor in conversations was carried out by Zimmerman and West (1975). They recorded a number of conversations in public places in a university community, and analyzed them for the occurrence of interruptions, overlaps (one speaker starting to respond before the other has completely finished), and silences. Their findings showed some dramatic differences between same-sex and cross-sex conversations. Although in same-sex conversations, the overlaps and interruptions were distributed fairly evenly among speakers, in cross-sex conversations virtually all the interruptions (98 percent) and overlaps (100 percent) were by male speakers. In fact, in contrast to the talk patterns of same-sex pairs, interruption seemed to be normal rather than exceptional for female-male pairs. Notably, none of the women in these conversations ever protested about being interrupted. The researchers found, however, that in cross-sex conversations, women more often fell silent than men, and that these silences occurred most frequently after an interruption or after a delayed minimal response by the male (for example, long pause followed by a disinterested "mmhmm").

It appears that the tactics used by males in cross-sex conversations tend to discourage females and subdue their efforts at participation—allowing the males conversational control. Research by Fishman (cited in Parlee, 1979), on conversational control, points in the same direction. By analyzing more than 50 hours of spontaneous conversations between the members of three couples, she found that 96 percent of the topics introduced by the males "succeeded" (resulted in a conversation in which they were discussed), while only 36 percent of those introduced by the females did so. Men frequently did not respond or responded minimally to topics raised by women, while women almost always responded to those raised by men.

Not only who controls the conversation, but also the actual style of speech relates to power. Researchers have shown that persons low in power tend to use a speaking style that is filled with intensifiers, hedges, hesitations and questioning intonations, and powerful people do not (for example, Erickson, Lund, Johnson, & O'Barr, 1978). This power aspect of speech clearly has an effect on the impression formed of the speaker. Erickson and her colleagues found that people using "powerful" speech were better liked and seen as more credible than were those using "powerless" speech.

Some authors have suggested that men use more powerful speech styles than women do (for example, Lakoff, 1975). This may well be true in the many situations in which men hold more power than women, but when status differences are controlled sex differences do not necessarily appear. Erickson and her co-workers, for example, found that the use of powerless language was much more closely linked to social power and status than to sex.

Environmental Symbols of Dominance

Not only behavior, but also the accoutrements with which we surround ourselves and the way we arrange our environment may signify dominance to a greater or lesser extent. For instance, dominance can be communicated through height, and, therefore, having one's desk on a raised platform may reinforce a position of superiority. Dominance can also be conveyed through lack of accessibility, and barricading oneself behind a desk (the larger the better) can contribute to this impression. In the workplace, the size of the desk, the depth of the carpet, and the general luxuriousness of office furnishings are all thought to communicate status.

Much attention has been lavished recently on the role of the environment that is closest to our skin—our clothes—in establishing power relationships. We are told now that we can "dress for success" (Molloy, 1975, 1977). Molloy's research shows that, in the business world at least, people have learned to associate certain types of clothing with competence, power, and success, and his books will no doubt strengthen that association.

Sex differences in clothing styles may well reinforce power differences between men and women. Women's clothing tends to restrict their actions more than men's does (it is difficult to run in high-heeled shoes) and helps to channel their body movements and posture into "feminine" patterns. *The Radical Therapist* (1971) published a series of exercises for men that illustrate, among other things, the way in which clothing may affect womens' behavior. For example:

> Bend down to pick up an object from the floor. Each time you bend remember to bend your knees so that your rear end doesn't stick up, and place one hand on your shirtfront to hold it to your chest. This exercise simulates the experience of a woman in a short, low-necked dress bending over.*

A woman's clothing, which is often designed to be more revealing than that of a man, symbolically makes her more vulnerable than he, since status is related to difficulty of access. Moreover, in the manner of a vicious circle, clothing that is very feminine seems to convey low status simply because of its association with the cultural stereotype of femininity—a stereotype that emphasizes ineffectiveness and emotionality rather than competence and power. Thus, Molloy (1977) advises businesswomen to avoid frills and ruffles like the plague and never, *never* to dress in such a way that their nipples can be discerned under their clothes. The message is clear: women who want to be taken seriously in business can only hurt their chances by displaying obtrusive reminders of their femininity!

Willamette Bridge (Liberation News Service) 1971.

In summary, then, many human behaviors are seen to go naturally with dominance. Whether such behaviors serve as ways of establishing dominance (status indicators) or as ways of reinforcing a status difference that already exists (status reminders) probably depends on the overall status cues in the situation. For instance, research by Summerhayes and Suchner (1978), in which subjects rated the dominance of men and women pictured in situations where one was touching the other, suggested that "while touch diminished the power image of persons being touched in unequal status relationships, touch under equal status conditions did not seem to have any systematic effect" (p. 109).

Obviously, the signals of dominance and submission are many and varied, and they interact with one another, sometimes outside awareness. Where do the tendencies to use and respond to such behaviors come from? As we know, some people argue, particularly with regard to male dominance and female submission, that human beings are merely following an ancient evolutionary pattern. The following section examines an alternate perspective—the roots of such a pattern lie in cultural practices.

SOCIAL ROOTS OF DOMINANCE BEHAVIOR

Aggression

It was pointed out earlier that some, but not all, dominance behaviors are based on aggression. The debate has raged for years—is aggression a "natural" behavior for humans or is it learned (see, for example, Montagu, 1968; Fromm, 1973)? Similarly, many arguments have been made over the issue of the inevitability of greater male than female aggression among humans (see Josephson & Colwill, 1978, for a review). What emerges from these debates is that aggression is a multidetermined behavior, at least some of whose roots lie in the individual's experience.

Evidence for the social roots of both aggression and dominance is particularly compelling in cross-cultural data. Researchers such as Benedict (1934), Mead (1935), and Gorer (1968) have described cultures where there is little or no aggressive behavior. Interestingly, one cultural characteristic that seems to relate to nonaggression is minimal sex typing: less than the usual emphasis on differences between the male and female roles and on male dominance over females. Fromm (1973), in summarizing the research on various cultures, argues that "aggression is to be understood as part of the *social character,* not an isolated behavior trait" (p. 193) of a culture. The character of an aggressive society, he says, includes hierarchical relations, dominance, competitiveness, and often the devaluation of women. Yet, he asserts, these behaviors are not merely the expression of human instincts, but are responses to social situations in which the functioning of society depends not on mutuality, but rather on control of one group by another. Hierarchies of dominance and submission, whether of male over female, rich over poor, or one caste group over another are, according to Fromm, responses to the social order rather than its cause.

Another scientist, James Prescott (1975, 1979), has searched for the roots of aggression in the childrearing practices of societies. He uses anthropological data to show that in societies in which parents give high amounts of physical affection to infants, there is little incidence of inflicting pain on infants or of killing, torturing, or mutilating an enemy in war. On the other hand, in societies where pain is habitually inflicted on infants by their parents or caretakers, children develop little nurturant behavior, and dominance is likely to be evident in the practice of slavery and/or the subjection of women. Although this does not prove that adult aggression and dominance behaviors are *caused* by lack of physical affection toward children, Prescott puts forward an intriguing hypothesis. As a neuropsychologist, he suggests that early somatosensory deprivation causes changes in the brain and in the biochemistry of the body associated with aggressive behavior. (Obviously, this hypothesis postulates that the biological and social roots of aggression and dominance are intimately interconnected). Some research supports Prescott's ideas, but more needs to be done.

Research with animals, whose dominance depends highly on aggression and threat, provides strong evidence that experience plays an important role in dominance behavior. According to Hoyenga and Hoyenga (1979), the effects of hormones on aggression are mediated by experience, and experience tends to decrease the relationship between hormones and aggression. They cite research showing, for example, that injections of the male sex hormone, testosterone, will not restore dominance in castrated male mice once it has been lost, and that castration or the halting of testosterone injections will not stop aggressive behavior in male mice or in female monkeys *once they have successful fighting experience.* "Apparently," they argue, "the memory of winning has more important effects on behavior than the change of hormones" (p. 130).

From these diverse sources, then, come strands of support for the idea that aggressive dominance behavior has at least some of its roots in social experience. We turn now to theories that try to identify the particular social origins of human male dominance over females.

Male Dominance and the Mother-Child Tie

A number of theorists have concerned themselves with the origins of men's "need" to dominate women. Sociologists Jean Stockard and Miriam Johnson (1979) have reviewed the writings in psychoanalytic theory and the social sciences that pertain to this issue, and they conclude that "an important step in altering the development of the motive underlying male dominance would be to have men, as well as women, care for infants" (p. 199).

How can the early tie between mother and child possibly be connected to male dominance over females in adulthood? Stockard and Johnson, in attempting to demonstrate such a connection, make heavy use of the writings of the "gynocentric" branch of psychoanalytic theory—a perspective that puts primary importance on the child-mother relationship and assumes that children of both sexes initially identify with and orient themselves toward their mother. Two themes stemming from this perspective are considered important: the unconscious fear and envy that children of both sexes are said to feel toward the mother, and the alleged special problems encountered by males in establishing a secure sense of their gender identity.

Several theorists have tried to show that fear and envy of the mother plays an important role in the development of both sexes, but especially boys. Stockard and Johnson cite the work of psychoanalyst Melanie Klein, who argued that the boy's pride in and emphasis on the importance of his penis are compensations for feelings of anxiety, envy, and inferiority regarding the mother. Similarly, they note that both Ernest Jones and Karen Horney suggested the existence of an early male dread of the female vagina. Horney, in fact, felt that a general male fear of women arose from the boy's fear of being rejected by the mother. She saw this fear as the root of men's compulsion to prove their manhood, often by conquering or possessing women. Cross-cultural evidence, which may suggest a male fear of women's mysterious procreative capacities, has been collected by researchers such as William Lederer (1968).

Envy as well as fear of women's procreative power was thought by the theorists to exist in males. Horney, for example, argued that men unconsciously envy women their capacity for pregnancy, childbirth, and suckling, and suggested that men may achieve wealth and produce material goods as a compensation for their perceived inferiority.

The hypothesis that men have a fear and envy of women stemming from women's role as bearers and primary caretakers of children is an intriguing one. However, it would be difficult to prove or disprove. Assuming for a moment that such male unconscious fear and envy do exist, how might they lead to male dominance? Stockard and Johnson cite one psychologist, Dorothy Dinnerstein, who argues that society allows men to hold the power outside the mother-child relationship precisely because the power held by the mother over the infant is so all-encompassing and threatening. As the infant grows into an adult, he or she flees from the overwhelming power of the mother, and thus finds it easier to accept male than female authority. Furthermore, men especially are fearful of becoming overly dependent on women because of their childhood experiences. If men were to join women in caring for infants, she asserts, one of the basic motives for male dominance would disappear.

A similar conclusion is reached via a different route by theorists who emphasize the notion that our heavily maternal system of rearing children results in special gender identity problems for the male child. Some psychoanalysts have argued that males have a more tenuous gender identity than females because their first close relationship is with an adult of the other sex—the mother. Social learning theorists concur with this notion, pointing out that, while the female child has available an appropriate sex model with whom to identify (the mother), the male child has little access to an appropriate sex model (the father), and so is forced to construct a male gender identity and role largely from the prescriptions and prohibitions sketched out by the mother and other (usually female) adults (for example, Lynn, 1966). Often, they argue, the resulting male identity is based largely on an avoidance of "feminine" behavior and a denigration of femininity, since feminine behavior on the boy's part has been a source of ridicule and/or punishment (for example, Hartley, 1959).

Stockard and Johnson argue that:

> . . . societal arrangements which actually give prestige and authority to males provide the most effective and concrete support for masculine identity. The system of male dominance allows men to demonstrate concretely that they are not only different from but "better than" women. Furthermore, defining masculinity as superior, giving the

highest prestige to the things males do (very much a part of male dominance), is a way of inducing men to give up "femininity" and take on a masculine identity. The greater rewards and power of masculinity then act as an inducement to men to break with femininity (p. 209).

Nancy Chodorow (1978) is one theorist who has integrated both of the above arguments in a penetrating analysis of the contribution of the nuclear family to male dominance in society. If this analysis is correct, men may develop a motive to dominate women both as a way of defending against their dependency needs and unconscious feelings of fear and envy and as a way of asserting their masculine identity. Both conditions theoretically arise from the social situation in which mothers are the primary caretakers of infants. The solution—shared child care by both parents—may seem absurdly simple, yet Stockard and Johnson present an excellent discussion of why it is not. Our economy is structured so that it is more difficult for women than men to get jobs and to earn adequate wages to support a family. Flexible hours are not available to either women or men, and the concept of paternity leave is virtually unknown. Child care, both in the home and out, is a low-paid, low-status profession that attracts few men. The difficulties of involving men substantially in child care are great indeed, but the authors hold out the hope that, if it can be accomplished, one of the main underpinnings of the ideology of male dominance will disappear.

SUMMARY

Dominance, the capacity to impose one's will on another, has frequently been thought of as existing within a relatively stable framework of power relationships. Working with animals, scientists have often identified dominance hierarchies, within which lower status individuals reliably defer to those of higher status. Separate hierarchies often exist for each sex, but it is a common finding that females defer to males in conflict situations. It has been suggested, on the basis of such findings, that male dominance over females has a biological and evolutionary basis.

Research suggests that dominance behavior in human groups is somewhat more complex than is that among lower animals. Among humans, dominance is less frequently based only on aggression or the ability to aggress, and although dominance hierarchies may exist in specific situations (such as business organizations), they rarely exist in the same way in other situations in which the members of the group are involved. Although there is a tendency for males to dominate females in many situations, the strength of this phenomenon varies markedly across cultures and appears to be related to cultural practices. The idea that men's dominance of women is based solely on unchangeable human evolutionary heritage proves to be, in the final analysis, inadequate explanation of human behavior.

POWER & SEXUALITY
6

Nina L. Colwill and Hilary M. Lips

And even when her effort at seduction succeeds, the victory is still ambiguous; the fact is that in common opinion it is still the man who conquers, who has the woman.

Simone de Beauvoir 1952, p. 649

Potency means "powerful." Impotent means "without power" . . . My rejection—and, I must admit, fear—of the potency concept in a sexual encounter with a woman is based on the awful and awesome responsibility that is packaged with that power.

Sam Julty

The pairing of power and sexuality is an emotional issue, and rare is the woman or man who can read of it or write on it without responding emotionally. Thus, this chapter has undergone many revisions based on many reviews and much re-examination. The exercise was often frustrating, sometimes painful, but always enlightening. It would be ridiculous to try to pretend that this version is without bias, that it has been stripped of all loaded language and subjective evaluations. For such is the nature of power and sexuality.

Power and sexuality are intimately linked in so many complex ways that we are hard-pressed to describe them all, even superficially, in one chapter. We begin by looking at status and the double standard of sexuality. In considering sexuality as a power resource, we talk about the power that one person can wield over another by virtue of sexual attraction, a power that has been both bewailed and celebrated in centuries of great literature and popular songs. We examine other ways in which sexuality may give one person power over another: prostitution, childbearing, and sexual blackmail. We consider sexuality as an expression of male dominance; a function that is often served by the idea of sexual activity as a conquest or victory for men and a loss or humiliation for women. In this context we examine pornography and forced sexuality. In a more positive vein, we look at sexual experiences, sexual relationships and sexual responsibility as sources of strong personal power.

SEX ROLES, STATUS, AND THE DOUBLE STANDARD

To most adults in our culture, the term "double standard" automatically implies sexuality. It conjures up a host of images and associations: man the sexual pursuer, "sowing his wild oats;" woman, dressed in white at her wedding to symbolize virginity; man the sexual aggressor; woman the gatekeeper. But the double standard has implications for more than just sexual behavior; it is integrally related to power and control.

One of the assumptions that maintains the double standard is that sexual activity is seen as more important for men than for women (Gross, 1978). Men's supposed greater need for sexual release lends legitimacy to their role as sexual aggressors. Armed with the power of legitimacy, men adopt a role in which they initiate and direct sexual activity. Women, likewise armed with legitimacy by the double standard, adopt a role in which they limit and restrict sexual activity. Men and women, both wanting relationships that include sexuality, work frantically at cross purposes to control them. An impartial observer of these power struggles would probably conclude that someone had played a huge joke on the human race!

Although both sexes use power in sexual encounters, the male sexual role of initiator, leader, expert, and teacher presents a more powerful image than does the female role of follower and gatekeeper. Men sometimes become trapped in this image of the powerful controller of sexuality, and in a charade that is reminiscent of the old fable "The Emperor's New Clothes," women cooperate in maintaining this image. In the fable, no one dared tell the emperor, parading naked down the street, that his new suit of clothes was so invisible as to be nonexistent. In the sexual context, women can rarely bring themselves to let men know that the male cloak of sexual expertise is similarly invisible.

Men themselves, caught in a role that allows no revelation of ignorance or uncertainty, often discover important sexual information only by chance. Both research and personal accounts indicate that men find it more difficult than women do to seek sexual information from others (London, 1974; Skovholt, Nagy, & Epting, 1976; Singer, 1976). The man's refusal to seek information and the woman's refusal to challenge his role as expert often combine to keep couples from the kind of open discussion that would improve the sexual interaction for both parties. Indeed, many women even fake orgasm, providing their male partner with false feedback about what gives them sexual pleasure (Tavris, 1973; Hite, 1976). In these situations, both members of the couple are maintaining power and limiting their vulnerability by withholding information about themselves. In traditional fashion, men are playing expert while women play helpless, but the effect of both strategies is to avoid taking personal responsibility for an examination of the sexual relationship.

The role division of man as sexual initiator and woman as either follower or gatekeeper carries with it some of the same problems as attributing superior sexual expertise to men. Although most men and women still expect the man to want and take the lead in sexual activity (Carlson, 1976; McCormick, 1979; Peplau, Rubin, & Hill, 1977), both sexes may experience dissatisfaction if this role division is too rigidly observed. Women compelled to be sexually passive and receptive are deprived of the positive experiences of giving pleasure, choosing to engage in sexual activity when they feel like it, and experimenting with new sexual behaviors; men are deprived of the positive experience of relaxing and receiving pleasure. Indeed, there is some evidence that neither men nor women are entirely happy with the traditional active-passive role differentiation (Carlson, 1976; Hite, 1976).

Although both sexes are restricted by the norm that men initiate and direct sexual activity, changes in the norm produce discomfort. Data collected by Komarovsky (1976) suggest that men are ambivalent about sexually active women and have difficulty accepting sexual invitations from them. It has even been suggested that the loss of male sexual control produced by the rising numbers of women who take sexual initiative and assert their own needs and preferences is creating an increase in impotence among men (Ginsburg, Frosch, & Shapiro, 1972). Must a change in the way women use sexual power have such dire consequences for men? Gross (1978) contends that, if such a pattern is indeed occurring, neither the women's liberation movement nor the sexual demands of individual women should bear the blame: "... it seems more appropriate generally to attribute 'new' male impotence to restrictive socialization and sex typing which has made it difficult for men to relinquish control, to accept and enjoy less structured and more egalitarian sexual relationships" (p. 100).

The issues raised here concern the control of sexual behavior. Such control is not exerted in an abstract fashion, however; it involves the exertion of power over specific individuals—one's partner and oneself. This control extends beyond the realm of specifically sexual behaviors, as we discuss in the next section.

SEXUALITY AS A POWER RESOURCE

In Chapter 3, a power resource was described as that which the power user has at his or her disposal to back up influence attempts. Such resources, can vary from the very concrete (money, strength) to the very personal (love, approval), where the degree of concreteness of a resource is defined as the degree to which it is independent of any specific personal relationship(s). This section examines the use of sexuality as a power resource.

Sexual Attraction and Sexual Activities
Someone who is sexually attractive to another person holds a powerful resource that can be distributed as a reward or bribe in either the personal or the concrete sense. As with other kinds of resources, the more the in-

fluencer wants what the power holder has, the more she or he will be willing to do to get it. At the personal end, someone who is strongly drawn sexually to another person may be willing to make many sacrifices for the privilege of being with that person, even though other opportunities for sexual relationships exist. This renders the "attracting" individual very powerful in the relationship, particularly if she or he is not as strongly pulled toward the other person. As a stereotype, popular literature tends to picture this scenario with a woman as the irresistible seductress and a man as the helpless victim of her manipulations. However, many people will testify that it works both ways.

Sex as a power resource is a mixture of the concrete and the personal in situations where a person is sexually attracted to another *and* sees no other opportunities for sexual activity. In this case, both the personal sexual attraction and the more general desire for sexual activity render the sexually attracted person susceptible to the power of the other. Examples of this are seen in certain marital situations where one partner punishes or manipulates the other by "holding out" sexually. Again, the stereotype example is female: a wife ordering her husband to sleep on the couch—colloquially known as "cutting him off." However, a scanning of the advice columns in newspapers and magazines suggests that plenty of men also "hold out" on their wives.

Prostitution: Women on the Bottom Again?

The most concrete use of sex as a power resource occurs in situations where impersonal sexual activity is exchanged for money. Among heterosexuals, prostitutes are almost invariably female and clients male. There is, in fact, another word used to describe a man who sells sexual activity to women—gigolo.

In prostitution, sexuality is a resource that can be used in a variety of different encounters to bargain for money. Within a given interaction, the prostitute has power over the client in certain respects to the extent that the client wants what she or he has. Power is easily measured by the amount the client is willing to pay and is strongly influenced by the availability of other sources of sexual satisfaction. However, the balance of power may well be more than equalized in other respects by factors such as the prostitute's need for money or the client's physical strength. Moreover, outside the specific interaction with a client, the prostitute is often in a position of very little power. The female prostitute, in particular, is usually attached to a pimp who takes a large portion of her earnings. She is also harrassed by police, frequently jailed, and usually regarded with contempt by other people, even the very people who pay for her services (Laws & Schwartz, 1977). Thus, although prostitutes can use sex very effectively as a power resource, they can rarely use it to accrue large power advantages over others. Instead, they are frequently in a position where sexuality becomes their *only* source of power, a situation in which they are more desperate for their client's money than the client is for sexual release.

Who Uses Sexuality as a Power Resource?

In reviewing the above examples, one cannot help but be struck with the fact that it is women rather than men who are usually thought of as using sexuality as a power resource. This is congruent with Johnson's (1976) finding, discussed in Chapter 3, that use of sexuality as a power base is seen as characteristic of women. In general, men are not viewed as exploiting this particular source of power. Why not? The stereotype derives partly from our mistaken notions about male and female sexuality. For centuries we have been taught not only that men wanted and needed sexual release more than women did, but even that women did not want it or need it at all. Thus, we have formed the image of the woman, unmoved, shamelessly manipulating the man caught up in his sexual passion or drive. (Many women probably wish life were that simple!) However, now that it has been shown that women want and enjoy sexual activity and have a strong sexual drive, it should also be clear that they have no monopoly on the use of sexuality as a power resource. The stereotype persists, however, and a little reflection indicates another reason for its strength: for many women, sexuality is the major or only power resource at hand.

In relating to women, men can often use physical strength and/or money as a power resource. A woman frequently is cut off from use of these resources because she is often physically weaker than and financially dependent on the man. Thus, she is more dependent than he on other power resources such as sexuality. In the case of young, attractive, single women, a dependence on sexuality may not be looked at as a disadvantage. Indeed, such women may feel very powerful relative to the men who court their favor. However, with rare exceptions, this sense of power tends to fade somewhat as the woman becomes defined as less sexually attractive with age. At the same time, the man's sense of power, based on income, status, and expertise is probably growing. Clearly, a total long-term reliance on sexuality or any other single power source puts a person at a disadvantage relative to others with more diverse power resources.

Childbearing: Women's Power or Man's Power?

There is, of course, an aspect of sexuality having little to do with attractiveness or eroticism that can serve as an important power resource: the ability to bear children. There was a period in history during which the male contribution to conception was not understood, and childbearing women were held in awe and reverence (Davis, 1971). Once the relationship between intercourse and childbirth was established, women lost the full strength of this power resource, but they still retained its vestiges in societies where pregnant women and mothers were cherished and adored. Rare is the woman, even today, who gains no interpersonal power through pregnancy, even if it is only to have her husband pull on her winter boots or cut her toenails.

Impregnation requires at least minimal cooperation from two people, except in cases of rape, and therein lies its current potential as a source of interpersonal power. If a man wishes to have a child, he must have the co-operation of a woman, and vice versa. Thus, either party could use this necessity for cooperation as a source of power by threatening to withhold it. Of course, in many situations this balance of power can be disrupted by physical force, ingenuity, or technology. A man may rape his wife (or any other woman) to get her pregnant. A woman whose husband or lover refuses to impregnate her may have intercourse with others or may quietly stop using birth control without informing him. In the same vein, a woman who wants a child but not a husband may seek out a man, seduce him, and have him father her child without ever telling him. (This plot is, in fact, featured in Margaret Atwood's *The Edible Woman*—the discomfiture of a man who discovers he has been used to father the child of a woman he thought he had tricked into bed.) Finally, of course, the growing new technology of test tube babies and artificial insemination makes it potentially possible that, in some cases, the only persons whose cooperation an individual will really require to produce a baby will be the medical technicians. Should this happen, and should society show increasing tolerance toward single parenthood, it is difficult to imagine the changes that would be wrought in the power relationships between women and men.

At the present time, however, many women find that the problematic aspect of impregnation lies not in their ability to influence someone to cooperate in having a child, but rather in their ability to avoid pregnancy. The effect of years of male dominance in church and state institutions has been to create a social structure in which women are still not allowed complete control over their own reproduction. Man-made laws forbidding abortion, birth control, and the dissemination of birth control and other sex-related information, and affirming a husband's right to sex with his wife whether or not she consents, have forced women by the million to bear children by the million throughout history. Yet, women still support these laws of church and state, either implicitly by adhering to them without complaint, or explicitly by lobbying against availability of information about or access to birth control and abortion.

Sexual Blackmail

One final aspect of sexuality has considerable potential for use as a power resource: sexual information about another person. In a culture that places a high value on certain types of sexual behavior, "negative" sexual information about someone can be a powerful weapon. The person who publicly comments or "jokes" about her or his spouse's lack of sexual interest or responsiveness can do considerable psychological damage. Similarly, the person who boasts far and wide that he or she has "slept with" someone may cause injury to the other's reputation. Finally, the individual who discloses the homosexual orientation, adultery, promiscuity, or other socially disapproved aspects of another's sexual behavior can cause serious problems for that person. Thus, people are often hesitant about sharing sexual information about themselves with other people. People who do have this type of knowledge about us have a potential source of power that increases according to our desire to keep the information private.

Information about sexual behavior can be used as a source of power over either men or women. However, our double standard of sexual morality decrees that specific types of sexual information are harmful to male and female reputations in different ways and degrees. Even though some data suggest that the male and female sides of this double standard are no longer as far apart as they once were (Perlman, 1979), there is still much evidence that women and men are not punished in the same way for violation of various sexual norms. On the one hand, female prostitutes suffer far more legal retribution than their male clients. Rape victims often experience as much social rejection as rapists. And it has often been documented that women pay a higher price than men for sexual indiscretion in the workplace (Williams, 1977). Thus, a woman is particularly vulnerable to certain types of sexual blackmail because she is thought to be "tarnished" by too much sexual activity. Joined with this attitude is the notion that any woman who would *allow* herself to be tarnished in this way is either a fool or very weak. So, the woman who breaks with the conventional sexual morality of the day is seen in a doubly negative light. Even though a man may be severely devalued for improper sexual behavior, he may also be regarded simultaneously as a sly devil.

If women are more easily victimized by information indicating that they are too active sexually, men can be more damaged by information that they are not doing *enough* (impotence) or that they are doing it with the wrong people (homosexuality). Indeed, the evidence suggests that homophobia (a social attitude of fear and disgust for homosexuality; Weinberg, 1973) is stronger in relation to male than to female sexuality (Anderson, 1974; Morin & Garfinkle, 1978). Homophobia is used to keep people, particularly males, in line, both sexually and in all aspects of sex role related behavior. In fact, Morin and Wallace's (1976) research indicates that sex-role attitudes are better predictors of homophobia than are sexual attitudes. Any display of "feminine" role behavior by a man is likely to arouse the suspicion of homosexuality. Thus, a man's reputation may suffer at the disclosure not just of homosexual interest or activities, but also of any preference or behavior that might be considered "effeminate."

Power based on information about sexual behavior, then, can be used against both women and men in different circumstances. Whatever the effect on individuals, the general effect of such power is to keep people adhering to sociosexual norms and to keep sexual information secretive. As a society we pay a high price for the power of sexual information in the form of the sexual rigidity, confusion, resentment, despair, and cynicism it generates and reinforces. Many individuals can ill afford to use sexual information as power for fear of equally damaging retribution, but a few others can ride to fame and fortune on it (witness the prostitute who "tells all" about her relationship with a senator). And yet, it is possible to envision a future in which a general attitude of openness and acceptance toward many aspects of sexual activity and sexual roles will render this type of sexual power obsolete.

SOCIAL EXPRESSIONS
OF MALE SEXUAL DOMINANCE

As discussed earlier, the male sex role in our culture includes leadership, dominance, and control in the area of sexuality. Certain factors of the social environment both reflect and reinforce this notion that part of being a man is the sexual dominance of women, while part of being a woman is sexual surrender to a man. In some cases, this message is so strong that researchers feel it may promote the ultimate in male sexual dominance—rape, discussed later in this chapter.

The Language of Sexuality

Language serves a crucial function in maintaining our male/female sexual roles. The words we use to describe male genitals are powerful words: prick, pecker, tool; while the words used to describe the female genitals—cunt and twat—are at best static, and at worst considered dirty and profane. In addition, we have a derogatory term—nymphomaniac—for a woman who desires inordinate amounts of sexual activity, but no comparable word to describe men. And what is the male equivalent of a "slut"? The language of intercourse is changing, however. Until very recently, men laid, screwed, fucked, and made love to women, never the reverse. In the past few years, however, the terms are beginning to be used to describe the sexual activities of either sex. Whether this reflects women's more active participation in sex is an interesting speculation.

Swearing is another use of language that is charged with power, perhaps because it is so often used in anger. A large number of profane words are sexual and antifemale in nature. Such profanity helps keep women in their place, both figuratively and physically, by reminding them of their lower status and by providing reasons to bar them from places where their delicate ears might be offended. Many women suspect that it is not profanity per se from which they are being protected, but from the knowledge of how men speak of women. Profanity serves two functions in maintaining the power status quo: keeping women in their place and keeping women out of places.

One of the ways in which the power of sexual language is often used effectively is in the form of jokes. As with profanity, aggressive power is a strong theme in sexual jokes, most often in the form of antifemale humor (Puner, 1974).

It is interesting to note that Freud believed humor, especially sexual humor, to be repressed aggression and that some of the neo-Freudians have considered humor a purely masculine domain. "Women are less fond of jokes than men," reports Grotjahn (1965), without data: "A witty woman is a masculine woman" (p. 121). This idea has not been supported empirically, however; it is merely that women prefer absurdity to aggressive humor (Groch, 1974; Landis & Ross, 1933; O'Connell, 1960). Even the finding that women take less pleasure than men in aggressive humor may be confounded, however, since most aggressive humor is antifemale in nature and females prefer antimale humor (Priest & Wilhelm, 1974). Recently, however, the feminist movement has been the spawning ground for aggressive antimale humor; witness the T-shirt slogans "A woman without a man is like a fish without a bicycle" and "When God made man she was only joking."

The Power of Pornography

What is pornography? In this analysis, pornography is defined as erotica that debases—erotica in which the theme is sexual degradation of another person.

What is the relationship between power and pornography? First, much of it reflects and reinforces the idea of male dominance and female submission in sexual behavior as erotic and desirable, and thus, it may be helping to maintain the belief that "sex in our society is construed as a dirty, low and violent act involving domination of a male over a female" (Herman, 1979, p. 59). Second, it may influence people's reactions to sexual coercion and assault in the "real world," possibly even enhancing the likelihood of such assault.

Malamuth, Feshbach, and Jaffe (1977) have argued that aggressive and sexual responses are both often taboo in this society and that disinhibiting one may disinhibit the other. Thus, the viewing of pornography may lower inhibitions for both sexuality and aggression. Since pornography is so often explicitly violent in nature, this association is often a blatantly obvious one. In fact, the incidence of sexual violence in such soft-core erotica as graces the coffee tables of America rose significantly between 1973 and 1977 as evidenced by Malamuth and Spinner's (1980) analysis of *Playboy* and *Penthouse.*

Brownmiller (1975), Clark and Lewis (1977), and Gager and Schurr (1976) have argued vehemently that the female degradation that turns erotica into pornography reinforces for males and females the fantasy that every woman wants to be raped, or at least possessed and dominated sexually, and that no real woman cares if she gets kicked around a bit in the process. In spite of the fact that women are gaining status as nonsex objects in many areas of their existence, this theme seems to be getting stronger rather than weaker. Violence against women is a common theme in hardcore pornography (Smith, 1976), and Brownmiller accuses *True Story,* a magazine read by millions of women, of handing out the same message of male power and female powerlessness under the rubric of romance.

To the extent that these magazines are guides to romance and sexual fulfillment, they perpetuate the model of male power and female powerlessness. But how direct is the influence of the pornographic message of violence against women? There are at least five lines of research that address this question.

1. The first set of studies shows a definite relationship between the viewing of sexual violence and subsequent aggression (Donnerstein, 1980; Malamuth, 1978). Aggression, in this research, was measured by subjects' willingness to shock others on a shock machine.

2. Since the first line of research measured willingness to shock rather than sexual arousal, a second line of research was necessary. Thus, Malamuth and Check (1979) asked male undergraduates to listen to one of three stories: a rape story in which the victim continuously abhorred the experience (rape-abhorrence), a rape story in which the victim became involuntarily aroused (rape-arousal), and a story of mutually desired intercourse. All subjects then listened to a depiction of a male student waylaying and raping a terrified female student in an alley. Subjects in the mutually desired and rape-arousal conditions were more sexually aroused (as measured by swelling, or tumescence, of the penis) by the subsequent rape story than were subjects in the rape-abhorrence condition. The consistent portrayal of rape as a singularly negative experience for the victim, then, served to inhibit sexual arousal during the reading of the rape story.

3. The third line of research goes beyond mere aggressive and sexual arousal to laboratory-presented stimuli, to the realm of self-generated fantasy. In this line of research, Malamuth (1979) exposed male undergraduate students to an erotic slide and talk show, which differed only in one slide and a short script insert to yield two conditions: rape versus mutually desired sex. All subjects were then exposed to a tape of a female describing a rape scene. The two experimental conditions themselves produced no difference in penile response—subjects in all conditions were equally sexually aroused. However, subjects were then asked to generate sexual fantasies, and herein lay the difference. Subjects who had been exposed to the rape slides followed by a verbal depiction of rape generated more sexually violent fantasies than did subjects in the mutual consent condition.

4. The pornography research reviewed to this point was measuring shocks, sexual fantasies, and penile tumescence, or erection, rather than attitudes

toward rape. The fourth line of research examined perceptions about male proclivity to rape. Subjects in one such study (Malamuth, Haber, & Feshbach, 1980) believed that close to half the male population would rape if they could be assured of no legal consequences. And, more dramatically, over half the male subjects in this study, and 69 percent in the Malamuth and Check (1979) study, thought that there would be some possibility that they themselves would perpetrate rape under those circumstances. These students were answering a questionnaire, however; they were not faced with the actual rape. We know from these data only that rape does not seem to be viewed as the crime of a statistical deviant.

5. The research reviewed so far has been concerned with a broad cultural concept—male sexual power and female sexual powerlessness, sexual awakening, and eventual sexual submission, the "every woman secretly wants to be raped" myth. The fifth line of research attempts to identify the segment of this broad cultural milieu most affected by pornography. Toward this end, male undergraduates in Malamuth's (1979) study were preclassified as sexually force-oriented or sexually nonforce-oriented on the basis of responses to a questionnaire about their sexual preferences. Irrespective of the experimental conditions described above, nonforce-oriented subjects created more sexual fantasies in forced-sex condition.

As noted in 4 (Malamuth & Check, 1979), 69 percent of male undergraduates felt there was some possibility that they would rape if they could be assured of not being caught and punished. There was a connection between this "proclivity to rape" and the belief that the woman in the story derived pleasure from her rape. "Rape proclivity" also is connected with sexual arousal to the rape-abhorrence story, but not to the rape-arousal or mutually desired intercourse story.

In short, three sets of interrelated attitudes and behaviors characterized 37 to 69 percent of subjects in four Canadian and American studies in university and junior college (Malamuth & Check, 1979; Malamuth, Haber, & Feshbach, 1980; Malamuth, Reisin, & Spinner, 1979; Tieger, 1979).

1. Stated "proclivity to rape."
2. Sexual arousal to sexual violence rather than to erotica, per se.
3. Acceptance of the myth that women enjoy rape, coupled with a callous attitude toward rape and rape victims.

Such data do not allow us to conclude that certain attitudes toward women *cause* these men to become sexually aroused to sexual violence or to believe themselves capable of rape. Much less able are we to conclude that any of these related attitudes and behaviors cause actual rape. Still, the interconnection among the three sets of attitudes, at least for certain men, raises serious questions about the "harmlessness" of violent pornography. To the extent that violent pornography promotes any of the three attitudes, it should be viewed with alarm. To those who recoil at the word *censorship,* these data may present a real dilemma.

Rape

In discussing sexual assault with students and colleagues, we frequently pose the question of why men have a virtual monopoly on rape. Invariably at least one person laughs at the absurdity of the question and reminds us that it is easier to rape a woman than to rape a man; women are physically weaker than men, and a man must attain an erection for sexual intercourse to take place, while a woman need not even be sexually aroused.

There are obvious arguments against this position. Penile erection is not under strict conscious control, especially in young males. Sexual assault need not even include penile-vaginal penetration. Men rape other men. Furthermore, in a large percentage of sexual assault cases, the method is forced oral sex (Selkin, 1975), which women could also perpetrate. The assailant need not even be larger and stronger than the victim. Most male rapists do not use excessive force, but intimidation—threat of death to or maiming of the uncooperative victim. In fact, Amir (1971) reports that in 87 percent of rape cases, the rapist used only verbal coercion to subdue his victim. And certainly gang rape could be as easily carried out by women as by men. It has not always been easy for men to rape women, yet over the centuries millions have managed. Surely something more complex than penile erection and physical strength accounts for the overwhelming sex difference in sexual assault.

More than one feminist author has suggested that rape is but one point on the continuum of male-female sexual relationships, that rape is consistent with a prevailing sexual ideology in which men are "supposed to seduce, to cajole, persuade, pressurize and eventually overcome" (Greer, 1977, p. 289), that the rapist is not a deviant, but an overconformer (Russell, 1975). He has learned his sex role too well, Russell contends, and has drawn the notion of male sexual dominance to its logical conclusion.

To most people, placing rape in the same category as mutually desired sex is an abhorrent association. Why would anyone be willing to reduce something as personally satisfying as mutually desired sex to an act of violence? Why does rape occur? Why would one person want to force another into sexual contact? Why is rape chiefly perpetrated by men upon women? It is possible, as many feminist journalists and academics have suggested, that there is one answer to all these questions: that rape is a crime, not of passion, but of power (Brownmiller, 1975; Clark & Lewis, 1977).

Brownmiller considers rape to be man's most efficient means of controlling woman. By raping women, by threatening to rape women, and by protecting women from the rape attempts of other men, she contends, men have held women in fear and have imposed upon them a double standard of chastity and monogamy. Historically, women became the property of the men whose name they bore, and early rape laws were property laws. Men were compensated for the loss of their daughter's chastity and their wife's monogamy with financial payment or the opportunity to rape the rapist's woman. In Anglo-Saxon law, in fact, the payment extracted from a rapist was determined by the sexual worth of his victim, which, in turn, was determined by the financial worth of her husband, brothers, and father.

Although present rape laws do not make explicit mention of a woman's sexual worth, Clark and Lewis (1977) contend that court decisions are still based on the early Anglo-Saxon model. Thus, an attempt is often made in the courtroom to minimize the personal value of a rape victim by establishing that she was sexually active before the rape. Despite recent legislation aimed at preventing this procedure, her sexual history may still, at the judge's discretion, be admissable evidence in many North American courts (McTeer, 1978). Women of high socioeconomic status, who can establish themselves as virgins or monogamous wives, are more likely to win rape cases than are women of low status or those whom the defense has established as sexually active and/or not sexually monogamous (Clark & Lewis, 1977).

There have been occasional reports of societies in which rape allegedly does not exist. Margaret Mead (1935) reported that the unaggressive Arapesh tribe of New Guinea, for whom few behaviors and abilities were sex-differentiated, had no comprehension of rape. Also, Brownmiller's (1975) sources in Vietnam contended that rape did not occur among the Viet Cong. They claimed that Viet Cong women were the first women in history to fight equally with men, and that this equality changed the image of women and men enough to set the stage for the disappearance of forced sexuality. The relative status of men and women in any society may, indeed, be a crucial determinant of the incidence and the consequences of sexual coercion.

Status and Sexual Coercion

We have raised the possibility that the status differential between men and women may be an explanation for the male monopoly on rape. Homosexual rape of men in jail is a commonly reported phenomenon, but Brownmiller (1975) may have been the first to analyze it in terms of status and to relate it to the rape of women. She contends that the selection of rape victims is not a random process; rather the youngest and most feminine men are chosen, for cell-block status is determined by traditional masculinity, and rape only occurs downward in this status hierarchy. Thus, this male-male rape appears to be a violent power strategy that serves to maintain the status hierarchy and mirrors sexual coercion in the outside world.

In the past few years, psychologists have begun to use the differences in male-female status to analyze interpersonal power. This work may have implications for the analysis of the power of sexual coercion.

As discussed in Chapter 3 (Johnson, 1976), men and women are perceived by themselves and others to gain and maintain power in very different ways—men may be more likely to employ *direct* and open assertion of their wants by stressing *competence* and using *concrete* rewards and punishments; women may use *indirect,* manipulative expression, stress *helplessness,* and rely on the affection of others in *personal* relationships. These "feminine" power strategies, while often effective in the short run, may establish their users as weak and incompetent people in the eyes of others and in their own self-perceptions. Thus, women who rely on men to protect their bodies from sexual assault may be buying into what Clark and Lewis (1977) call the "protection racket," by establishing themselves as the weak and needy member of their male-female relationship.

Storaska (1976) suggests that women *should* use what we would call indirect, personal, and helpless power strategies if faced with the reality of rape—to plead, to manipulate, and to appeal to the gentler side of the rapist's nature. Yet, Brodsky and Klemack's (1976) research indicates that the options available to a potential rape victim are not that clear-cut. Although some particularly aggressive rapists report being turned on by direct verbal attacks and turned off or dissuaded by displays of personal weakness or distress, the opposite holds true for other, more timid rapists. Moreover, Bart's (1980) examination of the differences between women who were able to avoid attempted rape and those who had been raped indicates that women may well use a variety of power strategies, including direct assertive ones, when confronted with a rapist. Bart found that background differences involving women's autonomy, competence, and self-reliance were related to

125

the ability to avoid rape; for example, size and weight, never being married, regular sports involvement, knowledge of first aid and self-defense, and assertiveness training. Moreover, in the actual rape situation, women who used the most ways to avoid rape were the most successful; the likelihood of being raped increased when the woman relied on only one strategy to avoid it. Pleading with the rapist was used by 33 percent of the women who were eventually raped and by only 22 percent of those who avoided the crime. Reasoning with the rapist was used by 72 percent of the women who were raped and by 67 percent of those who avoided it. The women who avoided rape, in contrast to the others, reported that they had used reasoning only as a way to buy time while they prepared to use another strategy, such as running, screaming, or physical force. These data suggest that women should be prepared to use many methods of avoiding rape, and that over-reliance on only the "feminine" modes of influence may be a big mistake. A woman must assume the burden of her own safety. The cold, hard facts are that no one has greater interest in protecting a woman's body than she does, and no other guardian is likely to be so constantly available.

It is difficult to think of a single positive statement about the future of rape in North America. If rape is a crime of power, it should decrease when women achieve power equality through status equality. But there is certainly no evidence that rape is decreasing in North America as women gain higher status; to the contrary, rape—reported rape at any rate—is on the increase (Selkin 1975), and we cannot know how much of this change stems from increased willingness to report the crime. What does this mean? Must rape get worse before it gets better? Perhaps the new-found status that women are enjoying in some areas merely serves to accentuate the difference in power or to create an incongruity between woman's status and her lesser size and strength. Or perhaps, as Russell (1975) suggests, the rapist sees sexual assault as an effective way of putting uppity women in their place.

To this point we have discussed sexual coercion as though it always ends in rape. There are, however, many degrees of sexual coercion, ranging from terrifying to merely annoying, that fall in the general area of sexual harassment.

Consistent with the double standard of sexuality and with a power analysis of sexuality, sexual harassment is usually considered an occupational hazard of women. The harrasser in this case may hold power in the form of organizational rewards and punishments. For those who find it difficult to view sexual coercion as an act of power, sexual harassment in organizations may serve as a good example. Male secretaries are highly unlikely to sexually harass female corporation presidents—sexual harassment takes place from the power strongholds downward.

The most blatant form of sexual harassment is rape, followed by sexual favors bestowed at the threat of one's economic livelihood. There is a third level of sexual harassment, however, one that Henley (1977) calls tactile hostility: physical indignities visited on subordinates by superiors. It is the relationship between touching and power that is relevant here, and Henley offers ample evidence to support her position that we are all more likely to "touch downward," those below us in the status hierarchy. Yet, touch has many other connotations, including sexual ones, and the student touched by a professor or the employee touched by a boss may wonder if the touch is meant to signify friendship, power, or sexual advance. In a world in which intimacy, power, and sexuality are so intertwined, it may often be difficult to know.

The Myth of the Willing Victim

There still is widespread belief that women enjoy being sexually overpowered. The common defense of apprehended rapists is "she enjoyed it," and many rapists try to extract such assertions from their victims (Gager & Schurr, 1976). Women, the argument goes, are natural masochists.

The ideal of female masochism probably enjoyed its finest hour under Freud. He saw masochism as the normal female's aggression turned inward and a necessary part of all female sexual response. Masochism was not seen as normal in males, however.

Helene Deutsch (1944; 1945), one of Freud's pupils, was the strongest proponent of female masochism and one of the first to deal with rape as a psychological phenomenon. Deutsch made much of "defloration," pain, and blood, and saw rape as merely an exaggeration of normal intercourse. To Deutsch, the vagina was completely passive, waiting to be overpowered by the penis, and the woman was sexually passive, waiting to be overpowered by the man. A woman was considered mature in Deutsch's system only when masochism became an integral part of her sexuality. Deutsch considered sexual intercourse to be so naturally aversive to women that masochism was a necessary part of female psychodynamics—essential to the survival of the species. In Deutsch's system, it is for the satisfaction of their masochistic needs, then, rather than for warmth, closeness, or physical release, that women have sexual intercourse.

Research on masochism is sadly lacking. Although women do report fantasies during intercourse of being overpowered and sexually dominated (Hariton & Singer, 1974), we have no evidence that they enjoy the reality of sexual assault. To the contrary, although 25 percent of Malamuth, Haber, and Fesbach's (1980) female subjects thought that other women would enjoy being raped, not one felt that she herself would enjoy the experience. Although these women did not feel that they themselves were masochistic, one-quarter believed the myth of the willing victim applied to other women.

Perhaps the data on female fantasies of sexual dominance have been misinterpreted. It may well be that women fantasize, not of being forced into intercourse against their will, but of being swept away by passion and sexually aroused against their will—the old Sleeping Beauty story. The focus may be more on the removal of sexual responsibility than on physical violence. This may not be the healthiest of sexual perspectives, but it is a far cry from the relish of physical abuse. Moreover, men, too, fantasize about being sexually dominated. Stein (1974), who observed more than 1,200 men in sexual interactions with call girls, reported that more than 10 percent of these men, called "slaves" by Stein, asked the woman to act out dominance-submission fantasies in which she was dominant, and Friday (1980) has collected anecdotal evidence that some men fantasize about being dominated sexually.

PERSONAL POWER, SEXUALITY, AND RESPONSIBILITY

Running through this discussion of power and sexuality is the theme that each sex tries, in its own way, to exert power without acknowledging responsibility. Thus, a man may sexually coerce or harass a woman and evade responsibility by claiming that he was overwhelmed by his own sexual needs, that she "asked" for it by her dress or demeanor, or that she really wanted it despite her protestations. To counter this attitude, women are taught a good deal about the negative or avoidance aspect of sexual responsibility. They are cautioned against looking too sexual, staying out too late, hitch-hiking alone, accompanying a man to his apartment, or frequenting certain areas of town. The sum total of these cautions teaches women not how to be sexually powerful, but only how not to be rendered sexually powerless. In addition, the perspective may be a strong inhibitor, not only of female sexuality, but even of affection and free movement. Masters and Johnson

(1974) have suggested, in fact, that such cautions, which extend even to a caution against touching men, teach women to *avoid* rather than to *accept* responsibility—responsibility for initiating intimate relationships and sexual activity. Moreover, these cautions and restrictions encourage women to think of themselves as victims or objects in the sexual encounter, rather than taking positive responsibility for sexuality on their own terms.

Both men and women can potentially integrate sexuality and power in a more positive way than that encouraged by the double standard. Sex makes us feel good, and to experience our own sexuality is to experience personal power, an enhancement of self-concept and feelings of self-worth.

In spite of the volumes of poetry and prose that have been written on the power of sexuality, seldom has the personal power of individual sexuality been celebrated. To the contrary, the most personal individual sexual act—masturbation—has been variously defined as evidence for immaturity, for perversion, even for sinfulness, while sexual attraction to another person has been described as "falling under a spell"—a symbolic loss of strength and will. However, the good feelings generated by sexual activity often give us a source of energy and personal power, as can the sense of personal worth that comes from a sexual relationship in which we feel appreciated, respected, and valued.

With personal power comes responsibility. To end the battle of the sexes requires the responsible effort of both women and men. It requires individuals to examine their own beliefs about sexuality—their beliefs about dominance and submission and pornography and rape. It also requires them to assure themselves that the sexual training of their daughters and sons does not follow the patterns of male dominance and female subservience so familiar to anyone who learned about human sexuality in our youth. It requires teaching children that the vagina is a reproductive organ like the testicles and that women's sexual pleasure is focused on the clitoris, rather than the vagina. And part of the sexual training of children involves the conscious discrediting of a double standard of sexuality, however frightening that may sound to the parents of girls.

Can we, given the social context of male dominance and female passivity, form sexual relationships between women and men that build rather than drain our personal power? It appears that we can. Some women and men are slowly, often painfully, moving out of the world in which the power of sexuality is a force with which men seek to control women and women seek to control men, a world in which women wait and men pay. There will be setbacks. There will be backlashes. There will probably be periods when it appears that the whole process of coercive sexuality is being escalated. But if our sex roles, inextricably intertwined with our sexual roles, unravel, this awesome power that men and women have held over each other for centuries should dwindle. There will probably always be power struggles within individual relationships, but if our double standard of sexuality dissolves into a single sexual standard for humane people, these struggles will become individual differences and two-person dynamics, rather than the group differences that necessarily define men, women, and heterosexual relationships.

SUMMARY

Sexuality and power are linked in a variety of ways. For women and men, the linkage is mediated by the double standard, which decrees that men are the sexual experts, leaders, teachers, and aggressors, while women are the followers, the objects of men's desires, and the gatekeepers. Thus, men's power is directed in stereotyped fashion at obtaining more sexual gratification, while women's is directed at setting limits on this process. Various aspects of sexuality can, however, be used by both men and women as a power resource. Sexual attractiveness, sexual information about another person, and childbearing can all be used by one person to gain leverage over another.

Men's dominance over women is a recurrent theme in our culture's notions about sexuality. This theme, which emerges from the double standard, is reflected in pornography and is acted out most destructively in the sexual harassment and sexual coercion of women by men. It is probable that these behaviors will persist as long as the men and women of our culture continue to bow to the double standard.

Sexuality involves individual personal power as well as the power of one person or group over another. The power to achieve one's own sexual pleasure and to communicate one's desires and feelings to a partner form an important source of positive sensations and emotions and may contribute to an individual's self-esteem. As women and men take responsibility for sexuality in a positive sense, they may well find that an increase in this sense of personal power reduces the need for power over their partners.

POWER &
THE FAMILY
7

Lillian M. Esses

*Marriage today must . . . be concerned not with the inviolable
commitment of constancy and unending passion, but with the
changing patterns of liberty and discovery.*

Carolyn Heilbrun

There is a growing recognition among social scientists that familial power is a dynamic, interactive process, involving and being determined at any one moment by *all* members of the family. Most empirical research thus far, however, has restricted its scope to the marital couple, and, thus, in many instances, familial power and marital power have been treated synonymously.

A major focus of research on marital power has been control of decision-making in the couple. In this chapter, we review these decision-making studies, since studies and analyses of the variables that influence power in the family have relied heavily on the decision-making research. A number of factors that affect the balance of power in the family are considered: management of the family economy, stages of the family life cycle, the use of love as a power resource, and cultural ideology. These factors will be examined within the framework of resource-exchange theory, which is the major theory used to account for the dynamics and sources of family power. We will look at the strengths and weaknesses of this model, with special attention to the need for further consideration of a systems analysis of family power.

THE POWER TO MAKE DECISIONS

Research into power relationships within the "typical" family have most commonly been concerned with one question—who decides? In every family, somebody has to decide such matters as where the family is to live, how money is to be spent, and how children should be reared and disciplined. Although many couples discuss these matters, often the final decision is made by either the wife or husband. Investigators have assumed that the spouse who most often has the upper hand in deciding major family issues has the most power in the family.

    Balance of power between husband and wife may be determined by a number of factors, including the roles and tasks each takes on in the family, personal skills and resources that each brings to the marriage, and cultural norms and assumptions concerning which spouse has a legitimate right to assert authority. Women's increased access to employment and education as well as a more "liberated" cultural ideology allowing for greater flexibility of male-female roles and behavior have led some theorists to assume that the North American family has made a complete transition from a patriarchal to a more equal system (Blood & Wolfe, 1960). Many believe that one of the most outstanding changes is that the husband no longer rules the household, but shares power equally with his wife. And yet, despite a lessening of male domination in social, political, and economic spheres, in many circles it is still considered a gross violation of norms if the wife "wears the pants" in the family and the husband allows himself to be "henpecked."

Has the balance of power between men and women shifted to the extent that husbands and wives assert an equal voice in decisions that concern the entire family? Has research provided any definite answers to this question? Is measuring the outcome of decision-making an adequate means of assessing power in the family? We shall see.

In decision-making studies, investigation of power within the family has been restricted to the couple—husband and wife. Although the marriage partners studied invariably have children, the children have not been viewed as an integral part of the family power structure—either as being able to determine which parent wields power or as sources of power themselves. This bias is not seen only in the decision-making literature; it is a direct outcome of viewing power as a personal attribute rather than as an interactive process that depends on the involvement of at least two individuals.

Most studies concerning the outcome of husband-wife decisions as an indicator of relative power rely primarily on self-reports. Even though Blood and Wolfe's (1960) research was done many years ago, it remains one of the most comprehensive and influential studies of this kind of marital power. In the study, 731 Detroit married women responded to several questionnaires concerned with husband-wife relations; one questionnaire asked them to indicate who most often made the final decision about important family issues—their husbands or themselves. The eight decisions they used as a measure of marital power and the results are shown in Table 2. As we can see, four of the eight decisions came out generally evenly divided (insurance, vacation, house, and doctor); two were generally husband-dominated (his job and the car), and two wife-dominated (wife's work and food). On a 10-point scale, about half the families yielded a score of 4 to 6, which led the investigators to conclude that decision-making within the North American home is largely equal and democratic.

Later, when Safilios-Rothschild (1969a) conducted a similar survey, using seven additional items related to typically female domains of decision-making (such as rearing children, purchasing clothes, relations with in-laws), she too found that most Detroit wives claimed that they had the final say about important family matters as often as did their husbands. As she quite

TABLE 2: Allocation of Power in Decision-Making Areas* (731 Detroit families)

Who Decides?	Decision (in percentages)							
	Husband's Job	Car	Insurance	Vacation	House	Wife's Work	Doctor	Food
5. Husband always	90	56	31	12	12	26	7	10
4. Husband more than wife	4	12	11	6	6	5	3	2
3. Husband & wife exactly the same	3	25	41	68	58	18	45	32
2. Wife more than husband	0	2	4	4	10	9	11	11
1. Wife always	1	3	10	7	13	39	31	41
No answer	2	1	2	3	1	3	3	3
Total	100	99	99	100	100	100	100	99
Husband's mean power†	4.86	4.18	3.50	3.12	2.94	2.69	2.53	2.26

*The eight questions on marital power are listed below:
1. What job the husband should take.
2. What car to get.
3. Whether to buy insurance.
4. Where to go on vacation.
5. What house or apartment to take.
6. Whether the wife should go to work or quit work.
7. What doctor to have when someone is sick.
8. How much money the family can afford to spend per week on food.

†The mean for each column is computed on the basis of the weights shown, e.g., "husband always" = 5.

Source: From R. O. Blood, Jr., and D. M. Wolfe, *Husbands and Wives* (New York: Free Press, 1960), p. 19–21. © 1960 by Free Press.

rightly points out, however, the flaws inherent in such decision-making studies are serious, and conclusions should be drawn with caution from this material.

First, all too often when researchers have attempted to examine familial affairs, they have consulted with wives only. Is it valid to assume that the husbands would have agreed with their wives' opinions? Apparently not. When Safilios-Rothschild (1969a) presented both husbands and wives with the decision-making questionnaire, 55 percent of the couples seriously disagreed on several items. This finding should not be surprising in light of the fact that couples have been found to disagree radically when asked to report the facts about far more clear-cut shared activities (such as topics of conversation [Feldman, 1965] and frequency of coitus [Kinsey, 1953]). With regard to who has the final say in making decisions, de Lenero (1969) found that wives tend to attribute more decision-making power to themselves than husbands do. Husbands have a tendency to perceive more equality of power than their wives.

The perceptions of other family members may also contradict one another. In the rare cases where children have been questioned about their views of the family power structure, the majority report egalitarian-democratic decision-making patterns. However, when adolescents were asked who the "boss" in the family was, they more often perceived the father as being dominant (Elder, 1962). Hess and Torney (1962) showed that sex, age, and religious affiliation may influence patterns of adolescent response. Boys tended to see the father as the family authority more often than girls, and Catholics, more than Protestants, were prone to view one parent as dominant.

One might well ask to what extent family members' perceptions of who exerts greatest control over decision-making reflect the true situation. In one study, Olson and Rabunsky (1972) used several subjective measures of power as well as objectively monitoring couples' decision-making processes in the laboratory. None of the self-report measures adequately predicted who actually made decisions in real life. Kenkel (1961) found that the sex of the observer has an appreciable impact on the decision-making process, and consequently on the observed power structure. When the observer was a woman, wives played a more active and powerful role.

Perhaps, then, it is not possible to speak of an objective reality regarding who controls the family decision-making process. The subjective realities of husband and wife, although often discrepant, may carry the greatest import. Each spouse undoubtedly perceives the "facts" of the situation in light of his or her own needs, attitudes, and beliefs. These subjective perceptions of who exercises the most control over decision-making may have a far greater impact on marital behavior and happiness than any objective measure of what actually takes place. In any case, research efforts cannot rely solely on wives' answers or on the opinions of parents to fully understand the familial power structure. The family is a dynamic interacting unit that may consist of as many different points of view as there are members. These differing perceptions converge to affect the behavior of all family members.

A third criticism of decision-making studies (Safilios-Rothschild, 1969a) is that typically all decisions are given equal weight, even though not all may have the same importance. For instance, the question of which job the husband should take has multiple ramifications in terms of time spent away from home, where the family is to live, salary level, and amount of leisure time available, whereas a decision regarding which doctor to consult would generally have far less impact on the family. In addition, decisions vary in the frequency with which they must be made and the amount of energy and time required to carry them out. Safilios-Rothschild (1969a) found that husbands tended to see all "important" family decisions as being made either by themselves or jointly with their wives. On the other hand, they claimed that their wives' decisions prevailed most often when the task was repetitive, time-consuming, or not critical (such as purchasing food or clothing, interacting with relatives, raising children).

The term "orchestration power" describes the power of one spouse to make important and infrequent decisions that do not infringe upon time, but determine family life-style and major characteristics. The marital partner who orchestrates the relationship also has the power to relegate responsibility for unimportant and time-consuming decisions to his or her spouse (Safilios-Rothschild, 1976). Thus, familial power cannot be determined by merely examining the number of decisions over which each spouse has control, but must also take into account the relative importance and frequency of these decisions. Ascertaining relative importance, however, may be a tricky business, since not only couples but individuals may differ in the degree to which they value the power to make specific decisions.

A fourth and more serious problem with these decision-making studies concerns the degree to which the particular items commonly used in questionnaires adequately represent the range of family decisions that determine marital power. Research demonstrates that one can and does get a completely different picture of the power structure in the family depending on which questions are included and omitted. For example, Blood and Wolfe (1960), in an attempt to make their questionnaire applicable to all couples, including those without children, omitted several decisions related to child care. Thus, it is not surprising that their results yielded more husband-dominant responses than did Safilios-Rothschild's (1969a) data.

Ensuring validity of questionnaire items would be an exhaustive and impossible task; it would require obtaining a complete record of all decisions made by a large sample of families. Nevertheless, if they are to claim that their self-report questionnaires adequately measure family power, future researchers will have to do some monitoring of the familial decision-making process instead of merely guessing at what may be important universal family decisions. One way of doing this might be to ask spouses to list all the decisions that they have had to make over a limited time period as a pretest.

The last, but perhaps most important, criticism of decision-making studies concerns the very definition and measurement of familial power. Can a measure reflecting only *outcome* of family decisions be considered an adequate indicator of family power structure? More recent investigators have pointed out that other dimensions are evident in the *processes* with which family members bargain and negotiate with one another, solve problems, and handle conflict (Olson, Cromwell, & Klein, 1975; Osmond, 1978; Rollins & Bahr, 1976). In fact, measuring the process of problem-solving, conflict resolution, and decision-making yields different results than measuring the outcome of family decision tasks (Olson, 1969; Olson & Rabunsky, 1972; Turk & Bell, 1972).

Even within the area of decision-making, an analysis of the process itself points to other crucial dimensions of power. For example, how do spouses go about influencing one another? Are attempts to influence direct or indirect? Covert or overt? How successful is one partner in influencing the other when faced with initial opposition?

Sometimes finding out who, in fact, is influencing whom may be a difficult task. Consider, for instance, the silent, covert influencer who manages to let his or her opinions be known nonverbally or indirectly, and in addition makes it appear that the partner has the final say: "Well, you know how I feel about it, dear, but you decide what's best." Decision-making studies examine who "wins" a disagreement, but what about who "decides" who wins? In looking at influence techniques used by husbands and wives, Safilios-Rothschild (1969b) found that when decisions were husband-dominated, 75 percent of the women used some type of technique, typically nonverbal, to influence their husbands, but let them officially "make the decision." Husbands (68 percent) make use of influence techniques when decisions are supposedly wife-dominated. Thus, just monitoring decision-making outcomes and excluding how the outcomes are reached yield only one index of family power. Furthermore, perhaps the outcome of a difference in views is less important for understanding familial power than is the process by which that outcome is determined.

In summary, descriptive self-report studies to examine who makes important family decisions have most often suggested that husbands and wives share equally in the number of decisions they make. The conclusion, then, by investigators is that the North American family's power structure is democratic and egalitarian. These decision-making studies, however, have come under attack for numerous inadequacies in method. When husbands and children as well as wives are asked to report on their perceptions of decision-making in families, reports differ among family members. Furthermore, self-report data bear little resemblance to data gathered by more direct observations of behavior. It has been difficult to define and measure power in terms of who controls family decisions because we have yet to determine what decisions adequately represent the range of issues about which couples must agree and which issues they believe to have the greatest importance to the family.

It is important to point up the question about method that concern studies dealing with the outcome of family decisions because much of our present knowledge about what affects family power has been based on these kinds of studies. More recent efforts to understand power in the family stress family power as a process, and to understand that process we must examine the entire family system.

SOURCES OF FAMILIAL POWER

Basically, there are two theories to explain division of marital and familial power. The first proposes that cultural ideology or social norms largely determine the relative power of husband and wife within the family. For instance, in a patriarchal system, both husband and wife take for granted that the husband should make most of the decisions. Patriarchal values dictate that men, by virtue of their sex, have an automatic right to pre-eminence, authority, and, hence, legitimate power. But, if culture were the only factor determining who controls familial decisions, there would be little variation between couples in which partner exercises the most power. Since decision-making studies show that, in fact, wide variation does exist, there must be other sources of power apart from those that are based on culture.

The more popular theory to account for differences among couples in balance of power says that the resources husband and wife bring to the marriage determine which exercises more power over decision-making. A "resource" is defined as "anything that one partner may make available to the other, helping the latter satisfy his needs or attain his goals" (Blood & Wolfe, 1960, p. 12). It is assumed that the primary motive for marriage is to better satisfy some needs and to attain certain individual and common goals. Need satisfaction and goal attainment are presumed to occur through the continual exchange of specific resources. Possible resources include personal attributes such as knowledge, skills, physical appearance, and personality characteristics. Those that have received most attention are material possessions and status derived from occupational, educational, or social position (Heer, 1963). The legitimate power conferred on men in our society may itself be viewed as a resource which enhances the husband's power in the family. The balance of power is said to reside with the mate who possesses the greatest number of or most highly prized resources.

This resource-exchange model of familial power, originally proposed by Blood and Wolfe in 1960, has since been critically examined and elaborated on by several authors (for example, Heer, 1963; Olson, Cromwell, & Klein, 1975; Osmond, 1978; Rollins & Bahr, 1976; Safilios-Rothschild, 1970, 1976; Sprey, 1972, 1975). Despite the fact that it has been widely criticized and in no way offers a complete understanding of power in the family, this model remains the most widely used framework for the study of power. After reviewing studies of factors that may affect power distribution in the family, we will discuss the resource-exchange theory in depth.

WHAT AFFECTS
POWER IN THE FAMILY?

Managing the Family Economy

Resource-exchange theorists have paid particular attention to resources such as income, occupational status, and education, which determine the financial input of a family member, typically the husband's domain. To what extent do men gain power over decision-making in the family as a direct result of being the primary bread-winners? Does a man with a higher income and more prestigious occupation wield greater power in the home? Do women who work outside the home have a greater say in familial decisions? Is there evidence for the claim that division of power within the family is largely related to who controls the economic resources?

Research thus far provides very strong support for the idea that economic factors are an important source of marital power. When Blood and Wolfe (1960) attempted to examine and isolate these factors, they found occupational status and prestige, education, and income to significantly determine the degree to which husbands exercise more control over decision-making than their wives. Despite the fact that professional men who are well educated seem to espouse more liberal views concerning equality between the sexes, middle-class husbands were generally more powerful within the home than their working-class counterparts. Husband's income alone was found to be the most sensitive indicator of relative marital power. Having a working wife, however, decreases the husband's power considerably. Women who are employed have more power vis-à-vis their husbands than do nonemployed wives, regardless of race or class. Furthermore, their power in the family increases in proportion to the number of years they have worked outside the home, regardless of whether women continue to work after they have married (Blood & Wolfe, 1960). Higher levels of education and greater participation in organizational activities outside the home also increase the wife's decision-making power relative to her husband's. In fact, even working in a voluntary capacity gives women more power to make familial decisions (Gillespie, 1971). These findings confirm that income, education, and occupational status are important in determining the relative power of spouses. In addition, they support the notion that power and status outside the home are positively related to level of marital power.

Cross-cultural studies, however, suggest that economic factors alone are not sufficient to explain women's lack of relative power within the family. Contrary to popular belief, males are not largely responsible for the family's economy in most cultures. Aronoff and Crano (1975) reviewed data from 862 societies and found that women contribute appreciably to the family economy, accounting for 44 percent of subsistence. This high figure does not merely reflect a few societies in which women are primary contributors. Rather, in 45 percent of the societies surveyed, women's contributions accounted for over 40 percent of the society's food production. Yet, the relationship between women's relative contribution to the economy and their relative status in a society is not straightforward, but complex. Sanday (1974) found that when the percentage contributed by women is *either* very high *or* very low, female status is low, whereas societies in which women's economic input is equivalent to that of men give women the highest social status. There is little explanation for this puzzling finding. Perhaps when women exceed men in their power over economic production, status is taken away from them in other realms in order to maintain a husband-dominant ideology. Whether this reasoning has validity is hard to say since cultural ideology and its relation to family economy was not examined. It is interesting to note, however, that there is no society in which it is generally expected that women should dominate men in marriage (Reiss, 1971). In North America, some would claim that the major reason for breakdown in female-headed, single-parent families is poverty (Brandwein, Brown, & Fox, 1974).

To summarize, contribution to the family budget is an important resource that may affect the relative power exercised by husbands and wives. As the comparative financial resources of husband and wife become more equitable, so does the division of marital power. Cross-cultural studies lead one to speculate, however, that should the financial contribution made by women exceed that of men, their decision-making power and social status may decrease rather than continue to increase. Although presently the number of wives seeking employment outside the home is steadily on the rise in North America and their contribution to the family economy can no longer be considered marginal, still it is seldom the case, except in single-parent families, that women are in charge of meeting the family's financial needs.

The Family Life Cycle

Resources that can be contributed by each spouse outside the marriage play an important role in determining the division of power within it. But what of the influence on marital power of internal factors that concern the family's function? Contemporary research suggests that stages of the family life cycle also affect the power distribution. A wife's power to make familial decisions, relative to that of her husband, tends to decline with age and number of children (Blood & Wolfe, 1960). Her employment status may act as a third intervening factor, as whether she works outside the home may be largely determined by involvement as a parent.

According to Blood and Wolfe's (1960) data, the birth of children results in a substantial jump in differences in power, the husband universally gaining. After the first child is born, but before the oldest child is in school, husband power reaches its maximum. There seems to be more than a little truth in the old saying that the best way to control a woman is to "keep her barefoot and pregnant," for the power of the wife declines as the number of children grows (Heer, 1958). Among white women throughout the United States, powerlessness is directly related to number of children where women's age, education, husband's occupation, and family income are equal (Morris & Sison, 1974). Furthermore, these power dynamics seem more closely related to cultural than biological factors. Female powerlessness does not seem to increase the number of children; rather, large numbers of children generate powerlessness for women within the family (Unger, 1979). Heer (1963) explains this by suggesting that relative power is determined primarily by the value placed on the resources that are contributed by each spouse outside the marriage. If, for instance, a husband exerts more power outside the marriage through occupational and social involvements, he is creating attractive alternatives for the wife—higher status, more money—and these alternatives help him to continue control within the marriage. At the same time, his external involvements make him less dependent on the marriage.

Assessing a woman's relative power in the family means taking into account her age, past and present employment status, resources she has accumulated outside the family network, and stage in the family life cycle. For instance, a much larger percentage of black women than white women continue to work when their children are young, which may explain in part why the birth of children does not lead to a dramatic decrease in black women's relative marital power (Gillespie, 1971). To give a further example, parenthood may be especially critical for the wife whose first child is born later, as she has typically achieved greater power within the marriage because she has worked for a number of years.

Many women stop working when their children are below school age and consequently become isolated and almost totally dependent on their husbands socially, economically, and emotionally. Later on in the family life cycle, it is often difficult for wives to regain power, as the rearing of children often prevents them from upgrading their skills, gaining seniority in professions, and becoming involved in community organizations.

Given that the husband's power within the family is so heavily dependent on his occupational status and income, it is not surprising that retirement leads to a decline in his relative power. In contrast, Blood and Wolfe (1960) found that relative power for the wife, and wife-dominance, reach their peak at middle age. Perhaps this reflects the fact that many wives have coped with an "empty nest" by entry or re-entry into the work force and establishment of broader social involvements. The researchers do not provide any data that would clarify such results. Indeed, especially in light of research that has linked middle age and depression in women (Bart, 1974), it would be most intriguing to find out why women in their forties and fifties appear to achieve a strength and self-confidence that younger women seldom know.

Love as a Power Resource

We have seen that the woman's childbearing role in our society makes it difficult for her to engage in activities outside the family that would enhance her resources and prestige. Furthermore, discrimination against women means that even if she does gain employment outside the home, her work tends to be low status and low paid and does not allow her to contribute substantially to the family economy. As Safilios-Rothschild (1976) points out, however, one way for wives to have an advantage in the marital exchange, even in highly sexist societies, is for women to control emotional or affective resources that are highly valued and needed by husbands. Following the principle of least interest (Homans, 1974), when a husband is clearly more in love with his wife than she is with him (and she is aware of this), the wife controls a valuable resource, that is, the reciprocation of his love. The withdrawal of sex and emotional or expressive resources from a wanting husband can give the wife a basis for power despite her lack of socioeconomic control. Similarly, although emotional resources are commonly discussed as "goods" within the female domain, husbands may also make use of love as a power resource in the same way.

Examining how emotional resources are exchanged between spouses sheds further light on factors that may have significant impact on marital power, and emotional resources in some cases may account for the differences in stress among couples who otherwise are much alike, in terms of husband-wife inconsistencies in income and occupational prestige. Yet, only recently have researchers given consideration to the roles of love, sex, and companionship in affecting power within the family.

One who has made an important contribution to emotional resource research is Constantine Safilios-Rothschild (1970, 1975, 1976). In one paper (1976), she claims that love has been neglected as a possible power resource because: (1) it has been considered a vague, subjective feeling and it is difficult to express it in terms of rules or "how it works," (2) there is a strong belief that love is constant, that is, couples marry for love and remain equally in love throughout marriage, and (3) most research has been carried out by males, who tend to equate power with masculine stereotypes of wealth and prestige rather than soft "feminine" qualities such as love and companionship. She questions each of these assumptions in her study of power among couples in Greece (1969a). Both husbands and wives were asked which spouse they perceived to be more in love. She found that wives who perceived their husbands as more in love also saw themselves as having greater orchestration power in decision-making. Furthermore, when spouses perceived themselves to be equally in love, marital power was shared equally.

Another interesting result comes from a study documented by Wolfe (1959). Using a Detroit population, he found that wives in husband-dominant families appear to have a greater need for love and affection than wives in wife-dominant families. Perhaps if a wife is not seeking emotional support from her husband, she may feel freer to exercise power that stems from other sources such as career. Undoubtedly, further research is required before both the workings and impact of emotional resources are thoroughly understood.

Violence in the Family

Research in the area of family power has all but ignored the use of coercive power based on the resource of physical strength. Yet it is all too common that family members are "kept in line" through the use of brute force. Wives are beaten by their husbands, children abused by their parents. Estimates of the incidence of husband-wife violence in the United States range from 25 percent to 37 percent of married couples, and this violence occurs in all socioeconomic groups (Frieze, 1979). It would be simplistic to argue that such violence is always merely a conscious power strategy—something that is turned on and off at will for rational reasons. Yet in families where the threat of violence exists, its potential victims must constrain their behavior to try to avoid a situation where they will be physically hurt, and so the perpetrator of the violence does gain some control. Researchers are still trying to unravel the causes of family violence, but it seems safe to say two things at this point: (1) the threat of violence can be a strong source of power for one person over other family members, and (2) people often stay in potentially violent family situations because they have no alternative source of the resources we have been discussing in this chapter: money, status, affection, or companionship.

SOCIAL PRESCRIPTIONS OF POWER

Research findings argue strongly for the role of exchangeable resources in determining the relative power of husband and wife. Is this to say that cultural values and societal attitudes have relatively little impact on who controls decision-making in the family? For instance, do subcultures with more traditional values and norms grant husbands greater relative decision-making power vis-à-vis their wives? To what extent does the premise of male authority in marriage still pervade the North American family? In society at large, does our thinking about how men and women ought to behave have a significant impact on power dynamics in the family?

To find the extent to which patriarchal attitudes influence the balance of power between husband and wife, Blood and Wolfe (1960) examined separately the decision-making data of five subcultures of the Detroit population that were expected to hold more traditional values regarding male-female roles and behavior: farm, immigrant, and Catholic families, old couples, and uneducated couples. Contrary to prediction, the husbands were not more dominant in decision-making in these groups than in other families. This led Blood and Wolfe to conclude that the patriarchal family is dead in North America and that the power advantage in marriage is no longer determined by a belief that says just because a man is a man, he is rightfully the boss. They claim no support for the contention that ideology influences marital power and maintain that their decision-making results can only be understood by examining the concrete sources of power.

Results contrary to these, however, have been documented by others who have sought to explore the relationship between subcultural ideology and power in marriage. For instance, Feldman (1967) found that in Ghana, uneducated men and women reported a more traditional ideology and a more husband-dominated decision-making pattern than did educated, more liberal couples. The high incidence of husband dominance among oriental couples has also been linked to their patriarchal value system (Centers, Raven, & Rodrigues, 1971).

Richmond (1976), investigating families of recent Cuban immigrants to the Miami area, found division of power to be affected both by resources of the family and its ideology or attitudes. In Cuban families where the tradition of male authority was most strong, women had little control over decision-making even when they contributed significantly to the family economy. The

146

wife's income was more important in determining her relative power than was her occupational status. When only couples holding similar ideologies were compared, so that the effects of ideology could be disregarded, the correlation between the wife's salary and her decision-making power remained significant. At the same time, the husband's monetary resources became a much more important factor influencing his relative power. Regardless of whether wives were employed, couples with egalitarian ideologies had a more equal division of power within the family than did those with male-dominant orientations. Richmond concluded that both resources *and* authority are important sources of familial power and that, especially in households where the male holds a high social status position, ideology may have a moderating influence on the husband's power.

According to Blood and Wolfe (1960), husband and wife are potential equals, and the person with the greatest resources gains the greatest power. Thus, accordingly, a "henpecked" husband is a man who has brought few resources to the marriage and is consequently dominated by his wife. These authors, however, have been harshly criticized for ruling out ideology as an important source of familial power.

Reiss (1971) notes that culture determines to a large extent the very resources that couples deem important for exchange in a marriage and how partners define their needs and goals. For instance, a man may be a very skillful cook and a woman very adept at mechanical repairs, but these resources would not be sought out by potential marriage partners nor would they be central in maintaining a marriage. Thus, cultural tradition does affect familial power by defining what task areas are important and which are male and female.

A second criticism made by Reiss is one we have already discussed; that is, Blood and Wolfe's (1960) neglect in determining the relative importance of familial decisions. Cultural standards also dictate which decisions carry the most weight. Our society's value system stipulates that the decision of which job the husband should take is more important than deciding on daily meal planning. Men have different tasks and corresponding decisions assigned to them, and these are generally more highly valued in our culture. Reiss (1971) disagrees with Blood and Wolfe's description of our culture as egalitarian, claiming that "when the decisions seem to give the male the culturally defined more important choices to make, one would have to define the system as male-dominant or patriarchal, in part at least" (p. 207).

Gillespie (1971) argues that to discount the role of ideology would be to disregard the fact that social, legal, and psychological blocks combine to prevent women from gaining access to material and status-type resources.

> The major error made by Blood and Wolfe is in assuming that this control of competence and resources occurs in individual couples by chance rather than being structurally predetermined in favour of the male . . . the cards are already stacked against her, for women are structurally deprived of equal opportunities to develop their capacities, resources and competence in competition with males. (p. 448).

Considerable evidence now exists to indicate that, from early childhood on, men and women are socialized differently. Different treatment promotes attitude and behavior characteristics that reduce women's effectiveness in many spheres of activity when compared to men. Women and men are encouraged to develop or enhance different cognitive skills (Maccoby & Jacklin, 1974; Lips & Colwill, 1978; Tavris & Offir, 1977), and many of the skills encouraged in women are not those that lead to high-status occupations or other high-status activity. In addition, men are encouraged to develop skills that enhance their social desirability outside the family, whereas women, if they are married, tend to give priority to the needs of the family over career concerns. Poloma and Garland (1971) found this pattern even among highly successful professional women. Women's participation in spheres outside the family may be dramatically hindered by prejudice and discrimination in education and employment (Hochschild, 1973). Such discrimination, in addition to the socialization process, may operate to lower self-esteem and reduce the likelihood that women will vigorously participate in occupational and other nonfamily activities.

The sex-based differences in roles within the nuclear family tend to maintain and enhance attitudes and behaviors that have been learned by women and men through earlier socialization. In his examination of family functioning in almost 200 different cultures, Zelditch (1955) found that most societies adopt as ideal a pattern in which men take on an instrumental role (stressing achievement in the outside world) in the family and women assume an expressive role (focusing on nurturing within the family).* Studies indicate that senior high school students generally agree that the wife should

---

*Eichler (1980) argues rightly that the terms "instrumental" and "expressive" are inappropriate to describe the sex role difference in families, since *both* the male and female roles actually include instrumental and expressive behaviors. Yet the terms are still in common use.

take care of the home and children and that the husband should be the key financial support (Bott, 1957; Dunn, 1960). Although division of labor does not necessarily indicate power, Blood and Wolfe's (1960) findings do indicate that it is related to power by the associated delegation of decision-making to the person assigned the task. These studies are all somewhat dated, and more recent investigations (Aldous, 1974; Bernard, 1972; Rapoport & Rapoport, 1971) suggest that family roles, although still somewhat sex-specific and split along this dimension, have become less dictated by culture. Unfortunately, there are no long-term studies available that would indicate whether greater flexibility in sex roles has led to more equal division of marital power.

The wife's functioning primarily in an expressive role, in contrast to her husband's instrumental or provider role, involves domestic support and the maintenance of family morale, especially husband's morale (Parsons & Bales, 1955). Furthermore, it has been shown that when a wife focuses exclusively on enacting the expressive role, this directly encourages her to be submissive and nondominant toward her husband (Laws, 1971). Although the so-called instrumental-expressive role split is not as common today as in previous times, family role theorists have suggested that any type of rigid role differentiation in marriage as a function of sex is likely to hinder women more than men, both in their personal development and the range of activities available to them (Rossi, 1967; 1972; Safilios-Rothschild, 1972).

In summary, cultural attitudes may influence the balance of power between husbands and wives in addition to whatever exchangeable resources they contribute to marriage. Furthermore, culture generally determines which decisions are considered most important to the family and which resources are valued items of exchange for each sex. Social discrimination, traditional role socialization, and traditional marital roles tend to restrict women's participation in activities that would gain them greater social status and provide them with resources necessary to attain power in the family. It should be stressed, however, that wives' relative lack of marital power is not merely a result of limited participation in high-status occupations and organizations outside the family. Rather, attitudes and behaviors into which women and men have been channeled may importantly determine family power relations, as is evident from research studies indicating that even female professionals demonstrate behaviors that reflect the channeling, or socialization process (Poloma, 1972; Rapoport & Rapoport, 1971).

Perceived and Derived Status
Not only do marital partners gain power as a result of the roles society dictates for them and the social status accorded their accomplishments outside

the family, but a husband or wife may, in addition, derive status from his or her spouse.

Felson and Knoke's (1974) study demonstrates that married women in our society derive much of their status from their husbands. Surprising as it may seem, both husbands and wives place little value on the wife's accomplishments in assessing the social status of a married couple. Although in 27 percent of their sample, wives had more education than their husbands and in 42 percent of cases the spouses were of the same educational levels, women and men alike gave significantly greater weight to the husband's achievements. In another study, Rossi et al. (1974) examined the criteria used to assess social status of the family by presenting raters with hypothetical married couples in which occupational status and educational levels of husband and wife were varied. An entire range of combinations was used (such as female college professor married to a machine operator, male psychologist married to a cashier in a supermarket). They found that raters considered the husband's characteristics to be twice as important as those of his wife's in determining the household's social standing. Even if a female physician was described as being married to a male payroll clerk, the husband's job took greater precedence. Level of education was not as important a characteristic as occupation in determining husband's social status and, hence, perceived status of the family.

It has been suggested that wives who work outside the home may enjoy two sets of status lines: one individually achieved and the other derived through their husbands (Safilios-Rothschild, 1975). Women may gain greater personal status by pursuing careers despite the fact that judgments of family status remain unaffected. In Finland, female white-collar workers ranked wives in professional occupations (achieved status) higher in status than wives of men in comparable occupations (derived status). These rankings were reversed by married women manual workers, who seemed to admire women's ability to obtain high status through their husbands without having to go out and work (Haavio-Mannila, 1969).

Eichler's report, *The Prestige of the Occupation Housewife* (1976), sheds further light on the status accorded employed women as opposed to women who "stay at home." People were asked to rank 93 occupational titles according to their own personal evaluation of the social standing of each occupation. Sex of the person holding an occupation was either left unspecified or indicated as male or female. Raters gave housewives a medium social status standing (ranking of 52), the same accorded secretaries and stenographers, the most common female occupations in Canada. Female-designated occupations that were given a considerably lower prestige score included salesclerk, teller, auto worker, hospital attendant, elevator operator, and baker. When the "housewife" was specified as male, the occupation dropped to the eighth lowest rank in terms of prestige.

Eichler's data again demonstrates that women are judged on the basis of their husbands' achievements. When a woman's social standing was lower than her husband's, his prestige pulled hers up. But in the reverse situation, in which the wife's occupational status exceeded her husband's, his score lowered hers, although it was not lowered to the same level as his. These findings indicate not only that a housewife derives status from her husband's occupation, but that the occupation of housewife has an independent status as well. Eichler's work also suggests that women who give up being a housewife out of a desire to enter the labor force will, unless they enter a very prestigious profession, experience a loss in prestige.

It is becoming much more common for women to identify themselves and for the media to introduce women in terms of both their achieved and derived statuses. But the relationship between these two status lines is still unclear and needs investigation. Simply adding together the prestige that a woman has attained from accomplishments outside the family to that derived from her husband does not necessarily indicate her perceived social standing. In fact, research findings thus far suggest that if a woman's achieved status is much greater than that of her husband, she is often perceived as having low "erotic rank" (Zetterberg, 1966). It is assumed that if she were sexy and attractive enough, she would have been able to find a husband more her equal. Along the same lines, when Blood and Wolfe (1960) examined the unusual marital situation in which the wife's decision-making predominated, they found that women who have superior power acquire it not by virtue of their own resources and competence, but rather by default. Women who were dominant in the family often tended to cover it up in public, a characteristic not found among dominant men. Wife dominance seems to be regarded as undesirable and deviant in that it reflects the husband's inadequacy in providing sufficient familial resources. "So the dominant wife is not exultant over the 'victory' but exercises power regretfully by default of her 'no good' or incapacitated husband" (p. 45).

Do husbands ever gain status from their wives? It has been suggested that husbands gain "brownie points" for marrying an attractive and desirable woman. A man's status is enhanced in the eyes of others because the fact that he was able to get such a "good catch" is said to be indicative of his masculinity. However, there is no hard evidence available yet to indicate the extent to which a man's ability to marry an attractive wife enhances his overall prestige. Similarly, as already mentioned, the potency and utility of emotional, affective resources typically within the female domain, such as love, sex, and companionship, have yet to be adequately explored.

It is interesting that the status husbands might gain from their wives' accomplishments has not yet been considered worthy of attention. It appears that the wife's contribution to the family has generally been regarded as negligible. But it is no longer true that women enter the work force just "to have something to do" or for extra pocket money. Furthermore, they are rapidly gaining greater access to occupations traditionally reserved for men and are asserting their rights to equivalent salaries. We may even see the day when both the wife's and husband's derived statuses are given equal merit in determining social status and familial power.

Marital power and marital happiness. Although investigation of the relationship between power and marital happiness is still in its infancy, some of the findings are worthy of mention. Not all results are consistent, but reported marital happiness seems greatest in husband-dominated families and least in wife-dominated families. Centers, Raven, and Rodriques (1971), using three levels of overall marital satisfaction, found reported happiness to be significantly lower in wife-dominant relationships than in husband-dominant and equal-dominance marriages. Kolb and Strauss (1974) measured exercise of power in a competitive game situation and found that couples in which husbands were able to gain a high number of complaint responses from their wives in a direct way, such as giving orders, had marriages that were rated significantly more satisfying and were more effective problem-solvers. These authors maintain that when a family departs from norms of male dominance, it experiences conflict with expectations from other members of society, including friends, relatives, and employees, which can lead to marital strain.

It would be premature to conclude that husband dominance is the key to marital success. First, marital happiness is a difficult concept to measure. The study by Kolb and Strauss (1974) has been criticized for using children to assess their parents' happiness, since children's perceptions have been shown to differ markedly from their parents' perceptions (Larson, 1974). Second, it may be that happiness is determined by the form of power in a marriage rather than how power is distributed. Raven (1974) reports that couples who are most satisfied use "referent" power, power based on liking or admiring the influencer, whereas coercive power is used by very un-satisfied couples.

The findings that concern marital happiness among couples of dual-career marriages are also interesting. Wives who work outside the home report themselves happier then housewives (Burke & Weir, 1976), and, as we have seen, they gain relative power from such employment. Housewives, in con-trast to employed women, claimed poorer mental and physical health, more feelings of "being in a rut," and difficulties talking with their husbands about subjects apart from child issues. But despite the fact that employed wives report being happier and present a better picture of their marriage relation-ships, husbands of employed wives see themselves as less happy than husbands of homemakers. They claim greater job pressures and job dissatisfaction, poorer physical and psychological health, and more difficulties in showing affection and communicating with their wives. Perhaps these men are under greater stress than husbands of housewives because they contribute more time and effort to child care and household tasks. Furthermore, they may receive less emotional support from their wives, and employed wives may, in fact, demand attention to their own social and physical needs.

The data from studies concerning dual-career marriages are difficult to interpret because other uncontrolled factors may be operating (Unger, 1979). Partners of dual-career marriages tend to be younger and married for a shorter time. Also, husbands of employed wives earn significantly less income than husbands in one-career families. In a society that measures masculinity by the size of one's paycheck (Gould, 1976), this may be a powerful source of marital dissatisfaction. Furthermore, husbands of employed wives may be less traditional in their attitudes about sex roles, making them more attuned to communicating and demonstrating affection to their partners. These men may be more willing to admit shortcomings in their marriages than are husbands of women who maintain the traditional homemaker role. Certainly this area is worthy of further investigation.

RESOURCES-EXCHANGE MODEL OF FAMILIAL POWER

Thus far, resource-exchange theory, derived from the social-exchange theory (discussed in Chapter 3), provides the most comprehensive framework for understanding familial power. This model can incorporate the other, ideologi-cal, theories of power when authority itself is viewed as a resource.

Several authors have discussed essential characteristics of the resource-exchange model (Beckman-Brindley & Tavormina, 1978; Blau, 1964; Osmond, 1978; Safilios-Rothschild, 1976; Sprey, 1972; Thibault & Kelley, 1959). The major points of the theory are: (1) power is treated as a dynamic dimension of ongoing relationships rather than as a stable, individual trait, (2) when persons A and B enter a relationship, both bring resources as well as needs, (3) balance of power is determined in part by person A's resources and person B's need for them, (4) each person "pays" a certain price in resources brought to acquire goods that will meet his or her needs, (5) the degree of importance attached to a resource is influenced by the extent to which persons have direct access to alternatives that can provide the same resources at the same or lower cost, (6) the most important determinant of relative power is not the actual resources exchanged, but each person's perception of the exchange, and (7) relative power may vary over time as needs and resources fluctuate in a variety of situations.

Safilios-Rothschild (1976) has broadened previous perspectives by suggesting a more comprehensive list of resources that have potential influence on family power patterns (see Table 3). She claims that, to date, ideas about what constitutes a "scarce and desirable good" have been colored by a strong masculine bias, which has led to the neglect of such resources as affection, companionship, and sex.

Marriage has been viewed as an unequal exchange because the sexes have unequal access to socioeconomic resources deemed important by our society (Unger, 1979). The greater the gap between value to the wife of resources contributed by her husband and value to the husband of resources contributed by his wife, the greater is the husband's relative power. Rewards and costs do not carry with them any absolute external value; rather, value is subjectively appraised by each family member (Safilios-Rothschild, 1976). Family stability and marital satisfaction are said to depend on "perceived equity," a state in which each partner feels he or she is getting enough re-wards from the relationship to balance the costs and feels reasonably "even" with the spouse in terms of what both are getting and giving (Walster, Walster & Berscheid, 1978). We have seen that many couples in which husbands wield greater relative power also report being very satisfied with their marriages. When a host of possible goods that may be exchanged between marital partners is examined, this finding becomes more easy to interpret.

For instance, a traditional wife can make available or withdraw a host of resources, thus achieving considerable control over even the most occupationally successful husband. She can spend hours in the kitchen preparing

TABLE 3: List of Resources Potentially Exchanged Between Spouses

1. Socioeconomic	– Money
	– Social Mobility
	– Prestige
2. Affective	– Affection
	– Love (loving-being loved)
	– Feeling needed-needing the other
3. Expressive	– Understanding
	– Emotional support
	– Special attention
4. Companionship	– Social
	– Leisure
	– Intellectual
5. Sex	
6. Services	– Housekeeping services
	– Child care
	– Personal services
	– "Linkage" services
7. Power in the relationship	

Source: From C. Safilios Rothschild, "A Macro- and Micro-Examination of Family Power and Love: An Exchange Model" in *Journal of Marriage and the Family* (May 1976), p. 356. © 1976 by the National Council on Family Relations.

his favorite foods or serve him frozen dinners. She can keep a neat, attractive house or leave it sloppy and disorganized, thus embarrassing her executive husband in front of his business associates. She can be a responsive, affectionate sexual partner or turn off her sexuality when dissatisfied with other aspects of the marital relationship. Similarly, husbands influence power in the marriage by either helping or refusing to contribute to household tasks. A husband may spend considerable social time with his wife, taking her out to dinner and to visit friends, or he may rarely be home, caught up in job responsibilities and business trips.

SUMMARY AND FUTURE DIRECTIONS

Many resources are used by marital couples in negotiating family power. Money, affection, authority, and status all enter into the exchange. Researchers studying family power have given little attention to a number of critical questions. What are the dynamics involved in resource exchange? What factors determine the cost incurred by withholding resources? Assessing the available or potential alternatives to the present marital situation is a difficult task.

The degree to which each spouse loves and needs the other may be crucial in explaining the marital power structure (Safilios-Rothschild, 1970). Similarly, the quality and level of interrelationships and the way in which members define the family situation may be supremely important rather than specific resources exchanged.

Beckman-Brindley and Tavormina (1978) point out that resource-exchange theorists have focused on individual contributions to a relationship, but have neglected to examine the process of relationships, which involves continual reciprocal exchange among all participants. These authors claim that the type of resources exchanged and patterns of influence used may vary from time to time and task to task, but that each family develops a set of rules, which remains relatively constant and which underlies all interactions (for example, all exchanges must be mutually satisfying; I will allow you to satisfy me less than I satisfy you as long as the children are left to my domain). According to the authors, these unspoken rules, which can be understood only by examining the family unit as a system of interdependent, interacting parts, hold the key to understanding family power.

Several hypotheses follow from this additional new perspective. For instance, the more consensus there is among family members regarding rules of exchange, the greater stability should be observed in their interaction. Also, when dissatisfaction with the existing rule structure exists, conflicts should appear until new rules are negotiated and equilibrium is once again established. Future research directed toward understanding the pattern of family rules and reciprocal interactions may provide us with a better understanding of power in the family.

POWER IN THE ORGANIZATION

8

Gary W. Yunker and Hilary M. Lips

In most organizations, the informal system of relationships finds both its origins and present function in the male culture and in the male experience. Its forms, its rules of behavior, its style of communication and its mode of relationships grow directly out of the male developmental experience . . . Few women are a part of this system and most women don't even recognize it exists.

Margaret Hennig and Ann Jardim

In this chapter we look at power relationships in the structure of organizations. People in positions of power in organizations have to be more than leaders in the simple sense of being dominant or influential and persuasive. They must be able not only to exert power over others, but also to "empower" others. They must be managers—a role that includes leadership and a variety of other functions, many of which are power-related (Mintzberg 1973). As with all people in formal positions of authority, a manager's power is enhanced by the recognized legitimacy of his or her position, that is, being seen as having a *right* to make certain demands of others. However, even at the same organizational level, not all managers are equally powerful, and in this chapter we will examine some reasons why.

The emergence of a leader in unstructured situations is gradual, informal, and a matter of common general consent. Over time, a person gains the group's respect and allegiance and is deferred to increasingly. Thus, in a group of friends, an individual's influence may gradually increase as she or he is recognized by others as having good ideas and being able to get things done. In a more formally structured group, such an individual might be officially recognized as a leader through election or appointment to a leadership position. In a social service club, a well-respected individual may be pressed to stand for office as president. There, the emergence of a leader becomes formal and less gradual, but still agreed to by all. In the highly structured context of a business organization, however, the designation of leaders becomes more formal and less a matter of common agreement; people are promoted from above rather than elected from below. Even in this context, however, the would-be leader may go through a preliminary process of gradually gaining the respect of those by whom leadership decisions are made.

How does a person acquire the informal prestige and status that can lead to a formal position of power? Is this process different for women and men? Let us begin with a focus on these questions and then examine managerial power in the broader organizational context.

BECOMING A LEADER: IMAGE AND BEHAVIOR

Platitudes about "natural-born leaders" to the contrary, the emergence of an individual into a group leadership position is dictated by a complex mixture of situational and behavioral factors. In terms of situation, the group must need a leader and the individual must conform to the group's image of one. In terms of behavior, the individual must both act and speak in order to be noticed and to create a favorable impression and must also avoid behaviors that are seen as incompatible with leadership. On these counts, there is some experimental evidence that women often encounter more difficulties than do men.

The Leadership Image

Perceived competence. Clearly, for a person to emerge as a leader, he or she must be seen as competent by the rest of the group. Another's view of individual competence may be influenced by information about background, training, and previous accomplishments, as well as by such factors as age, sex, and race. In situations where a group is getting together for the first time, members may have no background information about one another and must form initial impressions solely on the basis of obvious factors. This may place members of certain groups, such as racial minorities, women, or the physically handicapped, at a disadvantage because of unfavorable stereotypes about their competence.

Laboratory studies overwhelmingly show that, in the absence of any other information but sex, women are considered less competent than men (for example, Rosenkrantz, Vogel, Bee, Broverman, & Broverman 1968; Sherriffs & Jarrett, 1953), and that male success is more likely to be attributed to ability than is female success (for example, Deaux & Emswiller, 1974). Furthermore, products and performance records attributed to women are often evaluated less favorably than the identical items attributed to men (for example, Goldberg, 1968; Mischel, 1974; Rosen & Jerdee, 1973). Thus, in mixed-sex groups where participants know little about one another, the women may be seen initially as less competent than the men, and thus they will be less likely to emerge as leaders. Any background information that has to do with competence may alter this effect, however. For example, with little other information, paintings attributed to women were rated less favorably than the same paintings attributed to men, but when other subjects were told that the paintings had won a prize, the sex of the painter was not a determining factor in their ratings (Pheterson, Kiesler, & Goldberg, 1971). In this case, subjects were no longer basing their evaluations only on the sex of the individual, but were also taking into consideration independent information about the artist's competence. In a similar vein, we might predict that an individual who comes into a group with a solid reputation for excellent performance will tend to be perceived as competent, regardless of sex.

The masculine image of the leader. As discussed in Chapter 1, for many people the image of the powerful person is inescapably male. Research suggests that the image of the leader is similarly masculine. In 1965, a *Harvard Business Review* survey of 2000 business executives found that 31 percent of the male respondents described women as "tempermentally unfit for management." In fact, "the ideal manager is perceived as male in character: competitive, aggressive, dominant, firm, vigorous, and rational. Against this standard, women are perceived as inadequate. They are characterized as not competitive, valuing social skills, person-oriented, emotional, intuitive, unambitious, and dependent" (Brown, 1979, p. 275). O'Leary (1974) argues that the managerial role coincides closely with male-stereotyped attributes of competence, such as problem-solving and decision-making ability. The findings of a variety of studies fit with these observations (for example, Bass, Krussell, & Alexander, 1971; Schein, 1973, 1975).

Leadership roles in areas other than business are similarly stereotyped. Educational administrators, politicians, and church ministers, for instance, are typically expected to be men. Thus, even if a woman is seen as competent, she may still not meet the image requirements of leadership.

Another problem with the leadership image for women rests in their lack of similarity to existing male leaders. In many situations, a new leader is appointed or designated by an existing leader. Leaders tend to pick others who are similar to themselves (Dalton, 1951; Pfeffer 1977; Wilson & Lupton, 1959), and usually this means picking men.

Ascribed status. The fact that the sexes are seen as unequal in competence, plus the tendency to stereotype leadership positions as masculine, may form part of a larger pattern, the general tendency, as discussed in Chapter 1, to ascribe higher status to males than to females. High-status individuals are expected to be more competent and are thus accorded more power and prestige in the group (Berger, Cohen, & Zelditch, 1972). If sex is used as a status characteristic, then, with males being more highly valued than females, males will be more likely to hold positions of power and prestige in mixed-sex groups.

A large body of evidence asserts that sex is, in fact, used in determining an individual's value or status, and that maleness is more highly valued than femaleness. Anthropologists find that although tasks designated as women's work may vary according to culture, work performed by females is almost universally considered less important and valuable than work performed by males (Rosaldo, 1974). In North America, male children are preferred over female children, particularly as firstborns (Markle, 1974), and in one study (Gordon, Gordon, & Gunther, 1961) the birth of a female child was associated with a higher incidence of postpartum depression! Studies in which college students rated large numbers of adjectives according to the degree to which they characterize adult male and females show that a considerably larger number of male than female traits are valued positively (Brovermen, Vogel, Broverman, Clarkson, & Rosenkrantz, 1972; Rosenkrantz et al., 1968). These and other findings suggest that, in general, males are accorded higher value than females—a status difference that generally gives males the edge in mixed-sex groups whenever power and prestige are being allocated.

To this point we have been discussing the effects of group initial perceptions of individuals on the likelihood that the individuals will become group leaders. These perceptions do not act in a vacuum, however. It is probable that they shape and are shaped by the behavior of the particular individual. If someone is seen as "nonleader" material, for instance, input from that person is likely to be ignored or discounted. In response, the person in question may provide less and less input to the group. On the other hand, if the person continually challenges the group's impression of him or her as a nonleader by contributing strong, incisive inputs, the group may eventually reconsider its initial impression of that person.

Behavior: Acting Like a Leader

Given that an individual meets the minimum "image" criteria for emergence as a group leader, how must he or she behave in order to attain a leadership position? Research in group dynamics suggests that both verbal and nonverbal behaviors are important.

Verbal participation. A large number of studies of small groups have found a positive connection between the amount of verbal participation and emergent leadership (Stein & Heller, 1979). Simply put, people who talk a lot in the group are more likely to become the leaders. This occurs whether participation is allowed to occur spontaneously or is manipulated by the experimenters. For example, Gintner and Lindskold (1975) showed that even when people suggested the same solution to the assigned problem in different groups, their leadership ratings by other group members were linked to how much they talked.

Although talking in itself seems to be important in establishing leadership, certain *kinds* of talk may be especially important. Stein and Heller (1979) showed that "task leadership behaviors," such as asking questions, helping to set up structures and procedures for the group, giving information and opinions, and identifying and solving problems, are especially important in attaining leadership.

It is still unclear exactly why there is a strong relationship between verbal participation and leadership status, but interpersonal power, the successful exertion of influence, seems to be part of the answer. It may be that a high degree of visibility, brought about by high participation, leads group members to attribute competence to the individual, which gives that person a base of social power (see the discussion of expert power in Chapter 3). Or it may be, as suggested by the leadership valence theory (Stein, Hoffman, Cooley & Pearse, 1979), that leadership status increases gradually with participation, being enhanced by each successful attempt to influence others (even if this influence only involves getting the others to listen).

Laboratory studies indicate that in mixed-sex groups the behavior of men and women tends to differ in ways that are related to verbal participation and leadership status. Men talk more than women, women are more likely to yield to a man's opinion, and a higher proportion of men's verbal behavior than women's is in task-related areas (Lockheed & Hall, 1976). These differences do not appear between all-male and all-female groups, and they must, therefore, stem from the mixed-sex interaction. Males, then, are more likely than females to emerge as leaders in mixed-sex groups.

Why do such sex-related differences occur? Lockheed and Hall (1976) suggest that the answer lies in the use of sex as a status characteristic. People in experimental groups of strangers, having no information about other participants except sex and approximate age, simply expect less competence from the women than the men. However, if expectations are changed by giving the women prior experience in the assigned task, then women show greatly increased verbal behaviors in subsequent mixed-sex groups. Thus, when participants are not total strangers to one another or have some information about the relative competence of group members, the effect of sex as a status characteristic can be diminished.

The impact of sex as a status characteristic is most apparent when participants have little other information about one another, and we know relatively little about its importance in real-life ongoing working groups. However, the research on verbal dominance described in Chapter 5 leads one to suspect that even in groups and relationships where people know one another, there is a tendency to accord women lower status then men. Remember that in naturally occurring groups or couples, men are much more likely to interrupt women and that even among married couples, men seem to have more conversational control. So, if leadership depends on verbal participation, and women are more frequently thwarted than men in their attempts to participate, they are at a clear disadvantage in an attempt to gain leadership status. Long-term research with ongoing working groups is needed to specify clearly the true impact of sex-related differences in participation, the conditions under which they occur and the mechanisms that underlie them.

Nonverbal behavior. From Chapter 5, we see that whether we view someone as having leadership status can be influenced by that person's nonverbal actions. Recent research suggests that nonverbal behavior can be as potent a cue as sex for ascribing status in certain situations. McKenna and Denmark (cited in Denmark, 1977) showed subjects videotapes without the sounds of interaction between pairs of actors. These pairs were either same-sex or cross-sex, and each actor behaved nonverbally in either a high- or low-status style. The results showed that the nonverbal behavior, but not the sex of the actors, significantly affected subjects' judgements about status. Women or men who used high-status or dominant nonverbal behaviors (smiled less, initiated more touching, acted more relaxed) were seen as having higher status than women or men who used low-status nonverbal behaviors. Under certain conditions, then, the emergence of an individual as a leader can probably be helped or hindered by the use of nonverbal behavior. One very specific instance may be choice of seating position. Some research shows that persons who sit at the head of the table are more likely to emerge as leaders and that high-status persons are more likely than low-status persons to choose this seating position (Stodgill, 1974).

The connection between seating position and leadership emergence, like most of the findings discussed in this section, comes from experimental research in a laboratory situation, with groups of volunteer subjects whose only contact with one another was in the experiment. Research of this type is carried out in carefully controlled situations to test the basic premise; it cannot possibly duplicate a real-life situation in which people are working together on an ongoing basis and where the emergence or appointment of one person rather than another as leader has real long-term consequences. Therefore, let us broaden our scope and examine leadership and the acquisition of power within a real-world management and organizational context. As we will see, leadership is an important part (but not the only part) of the manager's organizational role, and the manager's power in the organization has a significant impact on subordinates' satisfaction and their perception of his or her effectiveness.

MANAGEMENT AND POWER
IN EVERYDAY ORGANIZATIONAL LIFE

Katz and Kahn (1978) defined organizational leadership in terms of "influential increment" exercised by a manager over and above the formal authority and status that the organization gives to a particular position. In terms of French and Raven's (1959) bases of power (see Chapter 3), the organization gives managers the legitimate power to reward and punish by virtue of their role. Any influence beyond this power base is gained through referent power (gaining influence by becoming well-liked and respected) and expert power developed largely by the individual manager. The amount of extra influence a manager accrues affects not only personal advancement, but also managerial effectiveness and subordinate satisfaction.

This section explores managerial behavior in the organization with specific emphasis on the possession of power and its relationship to managerial effectiveness. The research cited first is largely based on samples of male managers. Several investigations of female managerial behavior and use of power are then examined, and comparisons and contrasts are drawn between male and female managerial behavior.

Mintzberg's Ten Working Roles
Henry Mintzberg (1973) became disenchanted with managerial textbooks that lectured readers about what managers *should do*. After reviewing research in which ongoing managerial behavior was actually studied and compiling data from his own observations of managers, Mintzberg concluded that managerial behavior consists of ten working roles. These roles define what most managers *actually do*. Mintzberg felt that the ten working roles could be

grouped under three main categories: interpersonal roles, transfer of information roles, and decision-making roles (see Table 4).

**TABLE 4: Mintzberg's Ten Managerial Roles
(adapted from Mintzberg, 1973).**

(Input) ———————————————————————————→ (Output)		
Interpersonal	*Informational*	*Decisional*
Formal	Figurehead	Monitor	Entrepreneur

(Input)			(Output)
	Interpersonal	*Informational*	*Decisional*
Formal	Figurehead	Monitor	Entrepreneur
Authority ⟶	Leader ——————⟶	Disseminator ⟶	Disturbance handler
and Status	Liaison	Spokesperson	Resource allocator
			Negotiator

The ten working roles are interdependent and closely related. The three interpersonal roles are based on the formal authority and status initially given the manager by an organization. The interpersonal roles, in turn, facilitate the informational roles, which allow the manager to make various types of decisions in the decisional roles. A systems framework would consider the formal authority and status given managers by the organization as input into the managerial system and managerial decisions as the output of the system.

Following are brief definitions of the ten working roles of management.

Interpersonal

1. Figurehead. The manager may be required to act as a symbol in carrying out ceremonial, social, legal, or inspirational functions.
2. Leader. This role is defined by interaction with subordinates and allows the most display of managerial power.
3. Liaison. The establishment of a network of contacts outside the organization for the mutual benefit of all concerned defines this role.

Informational

1. Monitor. The manager constantly seeks out and is exposed to information from both within and outside the organization.
2. Disseminator. The manager channels external information into the organization and shunts internal information to various subordinates.

3. Spokesperson. This role requires the manager to become a public relations person and to transmit information about the organization externally.

Decisional

1. Entrepreneur. In this role, the manager must design and take the first steps toward change in the organization.
2. Disturbance handler. When the manager's unit must contend with an unforeseen problem for which there is no set polity or response, the manager must assume this role.
3. Resource allocator. This role allows the manager the opportunity to portion out organizational resources such as money, manpower, and reputation over which control is exercised.
4. Negotiator. This role entails negotiation activity with other organizations.

The ten working roles explain not only the exciting aspects of managerial behavior, but also the more routine day-to-day functions that the supervisor performs.

Sayles's Strategies for Gaining Power

Leonard Sayles (1979), who observed managers in several large organizations, attempted to follow Mintzberg's lead in defining what effective managers really do on a day-to-day basis. The heart of Sayles's discussion of managerial leadership is based on a description of lateral relations among managers and the ways in which managers gain power in the organization. Lateral relations generally involve matters that require coordination among managerial peers—people at the same level in organizational rank. Some basis other than authority must be established to get things done in these "sideways" relationships. Much can be seen about a manager's degree of influence by the success with which such relations are handled.

Traditional management theorists lump lateral relations under the heading of informal organization because such relations are not "spelled out" on the formal organization chart of authority. Laterial relationships can be difficult for the manager for the following reasons: they generally involve different values and orientations among different work groups; they usually are irregular because they involve unanticipated problems; they often interfere with the regular routines and processes of the involved units; and the number of lateral relations needed to solve one problem that affects many groups can be quite large and may require repeated contact.

Sayles, observed that many managers and their work units had power far beyond their apparent formal status in the organization. He linked this acquisition of power to the successful handling of lateral relations, and he concluded that power could be gained in the following ways:

1. Avoid the routine. The task that is highly predictable and regular has less power.
2. Strive for visibility. In the organization, visibility can be gained through introducing innovation, acquiring critical skills, or being a manager of a critical department.
3. Become proficient at advocacy. The ability to sell one's ideas to top management through effective presentation is a source of power.
4. Seek coalitions for support. Trade-offs involving services and resources are effective ways to gain support from other individuals or work groups.
5. Initiate workflow for others. Don't have others initiate work for your position.
6. Have access to information. Power is gained through continued access to critical information flowing through the organization.

The link between managerial power, lateral relations, and managerial behavior can be seen particularly in suggestions 2, 4, and 6 listed by Sayles and is very important to note at this stage. As one might expect, powerful managers are more likely to have their wishes fulfilled and their efforts rewarded than are less powerful managers. In terms of effectiveness, the powerful manager's behavior is more likely to be effective for both the manager and the group that the manager supervises than are the behaviors of less powerful managers. Finally, one of the best ways for a manager to develop bases of power in the organization is through frequent and meaningful lateral relations with colleagues. Effective lateral relations invite increased individual visibility, foster coalitions for support, and allow access to current, valuable, "hot" organizational information.

The Informal Organization
The relationship of the informal network to effective managerial behavior as defined by Mintzberg's (1973) ten working roles is fairly straightforward.

Informal relationships can potentially enrich all of the working roles except the figurehead role, which has a more formal, symbolic basis. Informal relations serve to broaden the range of interpersonal contacts that the manager develops. These contacts broaden and enrich the range of information to which the manager has access, allowing the manager to make informed decisions that, because of interpersonal contacts, are more likely to be implemented.

The informal organization is often cited as one of the greatest stumbling blocks for female managers on the road to power and effectiveness. It includes lateral and other relationships and processes not governed by the rules and regulations of the formal organization. However, the informal organization is covered by rules of a different sort—rules that are clearly male-oriented and based on male behaviors, modes of communication, and common experiences (Hennig & Jardim, 1977).

Much of any manager's power and effectiveness is deeply rooted in the informal network of relationships with the manager's superiors, fellow managers, subordinates, and individual contacts outside the organization. The situation today is such that, except for subordinates, this informal network is usually dominated by men. The key characteristic of most informal networks is mutual trust, which is dependent on such factors as compatible attitudes and behavior, common previous experiences, and a certain amount of overt behavior that conforms to the informal norms. It follows, then, that a female manager who attempts to make use of informal organization is faced with a number of factors that tend to work against her: (1) she is "different" and will probably not be trusted as readily as a comparable male, (2) she probably does not have a background of experience similar to most of the males in the network, which again emphasizes her difference, (3) she may have difficulties forming informal coalitions with male superiors and peers because of the fear that others may think the relationship is based on sexual favors, (4) the informal network may have meeting places where females are excluded, which Bernard (1976) called the "stag effect," and (5) she may be unwilling to enter a relationship to "use" someone she dislikes, whereas a male would be more likely to do so because of prior team-oriented experiences where this was necessary. This list of factors is not all-inclusive, but the important point is that women are placed at a distinct disadvantage when they attempt to function effectively in a system where they are informally excluded and for which they lack training, experience, and knowledge of the "rules of the game."

Are we idealizing the male experience in organizations when drawing these comparisons? Anne Harlan and Carol Weiss (cited in Chan, 1980) argue that women's experiences have been compared to a "successful male" myth rather than to men's actual experiences. Their own data suggest that men and women in the retail industry have very similar experiences as managers in many respects: both groups have difficulty in understanding and planning their careers, obtaining useful feedback, and getting opportunities for developing new skills.

Harlan and Weiss did find some differences between men and women in their access to power, however, which relate to the use of the informal organization. Men had significantly more control over company assets than did women in their study, despite the fact that the two sexes were matched on level of management, responsibility, and area of functioning. There was also a tendency for men to seek out and obtain early information about decisions and policy changes more often than women. Men and women both reported using the informal network, but there was some tendency for men to have more social contact with top executives and persons outside the company. Although men and women both reported using informal contacts to get advice and help in their jobs, women reported that they had to make a deliberate effort to become part of the network, whereas men said they were brought into the network without any effort on their part.

Two Common Stereotypes

To the extent that women have difficulty relating to and using the informal organization, they are limited in the power they can derive from lateral relations, sponsor-protégé coalitions, and upward influence with superiors. Rosabeth Moss Kanter (1977, 1979) concludes that the relative powerlessness of women in managerial positions as compared to their male counterparts helps to explain two common stereotypes about women in management: (1) no one wants a woman supervisor, not even other women, and (2) female managers "go by the book," that is, are too strict and rules-oriented.

According to Kanter (1979), the first stereotype simply reflects the fact that power is important to effective management. Subordinates of either sex prefer to work under a powerful manager who can get things done in the organization. Subordinates of a powerful manager also receive "reflected" power or power through association. The second stereotype, again, is the result of lack of power. Powerless individuals expect resistance from subordinates and are unsure of their own effectiveness. These individuals compensate for felt powerlessness by coercive styles of supervision that are tied to conformity to the rules.

Competence and Career Planning

Male and female managers may differ in their attitudes toward gaining power and getting ahead in the organization. Many women managers in Hennig and Jardim's (1977) sample felt that the way for a woman to advance her career in management was to stress job competence; they had to be better at their jobs than any man available. Therefore, they concentrated their efforts on becoming perfectionists in their positions, largely at the expense of developing informal working relationships. These women also tended to be less mobile in their careers, with many remaining at a single company. Harlan and Weiss (cited in Chan, 1980) found that women aspired to positions lower in the organizational hierarchy than those aspired to by men.

According to Hennig and Jardim, male managers are more aware of the potential rewards available through informal relationships. They also are more likely to see the opportunities for career advancement through making company changes, which speed up their vertical climb to some "ideal position in an ideal organization." However, Harlan and Weiss found no differences between men and women in future goal planning. In their sample, little career goal setting was undertaken by either sex.

Fear of Visibility

Several of the strategies mentioned by Sayles (1979) for gaining power relate to making oneself a highly visible figure in the organization. In fact, all the strategies he listed are based on dynamic, aggressive behavior that is meant to be visible to everyone in the organization. In management jargon, these highly visible managers are the "movers" who cause others around them to "shake."

For several reasons, most women have preferred to play the role of shakers rather than movers in management. This phenomenon has been explained by various phrases such as "fear of success" (Horner, 1972), "fear of retaliation" (Kanter, 1977), and "fear of visibility" (Denmark, 1977). Horner (1972) felt that the fear of success was due to the belief that success in competitive, male-oriented activities leads to unpopularity and a loss of femininity in the eyes of others. Kanter (1977) attributed the fear of becoming too outstanding in performance to a belief by some women that men do not like a woman to make them look bad and will retaliate against her through various means. Denmark (1977), citing earlier research by Megargee

(1969) and Tresemer (1974), concluded that the fear of visibility is an attempt by women to keep a low profile in the organization by not drawing attention to themselves as special cases. This appears to be a more encompassing explanation of the phenomenon than the first two concepts.

Fear of visibility most certainly places severe limitations on the acquisition of power. In essence, these women become their own worst enemies by "playing it safe."

The Socioemotional Attribution

The woman's image in our society has traditionally been characterized as closely linked to the "mother" role, which could be described in such terms as "warm," "understanding," "passive," and "emotional." Many studies involving descriptions of female managers by male subordinates show that the socioemotional stereotype of women by men is strong (for example, Petty & Lee, 1975; Denmark, 1977; Adams, 1978; Haccoun, Haccoun, & Sallay, 1978). Unfortunately for women, violation of this stereotype by directing, authoritarian behavior can lead to dissatisfaction and resentment among subordinate males.

However, many researchers and management theorists believe that in some important situations the effective manager may have to be very task-oriented and directive with subordinates (Kerr, Schriesheim, Murphy, & Stodgill, 1974; Tannenbaum & Schmidt, 1958; Vroom & Yetton, 1973). This situation places the female manager of male subordinates in a "no win" position. If she conforms to the socioemotional stereotype, she may not be as effective, overall, as a comparable male; on the other hand, if she violates this stereotype, she risks alienating her male subordinates, who may in turn sabotage her best efforts.

The Lone Female Manager

Committee or group-oriented work within a department may lead to situations in which a female manager is the lone woman in a group. As Kanter (1975a) discovered, what is said or felt about the lone female's informal role in the group may ". . . put the woman in her place without challenging the male culture of the group" (p. 57). Kanter (1975b) found four major roles that might be attributed to the lone female: mother, pet or group mascot, sex object or seductress, and iron maiden—militant and unapproachable. These attributed roles can seriously inhibit the female manager's show of organizational power and competent behavior.

Mistaken assumptions about the female manager's formal role in the organization have been linked to "statistical discrimination" (Kanter, 1975a); these assumptions are usually based on the statistical rarity of women in management. Statistical discrimination occurs when those with whom the woman manager comes into initial contact make assumptions about her role in the organization based on what "most women do in organizations." An example is the female manager who is mistaken for a secretary whenever she performs some function similar to those most secretaries perform—answering a phone, making copies of material, sitting behind a desk (see Lynch, 1973 for other examples). Many would argue that there is little harm done by these mistaken attributions. However, they may inhibit the woman's performance over the long run by lowering her self-image and status in the eyes of others with whom she works, thus interfering with her direct use of power.

Kanter (1977) has argued that, as long as women make up less than 15 percent of managers, they are viewed as tokens—symbols of their sex rather than individuals. As tokens they are subject to greater performance pressures, isolation, exclusion from male groups, and stereotyping. Presumably, as the proportion of women in management increases, sex bias decreases; women become too numerous to be considered tokens and are instead regarded as individuals. However, some new findings show that things may not be this simple.

Harlan and Weiss (cited in Chan, 1980) found sex bias to be considerably greater in one retailing company where women held 19 percent of management positions than in a comparable company where women held only 6 percent of such positions. This finding is in direct contrast to Kanter's prediction. Harlan and Weiss suggest that resistance to female managers may indeed decrease in proportion to their numbers—but only up to a point. After that point, if the proportion of women continues to increase, their presence is more likely to be seen by men as a real threat. Under such conditions, male managers may make increasing use of stereotyping and sexist behaviors. This explanation is still being tested against other possibilities.

Male-Female Behavioral Differences

One of the most widespread differences in male-female managerial behavior is that female managers tend to behave in a more accommodative manner than male managers, especially when interacting with men (Chapman & Luthans, 1975). For example, Manhardt (1972), Schuler (1975), and Bartol (1976) found that female business majors and employees of a large manufacturing organization placed higher value on such factors as "opportunity to work with pleasant employees," "congenial associates," and "pleasant interpersonal relationships" than did comparable male respondents. Kanter (1975a) stated that this accommodative manner is one coping strategy for remaining unobtrusive and avoiding conflict. Thus, the female manager may emphasize "blending in" with her male colleagues by not creating disturbances that would highlight her uniqueness. This agrees with research discussed in Chapter 3, which shows that an indirect personal style of power is considered the appropriate influence method for women.

Another common conclusion reached by many investigators is that the female manager is more concerned than are male managers with the immediate work environment (Manhardt, 1972; Bartol, 1976). Male managers appear to place more importance on the opportunity to influence important decisions (Schuler, 1975), rate of advancement (Manhardt, 1972; Roussell, 1974), opportunity to earn more money (Schuler, 1975), and additional responsibility (Manhardt, 1972).

A final main difference appears to be that female supervisors are more likely than male supervisors to adhere strictly to company policies (Green & Melnick, 1950, Sashkin & Maier, 1971). This may be caused by insecurity due to striving for unobtrusiveness and conflict avoidance or by a general need for security.

An interesting situation arises when a female manager supervises a group of male subordinates. Whyte (1949), in a classic study of the restaurant industry, showed that restaurant managers try to avoid situations where female waitresses give orders to male cooks by using rotating order spindles, and by creating high counters between the kitchen and the dining room. Many organizations try to avoid the potential conflict between female managers and male subordinates by allowing more female supervisors in those sections or departments where female subordinates are predominant (Dawkins, 1962). In one of the few studies of its kind, Petty and Lee (1975) found that male subordinates of female supervisors in a nonacademic university setting saw their supervisors as very high on the initiation of work structure and work guidelines and very low on considerate, human relations oriented behavior. The higher the males rated initiation of work structure and work guidelines, the lower was their job satisfaction. However, the perceived high initiation of structure may have been due more to what the male saw as a violation of sex role than to the actual bahavior of the female supervisors.

Not much research has analyzed the situation in which a female supervises female subordinates. In one of the few studies, Bartol and Wortman

(1975) found that female subordinates in a psychiatric hospital preferred their female supervisors to place emphasis on getting the job done as opposed to other styles of supervision. A somewhat unsubstantiated finding is that female subordinates are less satisfied with a female supervisor than a male supervisor (Terborg, 1977). Staines et al., (1973) have attempted to explain this dissatisfaction by the "queen bee syndrome." The queen bee is characterized as a successful female manager who sees female subordinates as potential competitors for her position and thus may treat them differently than male subordinates. The queen bee syndrome needs to be confirmed through sound research before it is acceptable as a potential explanation for female subordinate dissatisfaction.

Four investigations (Bartol & Wortman, 1975; Petty & Lee, 1975; Petty & Miles, 1976; Petty & Bruning, 1980) used the two Ohio State Leadership dimensions of *Consideration* and *Initiating Structure* to analyze mixed-sex subordinate groups' descriptions of female supervisors. All four studies involved female managers in ongoing, formal organizations. Petty and his colleagues found a consistent positive relationship between Consideration and subordinate satisfaction. Bartol and Wortman found that their female supervisors were perceived as significantly higher on Initiating Structure than were their male counterparts, but found no relationship between either Consideration or Initiating Structure and subordinate satisfaction. Petty and Bruning, who examined subordinates' reactions to both male and female supervisors, concluded that Consideration and Initiating Structure were related to subordinate satisfaction for both male and female leaders.

Male-Female Behavioral Similarities

A great many studies have found more similarities than differences between female and male managers. For example, three studies that used the Ohio State Leader Behavior Description Questionnaire (LBDQ) to assess management behavior as seen by subordinates reached the same general conclusion of little or no significant differences between males and females. Day and Stodgill (1972) found that a sample of male and female civilian employees of the United States Air Force were described as similar on leader behavior and effectiveness. Bartol and Wortman (1975) found no significant differences between descriptions of male and female supervisors in a psychiatric hospital, except in the dimension of Initiating Structure, on which females were seen as significantly higher than males. Osborn and Vicars (1976) studied 73 male and female supervisors in two mental health institutions. They concluded that the sex of the supervisor did not relate either to LBDQ—Consideration and Initiating Structure—or to subordinate satisfaction either directly or for various subgroups of the sample based on supervisor or subordinate characteristics, supervisor behavior, or subordinate sex. Osborn and Vicars also concluded that their findings would probably hold true for "long-term, real-life field settings" where there is some long-term, realistic basis for subordinates to rate supervisory behavior, as opposed to laboratory studies where subordinate responses may be based on stereotypes, not real people.

Chapman and Luthans (1975) concluded, after reviewing the research literature, that there probably are no significant differences between male and female managerial styles. Since then, Chapman (1975), Brief and Oliver (1976), the Muldrow and Bayton (1979) have reached similar conclusions based on samples drawn from military, civilian, retail department store, and civil service supervisors. The results of two laboratory studies indicated that males and females in the same profession may have more in common in terms of job interests than same-sex members of different professions (Bartol, 1976) and that males and females equally enjoyed their group roles as leaders (Jacobson & Effertz, 1974).

Morrison and Sebald (1974) and Moses and Boehm (1975) concluded that male and female management personnel appear to have similar motivations and ability. In the assessment center technique used at American Telephone and Telegraph, Moses and Boehm found that the dimensions relating most strongly to subsequent promotion and the management levels attained were the same for both females and males.

Kanter (1976) summarized her findings by drawing attention to the importance of the organizational environment:

> I could find nothing about women in my own research, and that of others that was not equally true of men in some situations. For example, some women do have low job aspirations, but so do men who are in positions of blocked opportunity. Some women managers are too interfering and coercive, but so are men who have limited power and responsibility in their organizations. Some women in professional careers behave in stereotyped ways and tend to regard others of their sex with disdain, but so do men who are tokens—the only member of their group at work. (p. 56)

She concluded by pointing out: "The job makes the man—and the woman. People bring much of themselves and their histories to their work, but I think we have overlooked the tremendous impact of an organization's structure on what happens to them once they are there" (p. 89).

SUMMARY

The emergence of an individual into a leadership role depends partially on that person's image and behavior within the group. Experiments show that emergent leaders must be seen as competent, and they are often expected to be male. A general tendency to ascribe higher status to males than females ensures that in groups of strangers males will emerge as leaders more often than will females. Research also indicates that verbal participation in the group, particularly where such behavior is related to work, is positively related to emergent leadership. In mixed-sex groups, women tend to participate less than men, thus decreasing their chances for leadership. Nonverbal behavior is an important factor in establishing dominance relations; therefore, it can influence how and whether someone is seen as having leadership status. As discussed in an earlier chapter, more dominant nonverbal behavior from the male is often part of male-female interactions, and this may also favor males to emerge as leaders.

Leadership is one of the ten roles every effective manager should play in his or her everyday functioning. However, leadership involves only the interaction between a manager and subordinates. The other nine managerial working roles place the manager in interaction with colleagues or peers, superiors, and individuals outside the organization, in addition to subordinates. It is through these interactions that an informal lateral relations network emerges, which lays the basis for managerial power in the organization.

Men tend to be aware of informal relationships in the organization, and they attempt to use them to further personal power and career aspirations. Their ability to use the informal network is aided by the "maleness" that pervades this system. Women, on the other hand, are sometimes penalized by a general unawareness of or lack of access to the informal organization. Its almost foreign male subcultural atmosphere can make the informal network difficult for women to use, and sometimes this atmosphere is deliberately maintained by men. As compensation for this lack of access to organizational power, many female managers have emphasized competence in the job and a career in one company, where they can take more time to develop these informal interpersonal relationships. This may be changing, however.

Woman managers are also largely cut off from two other avenues to power: visibility and showing directive, authoritarian behavior in critical situations. Denmark (1977) used the concept "fear of visibility" to describe the strategy of not drawing attention to oneself as a special case in the organization. This fear is motivated by the wish to be treated just like everyone else. However, increased individual visibility is one of the major ways to gain organizational power. The other avenue is showing effective management behavior in critical situations. Many times the effective handling of a situation involves taking control in a task-oriented, directive way. However, a female manager violates the popular stereotype of women if she attempts to handle the situation in an authoritarian way. This may lead to sabotage, resentment, and ineffective performance by her male subordinates.

There are few, if any, significant behavioral differences between male and female managers. Females may be more accommodative, concerned with pleasant surroundings, and policy-oriented than comparable males—all probably more due to the male-dominated work environment in which women must "survive" than to innate differences.

POWER
RELATIONSHIPS
BETWEEN GROUPS

9

The subjugation of women to men being a universal custom, any departure from it quite naturally appears unnatural.

John Stuart Mill

The emphasis in many earlier chapters is on power in personal or individual relationships between women and men, or in limited social contexts such as families or organizations. Always in the background, never the major focus, are the broad social and economic contexts in which personal relationships occur. Women and men never relate merely as individuals. They are also always members of two large groups, each containing approximately one half of the human race, which stand in a certain relationship to each other in society. The power relationship between these two groups conditions the interpersonal relationships of their members. In this chapter the focus is on that intergroup power relationship between women and men.

WOMEN AS A MINORITY GROUP?

Early research by social psychologists showed that members of randomly formed groups would soon develop strong positive ingroup feelings and stereotypes. Furthermore, if another group, an outgroup, were placed in conflict with the ingroup, strong negative stereotypes and feelings of hostility developed between the two groups (Sherif & Sherif, 1956). Perhaps more surprising are the conclusions of a review that the very fact of being classified as group members, even without conflict, leads to stereotyping (Brewer, 1979). In other words, even without any supporting evidence, people who are randomly assigned to groups tend to form positive stereotypes about members of their own group. If such ingroup-outgroup feelings can be generated in groups that are virtually identical in composition, it is not surprising that members of the male and female sexes, who *are* distinguishable in a number of superficial and a few not so superficial ways, should subscribe to sexual stereotypes.

   Although stereotyping can be divisive and can help both to produce and to maintain hostility between groups, it need not necessarily lead to or imply the domination of one group by the other. If one group is larger, stronger, or has access to more resources (that is, has a greater power base) than the other, however, that group will tend to dominate or even to oppress the other, and the ingroup-outgroup phenomenon will take on the character of intergroup relationships in which power is unequally divided. In such a case, the dominant group will show the expected positive ingroup bias and negative outgroup bias, but this pattern will be much weaker in the subordinate group. Indeed, members of the subordinate group may accept as true the prejudices directed against them by the dominant group and may even tend to idealize the dominant group (Allport, 1954).

Helen Mayer Hacker (1951) applied this analysis to men and women in her classic article, "Women as a Minority Group." Although women outnumber men in the human population (51 percent to 49 percent), the formal and informal discrimination against women makes their position comparable in many ways to that of minority racial and ethnic groups (such as Blacks and Hispanics in the United States, French Canadians in Canada). In the economic sphere, women are largely restricted to low-paid, low-status jobs and tend to be occupationally segregated from men. In the status of wife, a woman often has little access to or control over family property, finds the economic value of her housework and care of children discounted, and is confronted by social pressures to subordinate her own interests to those of her husband. As a mother, she bears the chief responsibility for child care and the chief stigma for an illegitimate child. In addition, she must cope with very limited or nonexistent provisions in the work world for pregnancy/ maternity leave or adequate day care. She has less freedom of movement than men, having to deal with the threat of violence or at least unwelcome attention if she travels alone, walks alone after dark, or ventures unescorted into certain places. Hacker's analysis, although well over a quarter-century old, is not yet substantially dated.

Yet, as Hacker also notes, the intergroup relationship between females and males is in many ways unique, and a general social-psychological analysis of the relations between groups is limited in how well it explains this particular case. There is more frequent and more initimate contact between males and females than between most majority and minority groups (such as Whites and Blacks in many parts of the world). Marriage and cohabitation— the intimate form of relationship that is generally looked upon as unthinkable between members of many dominant and subordinate groups—is normal between men and women. The strong emotional bonds that often form between individual women and men may, in fact, dilute their feelings of identification with their own sexual groups and may obscure the "built-in" power differences between men and women as members of those groups. Obscured or not, however, these differences in power affect male-female relationships by affecting the options that are available to and the behavioral styles that are adopted by individual men and women.

Through marriage and the family, women and men are more personally interdependent than are most majority and minority groups. While racial groups can stay segregated from each other, as do Blacks and Whites in South Africa, men and women cannot really do this. They must cooperate in order to bear children, and in our economic system women frequently depend on men for financial support, while men depend on women for maintenance, support, and general "life-smoothing" functions. In addition, both men and women may rely heavily on their spouses for emotional support and nurturing. For a relationship based on such a complex set of interdependencies to function smoothly, the issue of power is often just taken as a fact rather than examined and challenged. Relations between the sexes are handled in a schizophrenic way, for individual relationships of love and interdependence must exist side by side with political and economic relationships of discrimination and exploitation.

The Complex Issue of Female Status

The socially structured confusion surrounding the intergroup relations of males and females has a concrete illustration in a study by Abigail Stewart and David Winter (1977), who tried to define a measure of female status. Using statistical data from the United Nations, they chose twenty-five measures that might reasonably reflect women's status relative to men's (such as voting status, illiteracy rate, median years of education, economic differences). Then, using all countries for which data were available on at least eight of the twenty-five measures, they tried to determine how the different measures related to one another. When these relationships were examined, the variables were seen to cluster into two main groups. Thus two clear factors, or independent dimensions, of female status emerged. The first, labeled *social-educational equality*, was made up of variables involving the legal and political status of women and their educational opportunities. Countries scoring high on this measure of female status were characterized by: the full vote for women for many years, a relatively high percentage of female pupils at all stages of education, a low ratio of illiterate women to illiterate men, and women's not having to adopt the nationality of their husbands. A second, independent factor, included all the variables related to women's economic status, and it was labeled *economic equality*. Countries in which a high percentage of married women were economically active (that is, working for pay), where sex differentiation in occupation or industry was relatively low, and where the ratio of economically active men to women was not overly high, scored high on this dimension. Although these two factors necessarily omit some variables that are crucial to assessing male-female status differences, they do provide a starting point for an objective analysis of the problem.

Stewart and Winter's research indicates that the relative status of females is not a single factor, but is composed of at least two independent dimensions. Herein may lie a clue to the type of double message about the male-female power relationship that a society can give to its citizens. In Stewart and Winter's scheme, for example, the United States has one of the two highest scores in the world (the other being the U.S.S.R.) for female social-educational equality, but its score for female economic equality is unimpressive, ranking well below nations such as Japan and Indonesia. Canada also scores considerably higher on social-educational equality than on economic equality for females. It appears, then, that North Americans are willing to give women certain rights and privileges nearly equal to those of men, provided that women stay out of the economic sphere. In other words, North American women are encouraged to get an education, but not encouraged to work for a salary.

In socialist countries such as the U.S.S.R. and Czechoslovakia, on the other hand, women's economic equality outstrips their social-educational equality. Women in these countries are expected and encouraged to work outside the home, and jobs are less segregated by sex than they are in the West. Yet these women have trouble shaking off their subordinate social status, as indicated by their complaints that they are still expected to do the bulk of the housework, and by reports that few women ever rise to the top ranks in the Communist party. (Nonetheless, the U.S.S.R. scores higher on both measures of female status than does the United States).

In some of the poorer Third World countries such as Cambodia and Haiti, there are huge gaps between the scores on the two dimensions, with social-educational equality for women being extremely low and economic equality extremely high. Do these scores mean that women in poorer countries have achieved great breakthroughs in terms of economic status? Probably not. It may be safe to assume, in some of these cases, that people of both sexes are in such dire economic straits that both men and women *must* be employed. Such equality on the bottom of the economic ladder may be little cause for feminist celebration. Furthermore, the economic status of these women does not seem to affect their subordinate social status, perhaps because they do not subscribe to the North American work ethic. In the description by Moses (1977) of the West Indian community of

Montserrat, for example, males are taught an ideology of male dominance that is translated into men's being treated as pampered guests in their own homes. Since men are expected to do only a minimal amount of work both inside and outside the home, women often cannot depend on men for economic survival, and must themselves be employed.

Stewart and Winter's analysis does not report on certain aspects of women's status where objective data in all the cultures were unavailable (such as frequency of rape and wife abuse, number of female candidates for political office), but it does give some clues to the complexity of male-female differences in access to power resources. Moreover, their research demonstrates, in a preliminary fashion, the kinds of factors that may be generally associated with (not necessarily cause) differences in female status on the two dimensions.

A regression analysis, which used fourteen independent variables for which data were available across cultures, indicated that the social-educational status of women was positively and significantly related to the percentage of Christians in a country's population, high overall level of education, socialism, and relatively high number of young children per woman. The economic status of women in a country, on the other hand, was positively and significantly related to socialism, high overall level of education, and high proportion of women in the population; it was negatively related to the number of both Christians and Moslems in the population and to the extent to which the economy concentrated on manufacturing as opposed to agriculture, service, trade and commerce, and public administration. The reasons for these associations can only be guessed at for the present. However, the great number of variables related to female status suggests, at the very least, that restructuring male-female intergroup relations in the direction of equality is not a simple task.

SOURCES OF MALE POWER

Faced with the evidence that women as a group have less power and status than men, many theorists have tried to identify the bases from which males derive their greater power. Millett (1970), for example, has written angrily and incisively of the ways in which society compels its members to "interiorize" the notion of patriarchy—male superiority and male dominance.

Sexual politics obtains consent through the "socialization" of both sexes to basic patriarchal politics with regard to temperament, role and status. As to status, a pervasive assent to the prejudice of male superiority guarantees superior status in the male, inferior in the female. The first item, temperament, involves the formation of human personality along stereotyped lines of sex category ("masculine" and "feminine"), based on the needs and values of the dominant group and dictated by what its members cherish in themselves and find convenient in subordinates: aggression, intelligence, force, and efficiency in the male; passivity, ignorance, docility, "virtue," and ineffectuality in the female. This is complemented by a second factor, sex role, which decrees a consonant and highly elaborate code of conduct, gesture, and attitude for each sex. In terms of activity, sex role assigns domestic service and attendance upon infants to the female, the rest of human achievement, interest, and ambition to the male. The limited role allotted the female tends to arrest her at the level of biological experience . . . . Were one to analyze the three categories one might designate status as the political component, role as the sociological, and temperament as the psychological—yet their interdependence is unquestionable and they form a chain. Those awarded higher status tend to adopt roles of mastery, largely because they are first encouraged to develop temperaments of dominance (p. 26).

It is Millett's contention that this internalization of patriarchal ideology by both males and females becomes the chief source of men's power over women.

In a later analysis, Polk (1974) outlined some of the specific sources of male power. In describing them, Polk was writing not necessarily about power relationships between individual men and women (although individual relationships can certainly fit this pattern), but about the sources of power more available to men as the dominant group than to women as the subordinate group. Much of her analysis could be applied intact to the relationship between *any* dominant and subordinate groups (for example, majority and minority racial groups), regardless of the affection, respect, and efforts toward equality that might exist between individual members of such groups. The sources of power described by Polk could be said to contribute to both the internalization and the externalization of the idea of male dominance.

1. *Normative power.* Men are in a position to define what is important and what is appropriate behavior. Thus, they can ignore or devalue women's

accomplishments, as in omitting women's contributions from history books, or they can discredit these accomplishments, as in attributing women's scientific discoveries to men.

2. *Institutional power.* Most social institutions are controlled by men. Male control of the media, religion, and the educational system has a strong impact on public opinion and behavior. Male dominance of economic institutions makes it difficult for women to have access to money and high-status jobs, and thus helps to keep them locked in traditional roles. Legal and political institutions, administered largely by men, have to be coaxed and harrassed to keep any of women's interests in mind. Male dominance of society's institutions in combination with the normative power discussed above effectively blocks a large number of life options for women. Society's response to the long struggle waged by many women for adequate child day care is an example of such a process. Lawmakers refuse to pass the legislation or grant the funds necessary for adequate day care (institutional power), while reminding women that it is their responsibility as mothers to stay home with their children (normative power). Historically, perhaps one of the most glaring and heartbreaking examples of this double-barreled use of male power against the interests of women was in the American refusal to make any type of birth control information available to women. Until 1936, it was illegal for anyone (even a doctor) to give out birth control information, and women who requested it were accused of being irresponsible and immoral for shirking or wanting to limit their motherhood role (Sanger, 1971). Without the fierce and prolonged struggle waged by Margaret Sanger and her cohorts to make family planning available to women, one wonders when women's basic rights in this area would have been acknowledged.

3. *Control of options through reward power.* Through their greater control of concrete resources and institutions, men are able to provide women with rewards for "appropriate" behavior. Thus, male religious leaders make approving statements about "purity" and "humility" for women; big expensive weddings are theoretically reserved for women who "waited"; and, if she is not too assertive, a woman who is blessed with the right shape can be crowned Miss America.

4. *The power of expertise.* The recognized experts in virtually every field are men. Male dominance of education and the media ensures that males will select which individuals become experts and which experts receive public exposure. A woman needing advice in almost any area, then, is likely to have

to turn to a man. This not only reinforces the woman's subordinate status relative to the man, but also means that the advice she receives may well be conditioned by male values and insensitive to female interests.

5. *Psychological power.* Since men control and have shaped society's institutions, they tend to fit into the value structure of such institutions better than women do. Thus, for example, the male sex role matches certain professional roles (lawyer, business executive, university president) better than does the female sex role. This sense of fitting in gives men an important advantage over women in confidence.

6. *Brute force.* Most men are stronger then most women, and many men have been trained to feel confident in their physical strength and to use it against others. Men can physically dominate women by beating their wives, girlfriends, daughters, and sisters. Rape and the threat of rape are also used as a coercive form of male social control over women.

Polk argues that these six sources of male power overlap and reinforce one another, making it necessary for women to wage a many-sided struggle if they are to establish themselves on a truly equal footing with men. Although her list of male power bases may not be an exhaustive one, it illustrates the extent to which the dominance of one group over another can pervade a society. As Millett (1970) argued, an ideology that is so pervasive tends to be perceived as natural, right, and fair.

SOURCES OF FEMALE POWER

It may be true that an ideology of male dominance is pervasive and gives men considerable power over women, but this is not to say that women as a group have no sources of power. As argued in Chapter 3, control over outcomes is usually reciprocal to some extent; rarely does one person or group have ultimate control over another. Although women are clearly at a power disadvantage relative to men, there are some bases from which they exert some power in this relationship.

1. *Norms of dependence.* In many cultures women are expected to be somewhat helpless and dependent on men. Thus, they can make legitimate demands for protection and support. Little boys are instructed not to hit

little girls, for example, and woe to the boy who ignores this dictum! In disaster situations there is an expectation that women and children will be rescued first, and in many countries women are not expected to fight in the army even in wartime emergencies. Husbands are expected to support their wives financially, but the reverse is rarely true. Although such dependence puts women at the mercy of men in some ways, it also compensates them with the power to escape a number of noxious situations. Unfortunately, this compensatory power is unreliable. Husbands do beat their wives and refuse to support them, and women in wartime are tortured, raped, and killed whether or not they are part of the military. Nonetheless, the norm that men should be protective of women does provide women as a group with one source of power.

2. *Legitimization of male power.* As discussed in Chapter 3, the worth of a power base often lies in the way it is seen by the person toward whom an influence attempt is directed. Thus, for example, power can be based on reward only if the person being influenced views the outcomes controlled by the power holder as, indeed, rewarding. Similarly, legitimate power must be based on acceptance by the other person of the power holder's right to make a certain demand or request. Janeway (1975) has argued that women have a potential source of power in their capacity to grant or fail to grant legitimacy to male power. If women refuse to make male power legitimate, the power base of legitimacy is destroyed, and men must fall back on other bases such as coercion. Janeway argues that it is less satisfying to rule through force than through legitimate authority, and this seems intuitively to be true although there is no experimental evidence at this point.

3. *Childbearing.* From Chapter 6, we know that the ability to bear children gives a potential power resource to individual women. On a group level, this capacity may also be a source of power for women if men as a group are interested in the continuation of the human race. Women of childbearing age must be kept at a certain minimum standard of health if they are to reproduce, and female infanticide must be limited, lest the population drop so drastically as to threaten genocide (Schrire & Steiger, 1974).

4. *Symbolic powers.* In many cultures women are symbolized as powerful and dangerous and as having mysterious capacities to affect men and their environment (for example, Janeway, 1975; Wadley, 1977; Washbourn, 1977). Such assumed powers are often connected to a fearful suppression of women by men in the material world. Nonetheless, this image of women as powerful

enough to be potentially dangerous may serve as a source of strength for women, and the caution it engenders in men may occasionally provide women as a group with extra leverage.

On the whole, female sources of power seem to be at best unreliable in the present situation. Some of them do, however, give women an edge over other minority groups when it comes to survival. Perhaps if these resources were exploited more fully by women, the power gap between the sexes would begin to close. Since some of these resources operate only because of women's subordinate status, however, their use alone will never guarantee equality between the sexes.

THE PERCEPTION OF JUSTICE

Social psychologists argue that people are motivated to see their social relationships as fair and the world as a just place (Lerner, 1970; Walster & Walster, 1975). Why, then, do people tolerate a situation in which one group suppresses another, as in male dominance over women? The answer lies in the human capacity to perform olympic feats of rationalization. If people see a situation as unjust, but are powerless to change it, theorists argue that they "justify" it instead. Thus, for example, Lerner's research (summarized in Lerner, 1970, 1974) shows that people who see a victim being hurt or punished for no apparent reason resolve their own discomfort at this by manufacturing reasons why the victim might have deserved the punishment. In some instances, the more apparently blameless the victim, the more she or he is derogated.

People often seem to satisfy their need to believe that the world is a just place and that people generally get what they deserve by seeing victims as, by definition, deserving of the harm inflicted on them. This theory explains why a woman who has been raped is often the one who receives the anger and accusation—why was she out at night alone? What was she wearing to provoke the rapist?—rather than sympathy, and why people who are trapped in a cycle of poverty are automatically termed lazy and shiftless. As Jones and Nisbett (1972) have noted, people tend to focus on personal, internal causes when explaining the behavior of others; the observer imagines the hidden personality characteristics or motives of the victim that may have led to the harm.

A general tendency to want to see the world as just may provide a partial explanation for accepting the subordination of women. Historically and currently, apologists for male dominance have manufactured comprehensive lists of female qualities that are said to make women undeserving of or unfit for equal status. These various qualities have included both the biological (smaller brains, insufficient testosterone, incapacity to form bonds in small groups) and the psychological (too emotional, lack of moral sensitivity, illogical). Most of these supposed female qualities have no factual basis whatsoever, but they are used repeatedly to justify women's lower status. The strong need to rationalize and explain women's position probably reflects the motive to believe in a just world.

A parallel explanation for accepting male dominance over women comes from the study of the relationship between power and perceived justice. Walster and Walster (1975) argue that the persons with the most power in a community will not only gain control of the community resources, but will also evolve a social philosophy that supports their right to monopolize these resources. In fact, research by Kipnis (1972) supports the notion that men in positions of power tend to develop an exploitative morality and an exalted view of their own worth, while becoming alienated from and contemptuous of their subordinates. But Walster and Walster also contend that the dominant group's philosophy will eventually be accepted by the entire community as justification for the status quo; if the entire group accepts the status quo, everyone avoids the discomfort of a relationship viewed as inequitable or unfair. Their research suggests, in fact, that both exploiters and victims can and frequently do convince themselves that even the most unbalanced of exchanges is perfectly fair (Walster, Berscheid, & Walster, 1973). Thus, it seems that the ideology of dominance is self-perpetuating in that the more power a group obtains, the more its members will convince themselves and others that such power is deserved and stems from superiority.

In the light of this analysis, it is perhaps not surprising that, despite the visibility of the women's movement, many men and women are still convinced that it is natural and right for men to be the leaders and women the followers in society. For many, challenging this proposition involves accepting the possibility that one's decisions and behaviors have been unfair or that one has accepted unfair treatment—a possibility that, according to the research, can result in considerable discomfort for exploiter and victim alike.

THE PSYCHOLOGY OF MINORITY
GROUP STATUS

Gordon Allport's (1954) book, *The Nature of Prejudice,* contains an entire chapter on what he called traits due to victimization. In it, he argued that people who lack power and are victims of prejudice develop qualities that are due to the prejudice and that serve, in a self-fulfilling way, to reinforce it. Psychologists analyzing the relationship between women and men have noted that women in our society show a number of the behaviors identified by Allport (for example, Frieze, Parsons, Johnson, Ruble, & Zellman, 1978; Hacker, 1951). For example, women sometimes show behaviors of self-hatred and identification with the dominant group. Women may say that they do not like other women and may accuse them of being "catty," untrustworthy, and uninteresting. If they themselves succeed in a male-dominated career area, they may think of themselves as exceptions and act to discourage other women aspiring to similar success. Female politicians may repudiate involvement in "women's issues" in an attempt to disengage themselves from the low-status group and blend in with the dominant group. Such behaviors do not constitute feminine traits, but they are characteristic of people with minority status. They indicate the psychological effects of accepting as fair and equitable a system that relegates women to a subordinate position.

People who are stereotyped in a certain way often respond to social expectations by acting out the stereotype. Allport (1954) referred to this process as a self-fulfilling prophecy. If women are expected to be weak and helpless, no one will place the kinds of demands on them that would help them to develop their strength and competence. Due to the treatment that is a result of the stereotype, women learn to accept the stereotype and to confirm it with their actions. In this way women become party to their own subordination.

The domination of one group by another, once set in motion, becomes an interactive process in which members of both groups contribute (consciously or not) to maintaining the status quo. The dominant group convinces itself of its superiority, while the subordinate group affirms its own inferiority. Although both groups incur some costs by maintaining this relationship, the larger proportion of the costs, in both a material and psychic sense, are borne by the subordinate group.

COMBATING MINORITY GROUP STATUS

The self-hatred and fear that occur in minority groups isolate the members from one another and make it difficult for them to join together to improve their situation. One essential part of combating minority status is breaking down barriers and developing trust and solidarity among members of the subordinate group. For relatively weak parties to exert power, they must form coalitions (Komorita & Chertkoff, 1973). A second part is developing more access to the bases of power monopolized by the dominant group. In recent years, women have attempted both of these things. Although some progress toward male-female equality of status has occurred, it would be extremely premature to assert that male dominance is in its death throes.

Coalitions Among Women

One of the most common manifestations of the emerging women's liberation movement in the 1960s was the appearance of the multitude of consciousness-raising, or C-R, groups. These groups provided a forum where women could explore their situation together and form the mutually supportive relationships necessary for collective action to change their status. This deliberate structuring of mutual support groups by women continues today in many forms. Besides the C-R groups, there are now women's caucuses in professional organizations and political parties, and formal networks of professional women, housewives, women on welfare, and others.

One inevitable consequence of these support groups is the growth of strong positive ingroup feelings and hostility toward outgroups (most often men). Such feelings could never emerge as long as women were isolated from one another and shared little group identity. A few groups have even espoused separatist philosophies and have decided not to relate to men. These developments signal the emerging recognition of injustice as well as the new sense of their own power experienced by women in these groups. Although such reactions may be frightening to men (and perhaps sometimes to the women themselves), they are an unavoidable part of the serious re-examination and restructuring of the power relationship between women and men. It would be naive, indeed, to suppose that an ideology as long-standing, universal, and pervasive as that of male dominance and superiority could be successfully challenged in a completely gentle and painless way. Nonetheless, should the two groups eventually achieve equal status, it is to be hoped that hostility between them would not persist. There are few precedents on which to base such a hope, since the struggles of most minority groups (such as blacks in the United States and South Africa and native peoples in the United States and Canada) have yet to result in equal status with their respective majorities.

Access to the Bases of Power

Since the early 1960s, more and more women at both individual and collective levels have been trying to increase their access to such bases of power as expertise, legitimate authority, and physical strength. Areas of expertise that formerly were virtually closed to women are now being opened up, as women flood into law, medical, business, and trade schools. Not only are they entering the traditional bastions of male expertise in the formal career sense, but large-scale movements are making specialized information available to all women who need it. The growth of self-help resources for women in the area of health is an example of this process. The publication of materials such as *Our Bodies, Ourselves* by the Boston Women's Health Book Collective and the Canadian women's journal *Healthsharing,* and the development of women-run clinics that teach women techniques of self-examination, contraception, and health maintenance have demystified the area of medical knowledge for many. This movement not only allows individual women to take more control over their own lives, but also gives women as a group the knowledge and confidence to demand changes in the health care system when it does not meet their needs.

In the area of health, then, progress is occurring on the three fronts that Bunch (1980) lists as important for the achievement of feminist goals: (1) maintaining and enlarging organizations and projects that give power to women, (2) extending feminist insights and perspectives to people outside the women's movement, and (3) working within existing institutions to orient their structures and priorities to the needs and rights of women.

Politics is another area in which the structure of male-female intergroup relations is being challenged in these three ways. Women have formed large associations that lobby politicians for change (such as the National Organization for Women, and Women's Equity Action League in the United States, and the National Action Committee on the Status of Women in Canada). They have developed formal training programs for women who want to become involved in the policy-making of political parties, and they are seeking political office. Despite all this activity, however, progress toward upgrading women's status in the political arena has been slow. In the United States, for example, by 1978 fewer than 100 women had been members of the House of Representatives and the Senate in the approximately fifty years since women gained the vote (Frieze et al., 1978). In both the United States and Canada, women candidates are more likely to achieve election at the municipal than at the regional or national levels (Gruberg, 1968; Vickers, 1978). A large percentage of female candidates for office are unsuccessful, both because of men's (and women's) frequent unwillingness to support a female candidate (Harris, 1972) and the tendency of political parties to run women in "lost cause" seats (Vickers, 1978).

Women who do get elected to office often have trouble consolidating enough power to have the impact they would like, for a number of reasons. Women in politics, as in other male-dominated areas such as business, are still "token" figures. As such, they tend to be judged harshly and may find it difficult to form coalitions with other politicians (see the discussion of tokenism in Chapter 8). Much of political policy-making goes on in informal situations from which women are informally or formally excluded (Bird, 1968). If women in sufficient numbers are elected to office at all levels, many of the problems attached to token status will disappear. Movement in this direction has begun to occur—albeit at a snail's pace—as the number of successful female candidates slowly increases.

Physical strength, another power base to which women have had relatively little access, is also being assailed by women. Females are increasingly winning access to training and facilities in a variety of sport and fitness activities that promote the development of strength, endurance, and coordination, and the self-confidence that accompanies them. Self-defense courses are teaching women not only how to defend themselves against attack, but how to stop thinking of themselves as victims.

Women are combating their minority status, then, through the formation of coalitions and through concerted efforts to increase their access to traditionally male bases of power. But the inequality of the power distribution is also disturbing to some men, who have become dissatisfied with the male-female intergroup relationship and have initiated efforts to change their own patterns of dominance.

COMBATING THE POWER HOLDER STATUS

Membership in a dominant group has some disadvantages as well as many advantages. Men may, for instance, feel discomfort with the idea that they are participating in an inequitable relationship—a discomfort that can be avoided only by rationalizing their position (Walster & Walster, 1975). But rationalization of their dominant position becomes more difficult for some men when confronted with feminist arguments.

Dominance can also include shouldering the responsibility for decisions, playing out a role of strength and courage under pressure, and avoiding certain low-status activities. Thus, men, in maintaining their dominant role, are expected to take on most of the jobs in society that involve certain types of stress and danger, to avoid showing fear, grief, or other "weak" emotions, to assume the position of provider in the family structure, and to avoid the low status, but potentially satisfying, activity of child care. Research indicates that maintaining the male role is not particularly healthy for men. Their mortality rate from such stress-related ailments as heart disease, respiratory problems, and cirrhosis of the liver is significantly higher than that for women, and researchers have placed much of the blame on the male sex role (Harrison, 1978).

Dominance over others is regarded as one of the central characteristics of the male role (Brannon 1976; Cicone & Ruble, 1978), as is a general expectation on the part of men that they will be able to dominate women (for example, Gross, 1978). A small but significant minority of men have, however, begun to recognize problems inherent in the continual necessity for dominance that their role entails. Some men have complained that the male role is dehumanizing and alienating. Sawyer (1970), for instance, argues that the emphasis on achievement and suppression of affect that is so central to the male role in North America is limited and destructive, and Fasteau (1974) asserts that men have been isolated from one another by their socialization toward individual dominance and competitiveness. Concerns voiced by such men have sparked a men's liberation movement in the United States and Canada. This movement has attracted far fewer active members than has its counterpart, the women's liberation movement, and this difference probably attests to the general attractiveness of power in North America. It is more prestigious to try to increase one's power and status than to try to get rid of them.

Many of men's efforts at trying to transcend their sex roles have centered on developing more open, less competitive, and less controlling relationships with women, with other men, and with children. As one means to this end, men, like women, have formed consciousness-raising groups. Members of these groups report real breakthroughs in understanding their own feelings and in forming friendships with other men (for example, S. Levine, 1974). Some men have also involved themselves more with their children (for example, J. Levine, 1976), and the success of the movie *Kramer vs. Kramer,* which centers on a father-son relationship, suggests that it is becoming more acceptable for fathers to make the rearing of children a major life priority.

Little direct political action has grown out of the men's movement. This may be due partly to its small size relative to the women's movement and to the points from which each group is moving. According to a traditional typology made explicit by Parsons and Bales (1955), the ideal male role is largely an instrumental one, while the ideal female role centers on expressiveness. Instrumental refers to an emphasis on tasks and goal orientation; expressiveness refers to behavior concerned with social-emotional interactions and relationships. If each sex is re-examining and trying to shed aspects of its traditional role, it is perhaps not surprising that men should focus on increasing their expressiveness as women emphasize instrumental goals such as political equality and access to resources and institutions. On the other hand, men may simply have no desire to change their positions of power in politics and institutions, but only to make their lives more satisfying by improving their relationships. As we know, however, personal relationships inevitably affect and are affected by the intergroup relationship between men and women.

SUMMARY

Personal relationships between men and women must ultimately be considered within the framework of intergroup relations between the sexes. The male-female intergroup relationship can be analyzed as one between two groups holding unequal power. This analysis is complicated, however, by the fact that on a personal level women and men often form intimate relationships of attachment and interdependence. Such relationships often blind people to the power differences in which they are embedded and provide a source of motivation for both men and women to ignore the issue of power.

At a collective level, men and women have preferential access to specific bases of power. Sources of men's power over women include the capacity to establish and maintain social norms, the control of institutions and rewards, expertise, the ability to fit more easily than women into male-defined professions and institutions, and physical force. Sources of women's power over men include the norm that men should protect women, the capacity of women to accord or withhold the legitimization of men's dominance, the ability to bear children, and the symbolic power of attributed mystery and danger. In general, men's sources of power are more pervasive and reliable than those of women.

Men's dominance over women is generally rationalized and accepted. People's need to believe in a just world and to convince themselves that their relationships are equitable provide an explanation for this acceptance. Men convince themselves that they deserve higher status than women; women acquiesce to the viewpoint that they themselves are inferior. In the process, women become isolated from one another and maintain little sense of positive group identity.

Groups of women and men have made and are making efforts to combat the inequality in their power relationship. Women work in groups to develop mutual support and positive ingroup feelings, and they are trying in a variety of ways to increase their access to the traditional male power bases. Men are re-examining their relationships with women, with children, and with each other in an effort to shed some aspects of their dominant role. Both groups can point to signs of progress on the road to the development of a culture that emphasizes the shared humanity of the sexes more than the dominance relations between them. Yet, the most active members of these groups would be the first to admit that the journey has only begun.

EPILOGUE:
WHERE DO WE
GO FROM HERE?

Although power is an issue that has intrigued people for centuries, psychologists have only begun a factual study of it since the late 1950s. Therefore, the subject is still surrounded with as many questions as answers. Yet, it is not too early to draw some conclusions from the research discussed in this book. It is common knowledge that two people, faced with the same data, can draw very different conclusions. The reader's conclusions may already be drawn. The author's are presented here.

Power is considerably more than a personal characteristic or trait. Although individuals differ in the degree to which they appear to want or need power, or the sense of having an impact on their environment, there seems to be a general need for at least a modicum of control over one's life and surroundings. Individuals differ in the degree to which they feel powerful, but these differences appear to reflect environmental realities as much as, if not more than, personal temperamental dispositions. The actual power that a person can exercise over others is always dependent on the situation: the resources controlled by both the influencer and the one who is influenced, for purposes of exchange, bargaining, and threatening; the influencer's status relative to those he or she is trying to influence; and how the influencer and his or her power resources are seen by those who are to be influenced. When power differences exist between individuals or groups, one must look at these factors for an explanation. And these situational factors may themselves arise in part from the broad cultural context.

Male-female differences in the access to and use of power can largely be traced to the differences in status between the sexes. Men, having higher ascribed status than women, are automatically granted a certain amount of legitimate power or authority over them. Men's higher status gives them first claim to concrete power resources, such as income-producing jobs and such positions of formal authority as legislator, pope, corporate policy-maker, and head of household. Their higher status also makes it easier for males to be viewed as experts, with all the influence that image implies.

All this is not to say that men always are or feel powerful. Since only a few people can be at the top of any hierarchy, many men are and feel powerless compared to other men, and some may feel that even their power relative to women is an empty charade. Nonetheless, other things being equal, our society grants more status, and therefore more automatic access to the power bases of legitimacy, concrete reward and coercion, and expertise, to men than to women. In this respect, men always have a socially constructed power advantage over women. Men also have something of a biological power advantage in that they are, on the average, bigger and stronger than women. This advantage is magnified by social norms that encourage men, but not women, to use and develop their physical strength.

Women's lower status position makes it more permissible for them than for men to use helplessness as a method of influence. Also, because the feminine role allows for more expression of emotion than does the masculine one, women may sometimes be able to use referent power and personal resources more successfully than men can.

Operating from positions of different status and the resulting different access to bases of power, women and men resort to different styles of influence when dealing with each other. Men's power styles are more often competent, direct, and backed by concrete resources, while women's tend to be more indirect and based on helplessness and personal resources. These differences in power styles reinforce the sex-role stereotypes that are intertwined with the differences in male-female status: men are strong, decisive, logical, and competent; women are weak, fickle, illogical, and incompetent. Whether the status differential or the sex-role stereotypes came first is difficult to say, but at the present time each of these factors clearly reinforces and perpetuates the other, and the behavior of both women and men supports the resulting system.

Deviations from the accepted norm of high-status, strong, tough men and lower status, weak, vulnerable woman are undesirable and upsetting to many people. As demonstrated repeatedly in this book, the powerful woman is often greeted with negative reactions ranging from uneasiness to panic, while a powerless man draws contempt and avoidance. A strong woman is frequently regarded as unwomanly, a weak man as unmanly. Examples of these negative reactions stand out in the areas of sexuality, the family, and organizations. Both men and women often experience discomfort when women take the initiative in sexual relationships. Both members of a "wife-dominant" marriage may feel embarrassed about the direction of the power difference, try to hide it, and attribute it to undesirable weakness or incompetence on the part of the husband. There are also difficulties inherent in the organizational situation in which a woman supervises male subordinates.

Sometimes these negative emotional reactions to powerful women and less powerful men occur despite good intentions and even intellectual acceptance of the desirability of more flexible sex roles. Such "nonrational" reactions may well be the result of strong, early conditioning of which the individual is unconscious. As Milgram (1974) has noted, we are often unaware of the degree to which social norms are an integral part of us until we try to violate them. The lessons taught by our culture about the necessity for male strength and female weakness are rooted in each individual's earliest experiences.

Perhaps one of the reasons that our culture invests the strong man-weak woman stereotype with such emotional intensity is our propensity to believe in dualities. Strength and weakness, like male and female, are thought to be opposites, their mutual presence incompatible in the same individual. There is a belief that toughness drives out gentleness, that vulnerability drives out power. Even as people try to move beyond the rigidity of their sex roles, there is an underlying fear that if women become strong and powerful, they will necessarily become hard and insensitive, losing the nurturing qualities for which society (and particular individuals) depends on them; and that if men allow themselves to be gentle and nurturing, they will lose the toughness necessary to fulfill their roles of breadwinner and protector.

Are such fears justified? Many would argue that they are not. The recent emphasis in sex-role research is on androgyny—a concept that implies not only the possibility but the desirability of the blending of masculine and feminine qualities in one individual. Proponents of androgyny (for example, Bem, 1974) would argue that a person can be strong and tough in one situation without losing the capacity to be soft and vulnerable in another. The idea is not new, but grows out of the notions of earlier theorists (for example, Bakan, 1966; Jung, 1951) that the personality of each person contains both a masculine and a feminine principle, which must be developed and integrated. These theorists, while emphasizing the importance of integrating the so-called masculine and feminine aspects of the personality, were not as optimistic as present-day advocates of androgyny about the ease with which such integration could be achieved. Jung, for example, observed that individuals frequently become dominated by one principle, often to their own detriment.

Perhaps people's uneasiness about the possibility of integrating power and gentleness is justified. Although we are certain that power need not necessarily drive out gentleness, nor gentleness power, we are equally certain, from observation and sometimes bitter experience, that such transformations frequently do occur. Even psychological research supports this uneasiness. Research by Kipnis (1972) shows that power holders become alienated from and contemptuous of their subordinates. On the other side of the issue, research in experimental game situations shows that cooperation does not always breed cooperation (for example, Gallo & McClintock, 1965), suggesting that people who have power over others, but refrain from using it, may be stereotyped as weak and may be exploited.

Clearly, the acquisition of power carries with it the danger of losing the "soft" qualities of sensitivity, sympathy, and nurturing; while, on the other hand, the inability or hesitancy to use power against others can result in a person's being stereotyped as weak, losing the respect of others, and, ultimately, losing the power. People such as politicians who are in public positions of power are all too aware of the difficulties inherent in appearing not to be corrupted or intoxicated by power, at the same time appearing willing and able to use their power. There *is* a culturally supported tendency for power and gentleness to be and to be perceived as incompatible, and the woman or man trying to break free of sex-role stereotypes must be aware of this tendency to challenge it creatively.

WHAT NEEDS TO BE STUDIED?

Probably the most complex and difficult set of questions faced by researchers of any sex role related phenomenon concerns the origins of the behavior. Where and how did human beings get the notion that men must be strong and women weak, that men should be granted higher status than women? And what is responsible for the persistence of these notions? The answers to the first question offered to date are still quite speculative. Kohlberg (1966), for instance, indicates that one of the first distinctions children learn is "large-small" and that they quickly learn to value large things more than small ones. He suggests that this early learning, along with the observation that men are bigger and stronger than women, may predispose children to attribute greater power and status to men. Although there is much evidence that young children do form stereotypes about men and women, the specific link between the learning of the large-small distinction and the greater valuing of males than females has not been demonstrated.

A second explanation for greater male than female status and dominance focuses on the mother-child relationship. The theory is that men develop a need to dominate women because they were under such absolute control by their mothers as children. Men supposedly assert both their independence and their separate identity as males in adulthood by devaluing and dominating women. Variations on this general theory are offered by Winter (1973) to account for the apparent link between male need for power and the tendency to exploit women (discussed in Chapter 2) and by Stockard and Johnson (1979) to account for the social tolerance for and perpetuation of male dominance (discussed in Chapter 5). To many feminists, one attractive implication of this theory is that, in order for status equality to be achieved between the sexes, men and women must take on an equal share of the child care. Such sharing would eliminate the situation in which so much of children's ambivalence about being controlled by and emotionally dependent on their caretakers is directed at women. Although such a change in the allocation of child care responsibilities would doubtless do much to equalize men's and women's status, there is little evidence as to whether the equalization could be attributed to the reasons cited by this theory.

Many researchers prefer to focus on the maintenance rather than the early origins of differences in status and power between the sexes. Here there are many issues to be investigated. What are the specific methods by which children are taught to exert power in sex role related ways? How can women move toward a more direct use of interpersonal power without being derogated as unfeminine? To what extent can men and women learn to change their nonverbal cues of dominance and submission? But one of the most critical, yet underresearched, variables in the maintenance of the male-female power difference is probably physical strength.

As discussed in Chapter 4, one important aspect of feeling powerful is the idea that one is able to accomplish things to make a difference in one's environment. This sense of personal power is exemplified by Heider's (1958) notion of the "attribution of can." Perhaps men, having learned from an early age to be *physically* able to accomplish tasks requiring strength and endurance, transfer this feeling of ability to many other areas of their lives. Women, having learned over the years to be physically incapable of many behaviors, from opening jars and carrying heavy loads to fighting off an attacker, may similarly translate this feeling of incapacity to other areas of their lives. The appropriateness of this sex difference is reinforced so strongly in our culture that we rarely think to question it. When was the last time a movie showed a woman dashing into a burning building to rescue a trapped man, for example? How often do we question the depiction on television of a fight scene in which a male-female couple is attacked and the woman stands by helplessly, perhaps screaming or crying, while her male companion fights to defend both of them?

Researchers should be examining the importance of real and perceived sex differences in physical strength for male and female conceptions of power.

A sense of physical weakness may contribute to women's use of indirect power methods as well as to verbal and nonverbal deference to men in many situations. A sense of physical strength may help to give men the confidence required to be dominant and directly assertive. To gain some understanding of the importance of this variable, researchers might profitably examine the behavioral changes that take place among women who *are* developing their physical strength, or they might look at the behaviors that parallel within-sex differences on this dimension.

WHAT NEEDS TO BE DONE?

Presuming that the goal is to equalize the status of women and men, a variety of actions toward this end are possible. At the individual level, people can search for ways to break out of power styles that reinforce male dominance and female subservience. Women can endeavor to be more direct and assertive; men can try to stop interrupting women and exerting dominance through conversational control, gesture, and touch. Such strategies will have only limited effectiveness, however, until women and men have more equal access to the resources on which power is based. A person without concrete resources on which to base power is in a much more precarious position when being direct in influence attempts than is one who controls many such resources. Thus, women must improve their access to power bases such as physical strength and expertise. An increase in physical strength, expertise, and other power bases would give women not only more leverage in terms of *interpersonal power* (capacity to influence others), but also a stronger sense of their own *personal power* (power for the self).

To make this whole process less frightening, people will find it helpful to work together to explore and challenge the notion that power and gentleness, strength and vulnerability are incompatible. Steps in this direction can be taken both by examining the apparently paradoxical combinations of power and gentleness that are all around us and by experimenting with our own behavior.

One concrete example of the blending of two supposedly incompatible qualities exists in the new-found popularity of weight training, body building, and powerlifting for women. The idea of women lifting weights generates either laughter or revulsion from many people. There is a belief that women are too weak to go for this sort of thing, or, conversely, that women who do lift weights will become "muscle-bound" and masculine in appearance. The experience of many women has proven that neither of these suppositions is accurate. Women lifting weights do become stronger, but do not become masculine in appearance. And the fact that they can combine strength and femininity is perhaps most strikingly attested to by powerlifter Cindy Reinhoudt, who after lifting a total of 975 pounds in three lifts at an international competition, philosophically explained her failure to achieve her personal goal of 1000 pounds by revealing that she was six weeks pregnant and "feeling a little nauseous!"

Other less dramatic examples of the blending of the supposedly incompatible qualities of strength and gentleness can be found in the behavior of that rare breed of successful administrators and politicians—male and female—who feel no necessity to continually demonstrate their power by "steamrolling" the opposition. These "tough but fair" leaders can and will resort to threat or coercion when an emergency calls for severe measures, but such strategies are used only as a last resort. In everyday situations, they rely heavily on reason, compromise, and compassion.

The ability to balance gentleness and strength is one to be highly prized. Generations of parents and teachers have sought this balance in their relationships with their charges, most of them never achieving it to their own satisfaction. But not until we learn to reconcile the two qualities will women and men be able to break out of the dichotomy that equates only masculinity with strength and power and only femininity with gentleness and weakness.

If the power relationships between women and men change, will the shape of the social world change? Or will the social system go on as before, with lessened sex segregation in many jobs and roles? At this point, the answers to these questions must be pure speculation. Feminists are fond of saying that women do not just want to "make it" in a system based on male values, but they want to change the system by introducing female values. In some respects, such changes are already taking place. Some (admittedly few) businesses are beginning to acknowledge the importance of their employees' parental roles, for example, and have begun to provide day-care facilities and grant parental leave for members of their staff. It is difficult to imagine this happening without the presence and power of increasing numbers of women at all levels of an organization. If women gain more access to formerly male bases of power, if people abandon a dichotomy that allows only women to be the nurturers and only men to be strong, will fundamental changes occur on a large scale in our institutions? Only time will tell. But for women and men caught up in the challenge of exploring and redefining their own sense of power and their power relationships with others, this is an exciting question— a question whose answer we will all help to shape.

BIBLIOGRAPHY

Abramson, L. Y., Seligman, M. E. P., & Teasdale, J. D. Learned helplessness in humans: Critique and reformulation. *Journal of Abnormal Psychology*, 1978, *87*, 49-74.

Adams, E. A multivariate study of subordinate perceptions of and attitudes toward minority and majority managers. *Journal of Applied Psychology*, 1978, *63*, 277-288.

Adams, K. A. & Landers, A. D. Sex differences in dominance behavior. *Sex Roles*, 1978, *4*(2), 215-223.

Adler, A. *Understanding human nature*. New York: Greenburg, 1927.

Aldous, J. The making of family roles and family change. *The Family Coordinator*, 1974, *23*, 231-325.

Allport, G. W. *The nature of prejudice*. Reading, Mass.: Addison-Wesley, 1954.

Amir, M. *Patterns in forcible rape*. Chicago: University of Chicago Press, 1971.

Anderson, N. *A stereotypical association between sex role appropriateness, sexual orientation and sex drive*. Unpublished B.A. thesis, University of Western Ontario, 1974.

Archer, J. Sex differences in emotional behaviour: A reply to Gray and Buffery. *Acta Psychologia*, 1971, *35*, 415-429.

Ardrey, R. *The territorial imperative: A personal inquiry into the animal origins of property and nations*. New York: Atheneum, 1966.

Are women executives people? *Harvard Business Review*, 1965, *43*, 14-16+.

Aries, E. Interaction patterns and themes of male, female, and mixed groups. *Small Group Behavior*, 1976, *7*(1), 7-18.

Aronoff, J. & Crano, W. D. A re-examination of the cross-cultural principles of task segregation and sexrole differentiation in the family. *American Sociological Review*, 1975, *40*, 12-20.

Bakan, D. *The duality of human existence*. Chicago: Rand McNally, 1966.

Bartol, K. Relationship of sex and professional training area to job orientation. *Journal of Applied Psychology*, 1976, *61*, 368-370.

Bartol, K. & Wortman, Jr., M. Male versus female leaders: Effects on perceived leader behavior and satisfaction in a hospital. *Personnel Psychology*, 1975, *28*, 533-547.

Bart, P. The sociology of depression. In Paul M. Roman & Harrison M. Trice (Eds.), *Explorations in psychiatric sociology*. Philadelphia: F. A. Davis, 1974.

Bart, P. Socialization and rape avoidance: How to say no to Storaska and survive. Paper presented at the National Conference on Feminist Psychology, Santa Monica, March 1980.

Bar-Tal, D. & Frieze, I. H. Achievement motivation for males and females as a determinant of attributions for success and failure. *Sex Roles*, 1977, *3*(3), 301-314.

Bass, B., Krusell, J., & Alexander, R. Male managers' attitudes toward working women. *American Behavioral Scientist*, November 1971, 221-236.

Beckman-Brindley, S. & Tavormina, J. B. Power relationships in families. A social exchange perspective, *Family Process*, 1978, *17*, 423-436.

Bem, S. L. The measurement of psychological androgyny. *Journal of Consulting and Clinical Psychology*, 1974, *42*(2), 155-162.

Benedict, R. *Patterns of culture*. New York: New American Library, Mentor, 1934.

Benedict, R. Synergy: Patterns of the good culture. *American Anthropologist*, 1970, *72*, 320-333.

Berger, J., Cohen, B. P., & Zelditch, Jr., M. Status conceptions and social interaction. *American Sociological Review*, 1972, *37*, 241-255.

Bernard, J. *The future of marriage*, New York: World, 1972.

Bernard, J. Women, marriage and the future. In. C. Safilios-Rothschild (Ed.), *Toward a sociology of women*. Lexington, Mass.: Xerox, 1972.

Bernard, J. Where are we now? Some thoughts on the current scene. *Psychology of Women Quarterly*, 1976, *1*, 21-37.

Bird, C. *Born female: The high cost of keeping women down*. New York: David McKay, 1968.

Blau, P. M. *Exchange and power in social life*. New York: John Wiley, 1964.

Blood, Jr., R. O. & Wolfe, D. M. *Husbands and wives: The dynamics of married living*. Glencoe, Illinois: Free Press, 1960.

Bott, E. *Family and social network*. London: Tavistock Publications, 1957.

Bond, J. R. & Vinacke, W. E. Coalitions in mixed-sex triads. *Sociometry*, 1961, *24*, 61-75.

Bonoma, T. V. A pilot application of a social influence rating scale to some White House tapes. Mimeographed manuscript, Institute for Juvenile Research, 1975.

Borden, R. J. & Homleid, G. M. Handedness and lateral positioning in heterosexual couples: Are men still strong-arming women? *Sex Roles*, 1978, *4*(1), 67-74.

Boston Women's Health Book Collective, *Our bodies, ourselves.* New York: Simon & Schuster, 1971.

Brandwein, R. A., Brown, C. A., & Fox, E. M. Women and children last: The social situation of divorced mothers and their families. *Journal of Marriage and the Family*, 1974, *36*, 498-514.

Brannon, R. The male sex role: Our culture's blueprint for manhood, and what it's done for us lately. In D. David & R. Brannon (Eds.), *The forty-nine percent majority: The male sex role.* Reading, Mass.: Addison-Wesley, 1976.

Brehm, J. W. *A theory of psychological reactance.* New York: Academic Press, 1966.

Brewer, M. B. In-group bias in the minimal intergroup situation: A cognitive-motivational analysis. *Psychological Bulletin*, 1979, *86*, 307-324.

Brief, A. & Oliver, R. Male-female differences in work attitudes among retail sales managers. *Journal of Applied Psychology*, 1976, *61*, 526-528.

Britain, S. Contribution to S. Britain & J. Douglas, *Beyond depression to power.* Panel presented at the Fifth National Conference on Feminist Psychology, Pittsburgh, March 1978.

Brodsky, S. L. & Klemack, S. H. Simulation and baseline research in rape prevention. Presented at *Symposium on Rape: Victimization and Prevention*, American Psychological Association Convention, Washington, D.C., September 1976.

Broverman, I. K., Vogel, R. S., Broverman, D. M., Clarkson, T. E., & Rosenkrantz, P. S. Sex-role stereotypes: A current appraisal. *Journal of Social Issues*, 1972, *28*, 59-78.

Brown, L. K. Women and business management. *Signs: Journal of Women in Culture and Society*, 1979, *5*(2), 266-288.

Brownmiller, S. *Against our will.* New York: Bantam Books, 1975.

Bunch, C. Woman Power. *Ms.*, July 1980, *9*(1), 45-46, 48, 95, 97.

Burke, R. J. & Weir, T. Relationship of wives' employment status to husband, wife, and pair satisfaction and performance. *Journal of Marriage and the Family*, 1976, *38*, 279–287.

Campbell, J., *The masks of God: Primitive mythology*. New York: Viking, 1959.

Cann, C. Sex role and social identity: Achievement and power. Paper presented at the National Conference on Feminist Psychology, Dallas, 1979.

Carlson, J. E. The sexual role. In F. I. Nye (Ed.), *Role structure and analysis of the family*. Beverly Hills, Calif.: Sage Publications, 1976.

Cartwright, D. (Ed.). *Studies in social power*. Ann Arbor, Mich.: Research Centre for Group Dynamics, Institute for Social Research, University of Michigan, 1959.

Castaneda, C. *The second ring of power*. New York: Simon & Schuster, 1977.

Centers, R., Raven, B. H., & Rodriques, A. Conjugal power structure: A re-examination. *American Sociological Review*, 1971, *36*, 264–278.

Chafetz, J. S., *Masculine/feminine or human? An overview of the sociology of sex roles*. Itasca, Ill.: Peacock, 1974.

Chan, J. What's wrong with the "success" books? *Working Woman*, 1980 (August), *5*, 38+.

Chapman, J. Comparison of male and female leadership styles. *Academy of Management Journal*, 1975, *18*, 645–650.

Chapman, J. & Luthans, F. The female leadership dilemma. *Public Personnel Management*, 1975, *4*, 173–179.

Chesler, P. *Women and madness*. New York: Avon Books, 1973.

Chodorow, N. *The reproduction of mothering: Psychoanalysis and the sociology of gender*. Berkeley: University of California Press, 1978.

Christie, A. *Agatha Christie: An autobiography*. London: William Collins, 1977.

Cicone, M. V. & Ruble, D. N. Beliefs about males. *Journal of Social Issues*, 1978, *34*(1), 5–16.

Clark, L. & Lewis, D. *Rape: The price of coercive sexuality*. Toronto: Women's Press, 1977.

Collins, B. E. Attribution theory analysis of forced compliance. *Proceedings, 77th Annual Convention, American Psychological Association*, 1969, *4*, 309–310.

Collins, B. E. & Raven, B. E. Group Structure: attraction, coalitions, communication, and power. In G. Lindzey & E. Aronson (Eds.) *Handbook of social psychology*, Vol. 4. Reading, Mass.: Addison-Wesley, 1968.

Colwill, N. L. *The new partnership: The psychology of women and men in organizations*. Santa Cruz, Calif.: Mayfield, in press.

Dalton, M. Informal factors in career achievment. *American Journal of Sociology*, 1951, *56* 407–415.

Daly, M. *Beyond God the father: Toward a philosophy of women's liberation*. Boston: Beacon Press, 1973.

Daly, M., *Gyn/Ecology: The metaethics of radical feminism*. Boston: Beacon Press, 1978.

Davis, E. G. *The first sex*. New York: Putnam, 1971.

Dawkins, L. Women executives in business, industry, and the professions. Doctoral dissertation, The University of Texas. Ann Arbor, Mich: University Microfilms, 1962, No. 62-4832.

Day, D. R. & Stodgill, R. M. Leader behavior of male and female supervisors: A comparative study. *Personnel Psychology*, 1972, *25*(2), 353-360.

de Beauvoir, S. *The second sex*. New York: Alfred A. Knopf, 1952.

de Lenero, D. C. E. Hacia donde va la mujir mexicana. Mexico: Instituto Mexicano de Estudios Sociales, A.C., 1969.

Deaux, K. *The behavior of women and men*. Monterey, Calif.: Brooks/Cole, 1976.

Deaux, K. & Emswiller, T. Explanations of successful performance on sex-linked tasks: What is skill for the male is luck for the female, *Journal of Personality and Social Psychology*, 1974, *29*, 80-85.

Deaux, K. & Taynor, J. Evaluation of male and female ability: Bias works two ways. *Psychological Reports*, 1973, *32*(1), 261-262.

Denmark, F. L. Styles of leadership. *Psychology of Women Quarterly*, 1977, *2*(2), 99-113.

Deutsch, H. *The Psychology of women*. Vol. I. New York: Grune & Stratton, 1944.

Deutsch, H. *The psychology of women*. Vol. II. New York: Grune & Stratton, 1945.

DeVore, I. (Ed.) *Primate behavior: Field studies of monkeys and apes*. New York: Holt, Rinehart & Winston, 1965.

Dworkin, A. *Woman Hating*. New York: Dutton, 1974.

Dobbs, Jr., J. M. *Sex, setting and reactions to crowding on sidewalks.* Paper presented at the meeting of the American Psychological Association, Honolulu, August 1972.

Donnerstein, E. Aggressive erotica and violence against women. *Journal of Personality and Social Psychology*, 1980, *39*(2), 269–277.

Downs, J. F. *The Navaho*. New York: Holt, Rinehart & Winston, 1972.

Dunbar, R. I. M. & Dunbar, E. P. Dominance and reproductive success among female gelada baboons. *Nature*, 1977, *226*, 351–352.

Dunn, M. Marriage role expectations of adolescents. *Marriage and Family Living*, 1960, *22*, 99–111.

Eagly, A. H., Wood, W., & Fishbaugh, L. Sex differences in conformity: Surveillance by the group as a determinant of male nonconformity. In press, *Journal of Personality and Social Psychology*.

Eakins, B. W. & Eakins, R. G. Verbal turn-taking and exchanges in faculty dialogue. In B. L. Dubois & I. Crouch (Eds.), *Papers in Southwest English IV: Proceedings of the Conference on the sociology of the languages of American women*. San Antonio, Tex.: Trinity University, 1976.

Eakins, B. W. & Eakins, R. G. *Sex differences in human communication*. Boston: Houghton Mifflin, 1978.

Edelman, M. S. & Omark, D. R. Dominance hierarchies in young children. *Social Science Information*, 1973, *12*(1), 103–110.

Ehrenreich, B. & English, D. *Witches, midwives and nurses: A history of women healers*. Old Westbury, N.Y.: Feminist Press, 1973.

Eichler, M. *The prestige of the occupation housewife*. Paper presented at The Working Sexes Symposium, Vancouver, B.C., October 1976.

Eichler, M. The double standard: A feminist critique of feminist social science. New York: St. Martin's Press, 1980.

Elder, Jr., G. H. Structured variations in the child rearing relationship. *Sociometry*, 1962, *25*, 241–262.

Elig, T. W. & Frieze, I. H. A multidimensional scheme for coding and interpreting perceived causality for success and failure events: The coding scheme of perceived causality (CSPC). JSAS *Catalog of Selected Documents in Psychology*, 1975, 5, 313 (Ms. No. 1069).

Erickson, B. E., Lund, E. A., Johnson, B. C., & O'Barr, W. M. Speech style and impression formation in a court setting: The effects of "powerful" and "powerless" speech. *Journal of Experimental Social Psychology*, 1978, *14*, 266-279.

Erikson, E. H. Womanhood and inner space. In J. Strouse (Ed.) *Women and analysis*. New York: Dell, 1974.

Falbo, T. Relationship between sex, sex role, and social influence. *Psychology of Women Quarterly*, 1977, *2*(1), 62-72.

Fasteau, M. F. *The male machine*. New York: McGraw-Hill, 1974.

Feldman, H. *Development of the husband-wife relationship*. Ithaca, N.Y.: Cornell University Press, 1965.

Feldman, H. *The Ghanian family in transition*. Ithaca: Winneba Training College and Cornell University, 1967.

Felson, M. & Knoke, D. Social status and the married woman. *Journal of Marriage and the Family*, 1974, *36*, 516-521.

Feshbach, N. D., Dillman, A. S., & Jordan, T. S. Portrait of a female on television: Some possible effects on children. In C. B. Kopp (Ed.), *Becoming female: Perspectives on development*. New York: Plenum Press, 1979.

Finz, S. D. & Waters, J. An analysis of sex role stereotyping in daytime television serials. Paper presented at the meeting of the American Psychological Association, Washington, D.C., September 1976.

Fiorenza, E. S. Interpreting patriarchal traditions. In L. M. Russell (Ed.) *The liberating word*. Philadelphia: Westminster Press, 1976, 39-61.

Flora, C. B. The passive female: Her comparative image by class and culture in women's magazine fiction. *Journal of Marriage and the Family*, 1971, *33*, 435-444.

Franzwa, H. H. Female roles in women's magazine fiction, 1940-1970. In R. K. Unger & F. L. Denmark (Eds.), *Woman: Dependent or independent variable?* New York: Psychological Dimensions, 1975.

Freeman, J. The tyranny of structurelessness. *Ms.*, 1973, *2*(1), 76-78, 86-89.

French, Jr., J. R. P. & Raven, B. The bases of social power. In D. Cartwright (Ed.), *Studies in social power*. Ann Arbor, Mich.: Research Centre for Group Dynamics, Institute for Social Research, University of Michigan, 1959.

Friday, N. *Men in love: Men's sexual fantasies: The triumph of love over rage.* New York: Delacorte, 1980.

Friday, N. *My mother/my self.* New York: Delacorte, 1977, © 1977 by Nancy Friday.

Friedan, B. *The feminine mystique.* New York: Dell, 1963.

Frieze, I. H. Perceptions of battered wives. In I. H. Frieze, D. Bar-Tal & J. S. Carroll (Eds.), *New approaches to social problems.* San Francisco: Jossey-Bass, 1979.

Frieze, I. H. & Ramsey, S. Nonverbal maintenance of traditional sex roles. *Journal of Social Issues,* 1976, *32*(3), 133-142.

Frieze, I. H., Parsons, J., Johnson, P., Ruble, D., & Zellman, G. *Women and sex roles: A social psychological perspective.* New York: W. W. Norton, 1978.

Fromm, E. *The anatomy of human destructiveness.* Greenwich, Conn.: Fawcett, 1973.

Gager, N. & Schurr, C. *Sexual assault: Confronting rape in America.* New York: Grosset & Dunlap, 1976.

Gallo, P. S. & McClintock, C. G. Cooperative and competitive behavior in mixed motive games. *Journal of Conflict Resolution,* 1965, *9*, 68-78.

Gillespie, D. L. Who has the power? The marital struggle. *Journal of Marriage and the Family,* 1971, *33*, 445-458.

Ginsberg, G. L., Frosch, W. A., & Shapiro, T. The new impotence. *Archives of General Psychiatry,* 1972, *26*, 218-220.

Gintner, G. & Lindskold, S. Rate of participation and expertise as factors influencing leader choice. *Journal of Personality and Social Psychology,* 1975, *32*, 1085-1089.

Girvetz, H. K. *The evolution of liberalism.* London: Collier-Macmillan, 1963.

Goffman, E. *Relations in public: Microstudies of the public order.* New York: Basic Books, 1971.

Gold, M. Power in the classroom. *Sociometry,* 1958, *21*, 50-60.

Goldberg, P. Are women prejudiced against women? *Trans-action,* 1968, *5*(5), 28-30.

Goodchilds, J. Power: A matter of mechanics? *SASP Newsletter,* 1979, *5*(3), 3.

Gordon, R. E., Gordon, K. K., & Gunther, M. *The split-level trap*. New York: B. Geis, 1961.

Gorer, G. Man has no "killer" instinct. In M. F. Montagu (Ed.), *Man and aggression*. New York: Oxford University Press, 1968.

Gould, R. Measuring masculinity by the size of a paycheck. In D. S. David & R. Brannon (Eds.), *The forty-nine percent majority: The male sex role*. Reading, Mass.: Addison-Wesley, 1976.

Green, A. & Melnick, E. What has happened to the feminist movement? In A. Gouldner (Ed.), *Studies in Leadership: Leadership and democratic action*. New York: Harper, 1950.

Greer, G. Seduction is a four-letter word. In E. S. Morrison & V. Borosage (Eds.), *Human sexuality*, Palo Alto, CA.: Mayfield, 1977.

Groch, A. S. Generality of response to humor and wit in cartoons, jokes, stories and photographs. *Psychological Reports, 1974, 35,* 835-838.

Gross, A. The male role and heterosexual behaviour. *Journal of Social Issues,* 1978, *34*(1), 87-107.

Grotjahn, M. Interview in L. Freeman & M. Theodores (Eds.), *The why report*. New York: Pocket Books, 1965.

Gruberg, M. *Women in American politics: An assessment and sourcebook.* Oshkosh, Wis.: Academia Press, 1968.

Haavio-Mannila, E. Some consequences of women's emancipation. *Journal of Marriage and the Family*, 1969, *31*, 123-134.

Haccoun, D., Haccoun, R. & Sallay, G. Sex differences in the appropriateness of supervisory styles: A nonmanagement view. *Journal of Applied Psychology*, 1978, *63*, 124-127.

Hacker, H. M. Women as a minority group. *Social Forces,* 1951, *30*, 60-69.

Hall, E. T. *The hidden dimension*. New York: Doubleday, 1966.

Hall, K. R. L. & Mayer, B. Social interactions in a group of captive patas monkeys *(Erythrocebus patas)*. *Folia Primatologica,* 1967, *5*, 213-236.

Hariton, B. E. & Singer, J. L. Women's fantasies during sexual intercourse: Normative and theoretical implications. *Journal of Consulting and Clinical Psychology*, 1974, *43*, 313-322.

Harrison, J. *Mythology*. New York: Harcourt Brace, 1963.

Harrison, J. Warning: The male sex role may be dangerous to your health. *Journal of Social Issues*, 1978, *34*(1), 65–86.

Harris, L. and Associates. *The 1972 Virginia Slims American Women's Opinion Poll.*

Hartley, R. E. Sex-role pressures and the socialization of the male child. *Psychological Reports*, 1959, *5*, 457–468.

Heer, D. M. Dominance and the working wife. *Social Forces*, 1958, *36*, 341–347.

Heer, D. M. The measurement and bases of family power: An overview. *Marriage and Family Living*, 1963, *25*, 139–153.

Heide, W. S. Feminism for a sporting future. In C. A. Oglesby (Ed.), *Women and sport: From myth to reality*. Philadelphia: Lea & Febiger, 1978, 195–202.

Heider, F. *The psychology of interpersonal relations*. New York: John Wiley, 1958.

Henley, N. M. *Body politics: Power, sex, and nonverbal communication*. Englewood Cliffs, N.J.: Prentice-Hall, 1977.

Hennig, M. & Jardim, A. *The managerial woman*. New York: Doubleday, 1977.

Herman, D. The rape culture. In. J. Freeman (Ed.), *Women: A feminist perspective* (Second Edition). Palo Alto, Calif.: Mayfield, 1979.

Hess, R. D. & Torney, J. V. Religion, age and sex in children's perceptions of family authority. *Child Development*, 1962, *33*, 781–789.

Hite, S. *The Hite report*. New York: Dell Publishing, 1976.

Hochreich, D. J. Sex-role stereotypes for internal-external control and interpersonal trust. *Journal of Consulting and Clinical Psychology*, 1975, *43*, 273.

Hochschild, A. R. A review of sex role research. *American Journal of Sociology*, 1973, *78*, 1011–1029.

Homans, G. C. *Social behavior: The elementary forms*. New York: Harcourt Brace Jovanovich, 1974.

Horner, M. Toward an understanding of achievement related conflicts in women. *Journal of Social Issues*, 1972, *28*, 157–176.

Horney, K. *Self-analysis*. New York: Norton, 1942.

Hoyenga, K. B. & Hoyenga, K. T. *The question of sex differences*. Boston: Little, Brown, 1979.

Hutt, C. *Males and females*. Harmondsworth, England: Penguin Books, 1972.

Jacobson, M. & Effertz, J. Sex roles and leadership: Perceptions of the leaders and the led. *Organizational Behavior and Human Performance*, 1974, *12*, 383–396.

Janeway, E. *Between myth and morning: Women awakening*. New York: William Morrow, 1974.

Janeway, E. The powers of the weak. *Signs*, 1975, *1*(1), 103–110.

Johnson, P. Social power and sex role stereotypes. Paper presented at the meeting of the Western Psychological Association, San Francisco, May 1974.

Johnson, P. Women and power: Toward a theory of effectiveness. *Journal of Social Issues*, 1976, *32*(3), 99–110.

Johnson, P. Feminist people and power: Are we copping out? *SASP Newsletter*, 1979, *5*(3), 3–4.

Jones, E. E. & Nisbett, R. E. The actor and the observer: Divergent perceptions of the causes of behavior. In E. E. Jones, D. E. Kanouse, H. H. Kelley, R. E. Nisbett, S. Valins, & B. Weiner (Eds.), *Attribution: Perceiving the causes of behavior*. Morristown, N.J.: General Learning Press, 1972.

Josephson, W. L. & Colwill, N. L. Males, females, and aggression. In H. M. Lips and N. L. Colwill, *The psychology of sex differences*. Englewood Cliffs, N.J.: Prentice-Hall, 1978, 197–223.

Jung, C. G. Aion: Researches into the phenomenology of the self. *Collected Works*, Vol. 9 (ii). Psychologishe Abhandlungen VIII. Zurich: Rasher Verlag, 1951.

Kahn, A. From theories of equity to theories of justice: An example of demasculinization in social psychology. *SASP Newsletter*, 1979, *5*(3), 12–14.

Kahn, A., Nelson, R. E., & Gaeddert, W. P. Sex of subject and sex comparison of the group as determinants of reward allocations. *Journal of Personality and Social Psychology*, 1980, *38*(5), 737–750.

Kanter, R. Women and the structure of organizations: Explorations in theory and behavior. In M. Millman & R. Kanter (Eds.), *Another voice: Femin-*

ist perspectives on social life and social science. Garden City, N.Y.: Anchor Books, 1975a.

Kanter, R. Women in organizations: Sex roles, group dynamics, and change strategies. In A. Sargent (Ed.), *Beyond sex roles.* St. Paul, Minn.: West Publishing, 1975b.

Kanter, R. Why bosses turn bitchy. *Psychology Today,* 1976, May, 56-60, 88-91.

Kanter, R. *Men and women of the corporation.* New York: Basic Books, 1977.

Kanter, R. Power failure in management circuits. *Harvard Business Review,* 1979, *57,* 65-75.

Katz, D. & Kahn, R. *The social psychology of organizations,* 2nd ed. New York: John Wiley, 1978.

Kawamura, S. Matriarchal social ranks in the Minoo-B group: A study of the social rank system of Japanese monkeys. *Primates,* 1958, *1,* 149-156.

Kenkel, W. F. Sex of observer and spousal roles in decision-making. *Marriage and Family Living,* 1961, *23,* 185-186.

Kerr, S., Schriesheim, C., Murphy, C., & Stogdill, R. Toward a contingency theory of leadership based upon the consideration and initiating structure literature. *Organizational Behavior and Human Performance,* 1974, *12,* 62-82.

Kesey, K. *One flew over the cuckoo's nest.* New York: Viking, 1962.

Key, M. R. The role of male and female in children's books - Dispelling all doubt. In R. K. Unger & F. L. Denmark (Eds.), *Woman: Dependent or independent variable.* New York: Psychological Dimensions, 1975.

King, M. G. Interpersonal relations in preschool children and average approach distance. *Journal of Genetic Psychology,* 1966, *109,* 109-116.

Kinsey, A. C. *Sexual behavior in the human female.* Philadelphia: W. B. Saunders, 1953.

Kipnis, D. Does power corrupt? *Journal of Personality and Social Psychology,* 1972, *24,* 33-41.

Knott, P. & Drost, B. A measure of interpersonal dominance. *Behavior research methods and instrumentation,* 1969, *1,* 139-140.

Kohlberg, L. A cognitive-developmental analysis of children's sex-role concepts and attitudes. In E. E. Maccoby (Ed.), *The development of sex differences.* Stanford, Calif.: Stanford University Press, 1966.

Kolb, T. M. & Strauss, M. A. Marital power and marital happiness in relation to problem-solving ability. *Journal of Marriage and the Family,* 1974, *36,* 756-766.

Komarovsky, M. *Dilemmas of masculinity: A study of college youth.* New York: Norton, 1976.

Komorita, S. S. & Chertkoff, J. M. A bargaining theory of coalition formation. *Psychological Review,* 1973, *80,* 149-162.

Lacey, H. M. Control, perceived control, and the methodological role of cognitive constructs. In L. C. Perlmuter and R. A. Monty (Eds.), *Choice and perceived control.* Hillsdale, N.J.: Lawrence Erlbaum, 1979.

Lakoff, R. *Language and woman's place.* New York: Harper & Row, 1975.

Lancaster, J. B. Sex roles in primate societies. In M. S. Teitelbaum (Ed.), *Sex differences: Social and biological perspectives.* New York: Anchor Press, 1976, 22-61.

Lance, K. *Getting strong: A woman's guide to realizing her physical potential.* Indianapolis, Ind.: Bobbs-Merrill, 1978.

Landis, C. & Ross, J. W. H. Humor and its relation to other personality traits. *Journal of Personality and Social Psychology,* 1933, *4,* 156-175.

Larson, L. E. System and subsystem perception of family roles. *Journal of Marriage and the Family,* 1974, *36,* 123-138.

Laws, J. L. A feminist review of the marital adjustment literature: The Rape of the Locke. *Journal of Marriage and the Family,* 1971, *33,* 438-518.

Laws, J. L. & Schwartz, P. *Sexual scripts: The social construction of female sexuality.* Hinsdale, Ill.: Dryden Press, 1977.

Lederer, W. *The fear of women.* New York: Grune & Stratton, 1968.

Lerner, M. J. The desire for justice and reactions to victims. In J. Macaulay & L. Berkowitz (Eds.), *Altruism and helping behavior.* New York: Academic Press, 1970.

Lerner, M. J. Social psychology of justice and interpersonal attraction. In T. Huston (Ed.), *Foundations of interpersonal attraction.* New York: Academic Press, 1974.

Levine, J. *Who will raise the children? New options for fathers (and mothers).* New York: Lippincott, 1976.

Levine, S. One man's experience. In J. Pleck & J. Sawyer (Eds.) *Men and masculinity*. Englewood Cliffs, N.J.: Prentice-Hall, 1974, p. 156-159.

Levinson, R. M. From Olive Oyl to Sweet Polly Purebread: Sex role stereotypes and television cartoons. *Journal of Popular Culture*, 1975, *8*, 561-72.

Levy, G. R. *Religious conceptions of the stone age*. New York: Harper Torchbooks, 1963.

Lewin, K. *Principles of topological psychology*. New York: McGraw-Hill, 1936.

Lips, H. M. Preliminary research on the experience of power. Unpublished data, 1979.

Lips, H. M. Gender and the sense of power: Where are we and where are we going? Paper presented at the Institute of the Section on Women and Psychology, Canadian Psychological Association, Toronto, June, 1981.

Lips, H. M. & Colwill, N. L. *The psychology of sex differences*. Englewood Cliffs, N.J.: Prentice-Hall, 1978.

Lockheed, M. E. & Hall, K. P. Conceptualizing sex as a status characteristic: Applications to leadership training strategies. *Journal of Social Issues*, 1976, *32* (3), 111-124.

London, I. Frigidity, sensitivity and sexual roles. In J. Pleck & J. Sawyer (Eds.), *Men and masculinity*. Englewood Cliffs, N.J.: Prentice-Hall 1974.

Lynch, E. *The executive suite—feminine style*. New York: AMACOM, 1973.

Lynn, D. B. The process of learning parental and sex-role identification. *The Journal of Marriage and the Family*, 1966, *28:* 466-470.

Maccoby, E. E. & Jacklin, C. N. *The psychology of sex differences*. Stanford, Calif.: Stanford University Press, 1974.

MacCormack, C. P. Biological events and cultural control. *Signs*. 1977, *3*(1): 93-100.

Malamuth, N. M. Erotica: Aggression and perceived appropriateness. Paper presented at the 86th Annual Convention of the American Psychological Association, Toronto, September, 1978.

Malamuth, N. M. Rape fantasies as a function of repeated exposure to sexual violence. Paper presented at the Second Annual Conference on the Treatment of Sexual Aggressives, New York, 1979.

Malamuth, N. M. & Check, J. V. P. Penile tumescence and perceptual responses to rape as a function of victim's response. Paper presented at Canadian Psychological Association Meetings, Quebec City, June 1979.

Malamuth, N., Feshbach, S. & Jaffe, Y. Sexual arousal and aggression: Recent experiments and theoretical issues. *Journal of Social Issues,* 1977, *33,* 110-133.

Malamuth, N. M., Haber, S., & Feshbach, S. Testing hypotheses regarding rape: Exposure to sexual violence, sex differences, and the "normality" of rapists. *Journal of Research in Personality,* 1980, *14*(1), 121-137.

Malamuth, N. M., Riesin, I., & Spinner, B. Exposure to pornography and reactions to rape. Paper presented at the Annual Meeting of the Western Psychological Association, San Diego, 1979.

Malamuth, N. M. & Spinner, B. A longitudinal content analysis of sexual violence in the best-selling erotic magazines. *Journal of Sex Research,* 1980, *16*(3), 226-237.

Manhardt, P. Job orientation of male and female college graduates in business. *Personnel Psychology,* 1972, *25,* 361-368.

Markle, G. E. Sex ratio at birth: Values, variance, and some determinants. *Demography,* 1974, *11,* 131-142.

Marks, J. "On the road to find out": The role music plays in adolescent development. In C. B. Kopp (Ed.), *Becoming female: Perspectives on development.* New York: Plenum Press, 1979.

Marks, J. B. Interests and leadership among adolescents. *Journal of Genetic Psychology,* 1957, *91,* 163-172.

Maslow, A. H. The farther reaches of human nature. *Harmondsworth, England: Penguin Books, 1971.*

Masters, W. H. & Johnson, V. E., *The pleasure bond.* Boston: Little, Brown, 1974.

McArthur, L. Z. & Resko, B. G. The portrayal of men and women in American television commercials. *Journal of Social Psychology,* 1975, *97,* 209-220.

McClelland, D. C. *Methods of measuring human motivation. In J. W. Atkinson (Ed.), Motives in fantasy, action and society.* Princeton, N.J.: D. Van Nostrand, 1958, 7-42.

McClelland, D. C. *Power: The inner experience.* New York: Irvington, 1975.

McClelland, D. C., Atkinson, J. W., Clark, R. A., & Lowell, E. L. *The achievement motive.* New York: Appleton-Century-Crofts, 1953.

McClelland, D. C., Davis, W. N., Kalin, R., & Wanner, E. *The drinking man.* New York: Free Press, 1972.

McClelland, D. C. & Watson, Jr., R. I. Power motivation and risk-taking behavior. *Journal of Personality,* 1973, *41,* 121-139.

McClung, N. *In times like these.* Toronto: University of Toronto Press, 1972. Originally published by D. Appleton, 1915.

McCormick, N. B. Come-ons and put-offs: Unmarried students' strategies for having and avoiding sexual intercourse. *Psychology of Women Quarterly,* 1979, *4*(2), 194-211.

McGillin, V. A. The sex role dimensions of social power in mixed and same sex interactions. Paper presented at the National Conference on Feminist Psychology, Dallas, 1979.

McGinnies, E., Nordholm, L. A., Ward, C. D., & Bhanthumnavin, D. L. Sex and cultural differences in perceived locus of control among students in five countries. *Journal of Consulting and Clinical Psychology,* 1974, *42,* 451-455.

McHugh, M. C., Duquin, M. E., & Frieze, I. H. Beliefs about success and failure: Attribution and the female athlete. In C. A. Oglesby (Ed.), *Women and sport: From myth to reality.* Philadelphia: Lea & Febiger, 1977.

McKee, J. P. & Sherriffs, A. C. The differential evaluation of males and females. *Journal of Personality,* 1957, *25,* 356-71.

McLaughlin, M. The doctor shows. *Journal of Communication,* 1975, *25,* 182-84.

McTeer, M. Let's make rape laws firm and fair. *The Globe and Mail,* July 22, 1978.

Mead, M. *Sex and temperament.* New York: William Morrow, and Mentor, 1935.

Mead, M. *Male and female.* Harmondsworth, England: Penguin Books, 1950.

Megargee, E. Influence of sex roles on the manifestation of leadership. *Journal of Applied Psychology,* 1969, *53,* 377-382.

Mehrabian, A. *Nonverbal communication.* Chicago: Aldine-Atherton, 1972.

Midelfort, H. C. E. *Witch hunting in southwestern Germany 1562-1684, the social and intellectual foundations.* Stanford, Calif.: Stanford University Press, 1972.

Milgram, S. (interviewed by C. Tavris). The frozen world of the familiar stranger. *Psychology Today,* 1974, *8,* 71-73, 76-78, 80.

Miller, J. B. *Toward a new psychology of women.* Boston: Beacon Press, 1977.

Millett, K. *Sexual politics.* New York: Doubleday, 1970.

Minton, H. L. Power as a personality construct. In B. A. Maher (Ed.), *Progress in experimental personality research.* Vol. 4. New York: Academic Press, 1967.

Mintzberg, H. *The nature of managerial work.* New York: Harper, 1973.

Mischel, H. N. Sex bias in the evaluation of professional achievements. *Journal of Educational Psychology,* 1974, *66,* 157-166.

Molloy, J. T. *The dress for success book.* New York: Warner Books, 1975.

Molloy, J. T. *The woman's dress for success book.* New York: Warner Books, 1977.

Montagu, M. F. (Ed.). *Man and aggression.* New York: Oxford University Press, 1968.

Morin, S. F. & Garfinkle, E. M. Male homophobia. *Journal of Social Issues,* 1978, *34*(1), 29-47.

Morin, S. F. & Wallace, S. Traditional values, sex-role stereotyping, and attitudes toward homosexuality. Paper presented at the Meeting of the Western Psychological Association, Los Angeles, April 1976.

Morris, D. *Naked apes: A zoologist's study of the human animal.* New York: McGraw-Hill, 1968.

Morris, N. M. & Sison, B. S. Correlates of female powerlessness: Parity methods of birth control, pregnancy. *Journal of Marriage and the Family,* 1974, *36,* 708-712.

Morrison, R. & Sebold, M. Personal characteristics differentiating female executive from female nonexecutive personnel. *Journal of Applied Psychology,* 1974, *59,* 656-659.

Moses, J. & Boehm, V. Relationship & assessment-center performance to management progress of women. *Journal of Applied Psychology,* 1975, *60,* 527-529.

Moses, Y. Female status, the family, and male dominance in a West Indian community. *Signs,* 1977, *3*(1), 142-153.

Muldrow, T. & Bayton, J. Men and women executives and processes related to decision accuracy. *Journal of Applied Psychology,* 1979, *64,* 99-106.

Murray, H. A. Techniques for a systematic investigation of fantasy. *Journal of Psychology,* 1937, *3,* 115-143.

O'Connell, W. E. The adaptive functions of wit and humor. *Journal of Abnormal & Social Psychology,* 1960, *61,* 263-270.

O'Leary, V. E. Some attitudinal barriers to occupational aspirations in women. *Psychological Bulletin,* 1974, *81*(11), 809-816.

Olson, D. H. The measurement of power using self-report and behavioral methods. *Journal of Marriage and the Family,* 1969, *31,* 545-550.

Olson, D. H., Cromwell, R. E., & Klein, D. M. Beyond family power. In R. E. Cromwell and D. H. Olson (Eds.), *Power in families.* New York: John Wiley, 1975.

Olson, D. H. & Rabunsky, D. Validity of four measures of family power. *Journal of Marriage and the Family,* 1972, *34,* 224-234.

Omark, D. R. & Edelman, M. S. A comparison of status hierarchies in young children: An ethological approach. *Social Science Information,* 1975, *14*(5), 87-107.

Osborn, R. N. & Vicars, W. M. Sex stereotypes: An artifact in leader behavior and subordinate satisfaction analysis. *Academy of Management Journal,* 1976, *19,* 439-449.

Osgood, C. E., Suci, G. J., & Tannenbaum, P. H. *The measurement of meaning.* Urbana, Ill.: University of Illinois Press, 1957.

Osmond, M. W. Reciprocity: A dynamic model and a method to study family power. *Journal of Marriage and the Family,* 1978, *40,* 49-61.

Parlee, M. B. Conversational politics. *Psychology Today,* 1979, *12*(12), 48-49, 51-52, 55-56.

Parsons, T. & Bales, R. F. *Family socialization and interaction process.* Glencoe, Ill.: Free Press, 1955.

Peplau, L., Rubin, Z., & Hill, C. T. Sexual intimacy in dating relationships. *Journal of Social Issues,* 1977, *33*(2), 86-109.

Perlman, D. The premarital sexual standards of Canadians. In K. Ishwaran

(Ed.). *Marriage and divorce in Canada*. Toronto: McGraw-Hill Ryerson, 1979.

Petty, M. M. & Bruning, N. S. A comparison of supervisory behavior and measures of subordinates' job satisfaction for male and female leaders. *Academy of Management Journal*, 1980, *23*(4), 717-725.

Petty, M. & Lee, Jr., G. Moderating effects of sex of supervisor and subordinate on relationships between supervisory behavior and subordinate satisfaction. *Journal of Applied Psychology*, 1975, *60*, 624-628.

Petty, M. & Miles, R. Leader sex-role stereotyping in a female-dominated work culture. *Personnel Psychology*, 1976, *29*, 393-404.

Pfeffer, J. The ambiguity of leadership. *Academy of Management Review*, 1977, January, 104-112.

Phares, E. J. Locus of control in personality. *Morristown, N.J.: General Learning*-external control. *Journal of Personality*, 1968, *36*, 649-662.

Phares, E. J. Locus of control in personality. *Moristown, N.J.: General Learning Press, 1976*.

Pheterson, G. I., Kiesler, S. B., & Goldberg, P. A. Evaluation of the performance of women as a function of their sex, achievement, and personal history. *Journal of Personality and Social Psychology*, *19*(1), 114-118.

Polk, B. B. Male power and the women's movement. *The Journal of Applied Behavioral Science*, 1974, *10*(3), 415-431.

Poloma, M. M. Role conflict and the married professional woman. In C. Safilios-Rothschild (Ed.), *Toward a sociology of women*. Lexington, Mass.: Xerox, 1972.

Poloma, M. M. & Garland, T. N. The myth of the egalitarian family: Family roles and the professionally employed wife. In A. Theodore (Ed.), *The professional woman*. Cambridge, Mass.: Schenkman, 1971.

Prescott, J. W. Body pleasure and the origins of violence. *The Futurist*, 1975, April, 64-74.

Prescott, J. W. Alienation of affection. *Psychology Today*, 1979, *13* (7), 124.

Priest, R. F. & Wilhelm, P. G. Sex, marital status and self-actualization as factors in the appreciation of sexist jokes. *The Journal of Social Psychology*, 1974, *92*, 245-249.

Puner, M. Will you still love me? *Human Behavior*, 1974, *3*(6), 42-48.

Rapoport, R. & Rapoport, R. N. Dual career families. Harmondsworth, England: Penguin, 1971.

Raven, B. H. Social influence and power. In I. D. Steiner & M. Fishbein (Eds.), *Current studies in social psychology*. New York: Holt, Rinehart & Winston, 1965.

Raven, B. H. Power relations in home and school. *Paper presented at the meeting of the Western Psychological Association, San Francisco, May 1974.*

Raymond, J. Women's history and transcendence. In F. H. Littell (Ed.), *Religious liberty in the crossfire of creeds*. Philadelphia: Ecumenical Press, 1978.

Reiss, I. L. *The family system in America*. New York: Holt, Rinehart and Winston, 1971.

Rich, A. *Of woman born*. New York: Norton, 1976.

Richmond, M. L., Beyond resources theory: Another look at factors enabling woman to affect family interaction. *Journal of Marriage and the Family*, 1976, *38*, 257–266.

Rodin, J. & Janis, I. The social power of health-care practitioners as agents of change. *Journal of Social Issues*, 1979, *35*(1), 60–81.

Rogers, C. *Carl Rogers on personal power*. New York: Dell Publishing, 1977.

Rollins, B. C. & Bahr, S. J. A theory of power relationships in marriage. *Journal of Marriage and the Family*, 1976, *38*, 619–627.

Rorbaugh, J. B. Femininity on the line. *Psychology Today*, 1979, *13*(3), 30–42.

Rosaldo, M. Z. Woman, culture and society: A theoretical overview. In M. Z. Rosaldo & L. Lamphere (Eds.), *Woman, culture and society*. Stanford, Calif.: Stanford University Press, 1974, 1–16.

Rose, R. M., Gordon, T. P., & Bernstein, I. S. Plasma testosterone levels in the male rhesus: influences of sexual and social stimuli. *Science*, 1972, *178*, 643–645.

Rosen, B. & Jerdee, T. H. The influence of sex-role stereotypes on evaluations of male and female supervisory behavior. *Journal of Applied Psychology*, 1973, *57*, 44–48.

Rosenblatt, P. C. & Cunningham, M. R. Sex differences in cross-cultural perspective. In B. Lloyd & J. Archer (Eds.), *Exploring sex differences.* London: Academic Press, 1976.

Rosenkrantz, P., Vogel, S., Bee, H., Broverman, I., & Broverman, D. M. Sex-role stereotypes and self-concepts in college students. *Journal of Consulting and Clinical Psychology,* 1968, *32,* 287-295.

Rossi, A. S. Equality between the sexes: An immodest proposal. In R. J. Lifton (Ed.), *The woman in America.* Boston: Beacon Press, 1967.

Rossi, A. S. Sex equality: The beginnings of ideology. In C. Safilios-Rothschild (Ed.), *Toward a sociology of women.* Lexington, Mass.: Xerox, 1972.

Rossi, P., Sampson, W., Bose, C., Jasso, G., & Passel, J. Measuring household social standing. *Social Science Research,* 1974, 3, 169-190.

Roth, P. Portnoy's complaint. New York: Random House, 1967.

Rotter, J. Generalized expectancies for internal vs. external control of reinforcement. *Psychological Monographs,* 1966, *80,* 1-28.

Roussell, C. Relationship of sex of department head to department climate. *Administrative Science Quarterly,* 1974, *19,* 211-220;

Rowell, T. E. Hierarchy in the organization of the captive baboon group. *Animal Behavior,* 1966, *14*(4), 430-443.

Ruether, R. R. *New woman, new earth: Sexist ideologies and human liberation.* New York: Seabury Press, 1975.

Russell, B. *Power.* London: Unwin Books, 1938.

Russell, D. E. *The politics of rape.* New York: Stein & Day, 1975.

Ryckman, R. M., Rodda, W. C., & Sherman, M. F. Locus of control and expertise relevance as determinants of changes in opinion about student activism. *Journal of Social Psychology,* 1972, *88,* 107-114.

Sacks, H. On the analyzability of stories by children. In J. Gumperz & D. Hymes (Eds.), *Directions in sociolinguistics.* New York: Holt, Rinehart & Winston, 1972.

Sade, D. S. Determinants of dominance in a group of free-ranging rhesus. In S. A. Altmann (Ed.), *Social communication among primates.* Chicago: University of Chicago Press, 1967, 99-114.

Safilios-Rothschild, C. Family sociology or wives' family sociology: A cross-cultural examination of decision-making. *Journal of Marriage and the Family,* 1969a, *31,* 290-301.

Safilios-Rothschild, C. Patterns of familial power and influence. *Sociological Focus*, 1969b, *2*, 7-19.

Safilios-Rothschild, C. The study of family power structure: A review 1960-1969. *Journal of Marriage and the Family*, 1970, *32*, 539-553.

Safilios-Rothschild, C. Instead of a discussion: Companionate marriages and sexual inequality: Are they compatible? In C. Safilios-Rothschild (Ed.), *Toward a sociology of women*. Lexington, Mass. Xerox, 1972.

Safilios-Rothschild, C. Family and stratification: Some macrosociological observations and hypotheses, *Journal of Marriage and the Family*, 1975, *37*, 855-860.

Safilios-Rothschild, C. A macro- and micro- examination of family power and love: An exchange model, *Journal of Marriage and the Family*, 1976, *38*, 355-362. Reprinted by permission.

Sampson, E. E. On justice as equality. *Journal of Social Issues*, 1975, *31*(3), 45-64.

Sanday, P. R. Female status in the public domain. In M. Z. Rosaldo & L. Lamphere (Eds.). *Woman, culture and society*. Stanford, Calif.: Stanford University Press, 1974.

Sanger, M. *Margaret Sanger: An autobiography*. New York: Dover Publications, 1971. Originally published in 1938 by Norton.

Sashkin, M. & Maier, N. Sex effects in delegation. *Personnel Psychology*, 1971, *24*, 471-476.

Sawyer, J. On male liberation. *Liberation*, 1970, *15*, 32-33.

Sayles, L. Leadership: What effective managers really do . . . and how they do it. New York: McGraw-Hill, 1979.

Schein, V. E. The relationship between sex-role stereotypes and requisite management characteristics. *Journal of Applied Psychology*, 1973, *57*, 95-100.

Schein, V. E. Relationships between sex-role stereotypes and requisite management characteristics among female managers. *Journal of Applied Psychology*, 1975, *60*, 340-344.

Schrire, C. & Steiger, W. L. A matter of life and death. *Man*, 1974, *9*(2), 161-184.

Schuler, R. Sex, organizational level, and outcome importance: Where the differences are. *Personnel Psychology*, 1975, *28*, 365-375.

Schutz, W. C. *FIRO: A three-dimensional theory of interpersonal behavior.* New York: Holt, Rinehart & Winston, 1958.

Seeman, M. Alienation and social learning in a reformatory. *American Journal of Sociology,* 1963, *69,* 270-284.

Seeman, M. & Evans, J. W. Alienation and learning in a hospital setting. *American Sociological Review,* 1962, *27,* 772-783.

Seligman, M. E. P. *Helplessness: On depression, development, and death.* San Francisco: Freeman, 1975.

Selkin, J. Rape. *Psychology Today,* 1975, *8*(6), 70-72, 74, 76.

Sherfey, M. J. *The nature and evolution of female sexuality.* New York: Vintage Books, 1966.

Sherif, M. & Sherif, C. W. *Groups in harmony and tension.* New York: Harper, 1956.

Sherriffs, A. C. & Jarrett, R. F. Sex differences in attitudes about sex differences. *Journal of Psychology,* 1953, *35,* 161-168.

Silveira, J. Thoughts on the politics of touch. *Woman's Press,* 1972, *1*(13).

Singer, M. Sexism and male sexuality. *Issues in Radical Therapy,* 1976, *3,* 11-13.

Skovholt, T. M., Nazy, F., & Epting, F. Teaching sexuality to college males. Paper presented at the meeting of the American Psychological Association, Washington, D.C., August 1976.

Smith, D. D. The social content of pornography. *Journal of Communication,* 1976, *26,* 16-33.

Sommer, R. *Personal space: The behavioral basis of design.* Englewood Cliffs, N.J.: Prentice-Hall, Inc., 1969.

Sprenger, J. & Kramer, H. *Malleus Maleficarum* (M. Summers, Ed. and Trans.). New York: Dover, 1971. Originally published 1486.

Sprey, J. Family power structure: A critical comment. *Journal of Marriage and the Family,* 1972, *34,* 245-238.

Sprey, J. Family power and process: Toward a conceptual integration. In R. E. Cromwell and D. H. Olson (Eds.), *Power in families.* New York: John Wiley, 1975.

Staines, G., Tavris, C., & Jayaratne, T. The queen bee syndrome. In C. Tavris (Ed.), *The female experience.* Del Mar, Calif.: CRM Books, 1973.

Stein, A. H. & Bailey, M. M. The socialization of achievement motivation in females. *Psychological Bulletin*, 1973, *80*(5), 345–366.

Stein, M. L. *Lovers, friends, slaves.* New York: Berkeley Publishing, 1974.

Stein, R. T. & Heller, T. An empirical analysis of the correlations between leadership status and participation rates reported in the literature. *Journal of Personality and Social Psychology*, 1979, *37*(11), 1993–2002.

Stein, R. T., Hoffman, L. R., Cooley, S. H., & Pearse, R. W. Leadership valence: Modeling and measuring the process of emergent leadership. In J. C. Hunt & L. L. Larson (Eds.), *Crosscurrents in leadership.* Carbondale, Ill.: University of Southern Illinois Press, 1979.

Sternglanz, S. H. & Serbin, L. H. Sex role stereotyping in children's television programs. *Developmental Psychology*, 1974 *10*, 710–715.

Stewart, A. J. & Rubin, E. The power motive in the dating couple. *Journal of Personality and Social Psychology*, 1974, *34*(2), 305–309.

Stewart, A. J. & Winter, D. G. Arousal of the power motive in women. *Journal of Consulting and Clinical Psychology*, 1976, *44*(3), 495–496.

Stewart, A. & Winter, D. The nature and causes of female suppression. *Signs*, 1977, *2*(3), 531–553.

Stockard, J. & Johnson, M. The social origins of male dominance. *Sex Roles*, 1979, *5*(2), 199–218.

Stodgill, R. M. *Handbook of leadership: A survey of theory and research.* New York: Free Press, 1974.

Storaska, F. *How to say no to a rapist—and survive.* New York: Warner Books, 1976.

Strickland, B. R. & Haley, W. E. Sex differences on the Rotter I-E Scale. *Journal of Personality and Social Psychology*, 1980, *39*(5), 930–939.

Sugiyama, Y. Social behavior of chimpanzees in the Budongo Forest, Uganda. *Primates*, 1969, *10*, 197–225.

Sullivan, H. S. *Conceptions of modern psychiatry.* Washington, D.C.: William Alanson White Psychiatric Foundation, 1947.

Summerhayes, D. L. & Suchner, R. W. Power implications of touch in male-female relationships. *Sex Roles*, 1978, *4*(1), 103–110.

Tannenbaum, R. & Schmidt, W. How to choose a leadership pattern. *Harvard Business Review*, 1958, *36*(2), 95–101.

Tavris, C. Woman & man. In C. Tavris (Ed.), *The female experience*. Del Mar, Calif.: CRM Publishing, 1973.

Tavris, C. & Offir, C. *The longest war: Sex differences in perspective*. New York: Harcourt Brace Jovanovich, 1977.

Tedeschi, J. T., Schlenker, B. R., & Bonoma, T. V. *Conflict, power and games: The study of interpersonal relations*. Chicago: Aldine, 1973.

Terborg, J. Women in management: A research review. *Journal of Applied Psychology*, 1977, *62*, 647–664.

Terborg, J. R. & Ilgen, D. R. A theoretical approach to sex discrimination in traditionally masculine occupations. *Organizational Behaviour and Human Performance*, 1975, *13*, 352–376.

Thibaut, J. & Kelley, H. *The social psychology of groups*. New York: John Wiley, 1959.

Tieger, T. Self-rated likelihood of raping and social perception of rape. Unpublished manuscript, Stanford University, 1979.

Tiger, L. *Men in groups*. New York: Random House, 1969.

Tillich, P. *Love, power and justice*. New York: Oxford University Press, 1954.

Tillich, P. *Political expectations*. New York: Harper, 1971.

Touhey, J. C. Effects of additional women professionals on rating of occupational prestige and desirability. *Journal of Personality and Social Psychology*, 1974, *29*, 86–89.

Tresemer, D. Fear of success: popular, but unproven. *Psychology Today*, 1974, *7*(10), 82–85.

Turk, J. L. & Bell, N. W. Measuring power in families. *Journal of Marriage and the Family*, 1972, *34*, 215–222.

Ulcman, J. S. A new TAT measure of the need for power. Unpublished Doctoral Dissertation, Harvard University, 1966.

Uleman, J. S., The need for influence: development and validation of a measure and comparison with the need for power. *Genetic Psychology Monographs*, 1972, *85*, 157–214.

Unger, R. K. The politics of gender: A review of relevant literature. In J. Sherman & F. Denmark, (Eds.), *Psychology of women: future directions of research*. New York: Psychological Dimensions, 1978.

Unger, R. K. *Female and male: Psychological perspectives*. New York: Harper, 1979.

Van Lawick-Goodall, J. The behavior of free-living champanzees in the Gombee Stream Reserve. *Animal Behavior Monographs*, 1968, *1*, 1-311.

Veroff, J. Development and validation of a projective measure of power motivation. *Journal of Abnormal and Social Psychology*, 1957, *54*, 1-8.

Vickers, J. M. Where are the women in Canadian politics? *Atlantis*, 1978, *3* (2, Part II), 40-51.

Vinacke, W. E. Sex roles in a three-person game. *Sociometry*, 1959, *22*, 343-360.

Vroom, F. and Yetton, P. *Leadership and decision-making*. Pittsburgh: University of Pittsburgh Press, 1973.

Wadley, S. Women in the Hindu tradition. *Signs*, 1977, *3*(1), 113-125.

Walster, E., Berscheid, E., & Walster, G. W. New directions in equity research. *Journal of Personality and Social Psychology*, 1973, 25, 151-176.

Walster, E., & Walster, G. W. Equity and social justice. *Journal of Social Issues*, 1975, *31*(3), 21-43.

Walster, E., Walster, G. W., & Berscheid, W. *Equity: Theory and research*. Boston: Allyn & Bacon, 1978.

Washbourn, P. *Becoming woman: The quest for wholeness in female experience*. New York: Harper, 1977.

Washburn, S. L. & Devore, I. The social life of baboons. *Scientific American*, 1961, *204*(6), 62-71.

Washburn, S. L., Jay, P. C., & Lancaster, J. B. Field studies of Old World monkeys and apes. *Science*, 1965, *150*, 1541-1547.

Watson, Jr., R. I. Motivation and role induction. Unpublished Honors Thesis, Wesleyan University, 1969.

Weinberg, G. Homophobia. In E. S. Morrison & V. Borosage (Eds.), *Human*

Sexuality: Contemporary Perspectives. Palo Alto, Calif.: Mayfield, 1973.

Weiner, B., Frieze, I., Kukla, A., Reed, L., Rest, S., & Rosenbaum, R. M. *Perceiving the causes of success and failure.* New York: General Learning Press, 1971.

White, R. W. Motivation reconsidered: The concept of competence. *Psychological Review,* 1959, *66,* 297–333.

Whyte, W. The social structure of the restaurant. *American Journal of Sociology,* 1949, *54,* 302–310.

Williams, M.G. *The new executive woman: A guide to business success.* New York: New American Library, 1977.

Wilsnack, S. The effects of social drinking on women's fantasy. *Journal of Personality,* 1974, *42,* 243–261.

Wilson, C. & Lupton, T. The social background and connections of top decision makers. *Manchester School of Economics and Social Studies,* 1959, *27,* 33–51.

Winter, D. G. Power motivation in thought and action. Unpublished Doctoral Dissertation, Harvard University, 1967.

Winter, D. G *The power motive.* New York: Free Press, 1973.

Winter, D. G. & Stewart, A. J. The power motive. In H. London & J. E. Exner, Jr. (Eds.), *Dimensions of personality.* New York: John Wiley, 1978.

Winter, D. G., Stewart, A. J., & McClelland, D. C. Husband's motives and wife's career level. *Journal of Personality and Social Psychology,* 1977, *35*(3), 159–166.

Wolfe, D. M. Power and authority in the family. In D. M. Cartwright (Ed.), *Studies in social power.* Ann Arbor, Mich.: Institute for Social Research, 1959.

Wynne-Edwards, V. C. *Animal dispersion in relation to social behavior.* Edinburgh: Oliver and Boyd, 1962.

Zanna, M. & Bowden, M. Influence of interpersonal relationships on justice. Paper presented at the Canadian Psychological Association, Vancouver, 1977.

Zelditch, Jr., M. Role differentiation in the nuclear family: A comparative study. In Talcott Parsons & Robert F. Bales (Ed.), *The family: Socialization and interaction process*. New York: Macmillan Company, 1955.

Zetterberg, Hans L. Den hemliga rangordningen. *Sociologisk forskning*, 1966, *3*(3).

Zimmerman, D. H. & West, C. Sex roles, interruptions and silence in conversation. In B. Thorne & N. Henley (Eds.), *Language and sex: Difference and dominance*. Rowley, Mass.: Newbury House, 1975.

INDEX